'To Walk in the Dark'

'To Walk in the Dark'

Military Intelligence during the English Civil War 1642-1646

1642-1646

John Ellis

SPELLMOUNT

'Who can love to walk in the dark? But Providence doth often so dispose.'
Oliver Cromwell

First published in 2011
by Spellmount, an imprint of The History Press
The Mill, Brimscombe Port
Stroud, Gloucestershire, GL5 2QG
www.thehistorypress.co.uk

British Library Cataloguing in Publication Data.
A catalogue record for this book is available from the British Library.

ISBN 978 0 7524 6023 9

Typesetting and origination by The History Press
Printed in the EU for The History Press.

Contents

Acknowledgements

As many people and organisations have assisted me with my research, it is invidious to place them in any particular order. I am particularly appreciative of the assistance provided so expertly by Nick Graffy and the other staff of the Southampton University library, along with the staffs of the British Library, the Bodleian Library and the National Archives, all of whom handled my requests quickly, cheerfully and efficiently. I am also extremely grateful to Professor Mark Stoyle of the University of Southampton for his supervision during my PhD.

As ever, I suspect, I am particularly appreciative of the help and guidance offered me by my editor, Miranda Jewess, and the other staff at The History Press. Without them, it is unlikely that this book would have seen the light of day!

I am especially grateful to Jo, my wife, not just for drawing up the maps and sketches and taking the photographs, but also for her patience and understanding. Indeed, the support of my family and friends has been a major factor and I am most appreciative not only of their interest in a subject that was not of their choosing, but also for their enthusiasm and encouragement during the writing of this book.

Introduction

Although much has been written about many of the aspects of the Civil War during the past 350 years, it is surprising that comparatively little information has been published about the conduct of intelligence operations during that conflict. This is even more remarkable when one considers just how many contemporary accounts of the Civil War provide strong and comprehensive evidence which reveals that a great deal of intelligence-gathering was carried out by both sides during the fighting.[1] It is, therefore, reassuring to note that some of the more recently published accounts of the Civil War have begun to explore the impact that intelligence information had upon the conduct and outcome of a few of the more important Civil War campaigns and battles.[2] As these more recent accounts have revealed that intelligence information did, in fact, play a significant role in the outcome of these battles, it seems that now is an appropriate time to evaluate the broader impact that intelligence operations had upon each campaign – and consequently upon the entire conflict. Accordingly *'To Walk in the Dark'* aims to explore the contribution made by military intelligence-gathering operations to the outcome of the English Civil War fought between 1642 and 1646. Following an extensive exploration of the contemporary accounts of the fighting, this book will challenge the long-held perception that intelligence-gathering during the English Civil War was amateurish and imprecise, and will show just how much impact this intelligence information actually had upon the final outcome of the conflict.

The long-standing perception that military intelligence-gathering was ineffective has often been attributed to statements contained in the principal contemporary account of the English Civil War, *The History of the Rebellion and Civil Wars in England,* written by the Royalist, Sir Edward Hyde, later ennobled as the Earl of Clarendon.[3] (Hyde was made Earl of Clarendon following the Restoration, and it is by this title that he will be referred to from now on.) As a key adviser to both Charles I and Charles II, Clarendon's account has been generally regarded as the most reliable contemporary record of the English Civil War. In the last century, however, its accuracy has been challenged by historians, such as the Victorian, Sir Charles Firth, and more recently Ronald Hutton. But, notwithstanding the concerns that they have raised, there appears to have been a marked reluctance to accept the validity of these criticisms – let alone act upon them. For example, even in the most recent account of intelligence operations during the Civil War and Interregnum, the author Julian Whitehead continued to cite *The History of the Rebellion* on numerous occasions, particularly when Clarendon described his perception of the effectiveness of Civil War intelligence-gathering.[4] The most damning – and the most frequently cited – criticism made by Clarendon appears in his account of the Edgehill Campaign, when he described the intelligence-gathering conducted before the battle in the following terms:

> The two armies, though they were but twenty miles asunder when they set forth, and both marched the same way, they gave not the least disquiet in ten days' march to each other; and in truth, as it appeared afterwards, neither army knew where the other was.[5]

Although this perception is not supported by the evidence of other contemporary sources, Clarendon's longstanding reputation as perhaps the greatest historian of the conflict has given his comments a credibility which has frequently led subsequent scholars to portray the military intelligence-gathering operations as ineffective and of no significance. For example, on the 350th anniversary of the English Civil War, historian Alan Marshall published an account of intelligence and espionage in the reign of Charles II, in which he affirmed that 'It was clear that intelligence activities [of the First English Civil War] were on a primitive level and that most civil war battles were more often the result of armies meeting accidentally rather than as any intelligence coup.'[6]

As many other scholars continue to reflect this view,[7] this book will try to show that the contemporary accounts do in fact provide conclusive evidence that military intelligence-gathering operations during the English Civil War were by no means as ineffectual as has so often been claimed. On the contrary, on the basis of the evidence presented, it will be suggested that the reverse is true, and that intelligence information made a decisive contribution to the outcome of the entire conflict.

In all that has been written about the English Civil War, most scholars have tended to focus their earlier research on the two great questions of *why* the War was fought and *why* people chose to support either Charles I or Parliament.[8] Exploring the political and social rationale of the Civil War has thus been considered to be generally much more meaningful than conducting re-evaluations of the sparsely described military campaigns. Although, more recently, English Civil War historians such as Peter Young, Glenn Foard, Malcolm Wanklyn and Jon Day have concentrated their research on the military aspects of the campaigns – seeking to establish exactly *where* these battles were fought and *what* happened – even some of these scholars have spent relatively little time in reviewing the impact that military intelligence had upon the outcome of the campaigns.[9] Although an exploration of the primary seventeenth-century sources shows that intelligence operations played a significant role in determining the outcome of so many of these campaigns, most historians have tended simply to echo the opinions of Clarendon. For example, Eliot Warburton, the nineteenth-century historian, writing in 1869, claimed that, at Edgehill, 'such was the scarcity of information, or the want of skill in collecting it, that the two great armies were in total ignorance of each other's movements.'[10] Clarendon's conclusions have also continued to be cited by more recent historians. In 1967, Peter Young cited Clarendon's account of Edgehill to support his claim that Robert Devereux, Earl of Essex, Captain General and overall commander of the Parliamentarian forces, was 'ill-served by his intelligence'.[11] Yet, as the more recent assessments of Day and Foard now assert, the contemporary evidence reveals that a great deal of intelligence-gathering was being conducted.

In order to establish as many of the facts of what occurred as is possible so long after the conflict, *'To Walk in the Dark'* sets out to review the subsequent historical assessments of these individual actions and to compare them with the primary and contemporary evidence of these battles. This evaluation should allow the reader to establish to what extent the outcome of the English Civil War was influenced by military intelligence operations. In order to assess the impact, this book will not only identify the wide variety of intelligence sources which were being used during the conflict, but it will also demonstrate just how effectively each side managed their intelligence-gathering – and how efficiently intelligence was subsequently integrated into each side's decision-making processes. It will then establish just how the opposing sides gradually developed their intelligence-gathering operations and thereby prove that military intelligence information *was* widely used during the conflict, and that this intelligence information did have a significant impact upon the outcome of the war. In order to highlight the differences between the evidence of the contemporary accounts and the accounts of the subsequent historians, this book will also seek to provide a brief evaluation of the validity of what subsequent historians have written about Civil War intelligence operations by examining the evidence of the contemporary accounts which they may have cited to support their assertions.

As any exploration of seventeenth-century intelligence-gathering needs to recognise that the word 'intelligence' had a number of different usages at that time, it is sensible to avoid any possible confusion by clarifying a few definitions of contemporary terms as early as possible. In contemporary accounts of the Civil War, the word 'intelligence' was used to describe many forms of information. For example, intelligence operations would have included what is now understood to be 'investigative journalism' as well as military scouting. During this period, the distinction between information and intelligence was often indistinct, the result being that the word 'intelligence' was used to describe the activities and the people who were engaged in all aspects of intelligence-gathering, ranging from spy to messenger. Thus 'intelligencers were pamphlets as well as people, [and] intelligence was the stuff of both the newshound and the spy.'[12] An example of this ambivalent meaning is provided by the fact that some of these early news pamphlets were called *The Spie* and *The Parliament Scout*. Further potential misunderstandings arise from the fact that contemporary accounts often used the word 'advertisements' to describe specific intelligence reports; on 22 March 1645, the Parliamentarian commander in the North West, Sir William Brereton, wrote to David Leslie, his ally in the Solemn League and Covenant and the Scottish General commanding the invading Scottish Army, describing how 'by several advertisements that came into my hand since I left you, I am further certified that both Princes and their forces are marched away.'[13] One final point of clarification of the military terms in use during the seventeenth-century should be included here: the words 'designes' and 'grand designes' were often used to describe what we would now term tactical and strategic plans.[14]

This book seeks to explore how intelligence information was gathered and used to inform commanding officers during the various campaigns of the First Civil War. It also seeks to demonstrate that intelligence information played a more significant part in determining the outcome of the battles – and hence the war itself – than has been acknowledged by subsequent historians. It therefore explores just what has been said about Civil War intelligence-gathering in contemporary and subsequent historical publications, examining primary evidence to ascertain exactly what intelligence information was available to the respective commanders during each campaign and considers the objectivity of each account.

Because intelligence is such a large subject, this book will only explore the impact of intelligence information on the main military actions fought in England between 1642 and 1646, considering the collection, assessment and use of information relating to the strengths, location, capability and intentions of the Royalist and Parliamentarian military forces. The gathering of international strategic or political intelligence will therefore not be explored, nor will the gathering of politico-economic intelligence by either side (except insofar as that intelligence had a military application as defined above). However, the content of news pamphlets (the number of which grew a great deal during the time period) will be assessed in order to establish the impact that their reports of the military situation may have had upon intelligence-gathering during the conflict. As there are so many contemporary descriptions of a comprehensive range of intelligence-gathering operations conducted during the First English Civil War, *'To Walk in the Dark'* will concentrate on the major actions and campaigns only.

Notes

1 See, for example, T. May, *A Breviary of the History of the Parliament of England* (London, 1655), pp.250–252, 319, and 343–346; and J. Sprigge, *Anglia Rediviva. England's Recovery* (London, 1647, reprinted Oxford 1854), p.27.

2 See, for example, G. Foard, *Naseby: The Decisive Battle* (Kent, 1995), pp.154–159 and 202; C. Scott, A. Turton and E. Gruber von Arni *Edgehill: The Battle Reinterpreted* (Barnsley, 2004), p.5; J. Day, *Gloucester and Newbury 1643: The Turning Point of the Civil War* (Barnsley, 2007), pp.142–145 and 217–218; B. Donagan, *War in England: 1642 – 1649* (Oxford, 2008), pp.100–106, 110 and 113; and J. Whitehead, *Cavalier and Roundhead Spies Intelligence in the Civil War and Commonwealth* (Barnsley, 2009).

3 E. Hyde, *The History of the Rebellion and Civil Wars in England, together with an Historical View of the Affairs of Ireland* (sixteen books, London, 1703–4), Book VI, p.79.

4 Whitehead, *Cavalier and Roundhead Spies*, p.235.

5 Clarendon, *History*, Book VI, p.81.

6 A. Marshall, *Intelligence and Espionage in the Reign of Charles II, 1660–1685* (Cambridge, 1994), p.18.

7 See, for example, B. Worden, *The English Civil Wars 1640–1660* (London, 2009), p.69.

8 See, for example, R.H. Parry, *The English Civil War and After: 1642–1658* (London, 1970), pp.22–24; C. Hill, *The Century of Revolution: 1603–1714* (London, 1975), pp.110–114; M. Stoyle, *Loyalty and Locality. Popular Allegiance in Devon during the English Civil War* (Exeter, 1994), p.255; and J. Kenyon, *The Civil Wars of England* (London, 1996), pp.30–32.

9 See, for example, Austin Woolrych, *Battles of the English Civil War* (London, 1961), pp.63–80; P. Young and R. Holmes, *The English Civil War: A Military History of the Three Civil Wars 1642 -1651* (London, 1974), pp.72–83; G. Foard, *Naseby The Decisive Campaign* (Barnsley, 1995), pp.329–343; S. Reid, *All the King's Armies: A Military History of the English Civil War 1642 – 1651* (Kent, 1998), pp.121–149; M. Wanklyn, *Decisive Battles of the English Civil War* (Barnsley, 2006), pp.35–42, 57–67, 136, 145 and 161–172; and J. Day, *Gloucester and Newbury 1643 The Turning Point of the War* (Barnsley, 2007), pp.140–145.

10 E.G.B. Warburton, *Memoirs of Prince Rupert, and the Cavaliers* (three volumes, London, 1869), Volume II, p.10.

11 P. Young, *Edgehill 1642* (first printed 1967, first reprinted Moreton-in-Marsh, 1995), p.70.

12 M. Nevitt, *Women and the Pamphlet Culture of Revolutionary England, 1640–1660* (Aldershot, 2006), pp.104–105.

13 R.N. Dore, *The Letter Books of Sir William Brereton* (two volumes, The Record Society of Lancashire and Cheshire, 1984 and 1990), Volume 1, pp.106–107.

14 See, for example, Clarendon, *History*, Book IX, p.11 and R. Bell (ed.), *The Fairfax Correspondence* (two volumes, London, 1849), Volume 1, p.218.

1

English Intelligence Gathering Before the War

Although the recent 'Troubles' in Northern Ireland may help us to envisage a situation where perceived threats to religious, social and political rights have led to a form of armed insurrection, it is nonetheless difficult for us to fully comprehend the political, military and social landscape of the early 1640s. During this time Charles I's determination to uphold the 'divine right' of the monarchy was opposed with increasing popularity and success by John Pym, the Tavistock MP and unofficial leader of the Parliamentarian party with followers in both the House of Commons as well as the House of Lords. Pym's single-minded ambition to give Parliament a greater role in the governance of England, coupled with a combination of regal ineptitude and duplicity from Charles, had split the country and had made some form of military resolution increasingly inevitable. Thus, as England moved inexorably towards civil war at the beginning of 1642, it is helpful to establish just what military expertise was available to the commanders of the opposing Cavalier and Roundhead forces and, consequently, just how effective would be their generals' understanding of the role to be played by military intelligence in any future conflict. There had been no major fighting on English soil for generations and, although some of the more restless spirits were involved in the Thirty Years' War in northern Europe, the recent Bishops' Wars fought against Scotland had shown with embarrassing clarity that England's military expertise was extremely limited. Accordingly, this chapter seeks to 'set the scene' so that we may better understand which events influenced English military thinking in the early years of Charles I's reign – and thereby understand how military intelligence-gathering operations contributed to the conduct and eventual outcome of the First English Civil War.

Before the Bishops' Wars and the Civil War, there had been no large-scale internal disturbances in England since the Tudor rebellions of 1535–36, 1549 and 1569. Although parallels with the English Civil War are difficult to draw as these earlier insurrections were not full-blown nation-wide conflicts, contemporary accounts of these rebellions provide evidence that both national and local intelligence-gathering operations nonetheless played a significant part in their suppression. During the Tudor period, the responsibility for the provision of intelligence lay with the monarch's chief ministers; thus, in 1535–36, Thomas Cromwell – as Henry VIII's chief minister – had directed an unrivalled intelligence network which had enabled him to send spies into the rebel-held areas. Cromwell had also gathered further intelligence from the interception of mail.[1] During the later uprising called the Pilgrimage of Grace, some of Henry VIII's commanders had used their own intelligence-gathering networks; for example, it was recounted how one of Henry VIII's commanders, called Davey, 'had many friends who acted as spies for him'.[2] At the same time, the rebel commanders had established their own 'scoutwatch' system to ensure continuity of reporting; we are told that the rebel commanders waited 'to hear the reports of the scouts and spies as they came in'.[3]

The central direction of intelligence networks continued after the death of Cromwell and Henry VIII, for whilst commanders had continued to rely upon scouts and local informants during the 1549 rebellion, the Privy Council had also undertaken to keep the local commanders informed of any intelligence information they could get their hands on. For example, in 1549 it was reported that the Lord Privy Seal (Russell) was 'undelayedly (sic) advertised from us [the Privy Council] of all occurrences of importance'.[4] Both sides made full use of spies and scouts to gather intelligence, and 'the rebels freely sent spies into Russell's camp' just as he 'was to send trusting men into theirs.'[5] The rebels also made effective use of local intelligence and were able to use this information to launch a number of delaying attacks on Russell's army as it moved to attack Exeter in the summer of 1549.[6] The importance of intelligence-gathering continued to be recognised during Elizabeth's reign; in 1569, one George Bowes was appointed 'to provide intelligence of the [rebel] Earles [Northumberland and Westmoreland] setting out'.[7] Bowes reported that the rebels had also established an effective intelligence-gathering system, recording that, although 'I keep as good spyall as I can, but not so good, I feare, as they have of me, for I am therebye watched.'[8] The rebels proved to be active gatherers of intelligence, intercepting mail so frequently that Bowes requested that senders should tell him of any messages sent 'least some of them be intercepted'.[9] Contemporary accounts of the rebellions show very clearly that, as intelligence-gathering was recognised as a priority task by the Tudor monarchs, a variety of intelligence networks were established by the ruler's senior ministers. Any possible means of obtaining intelligence were used and the deployment of spies and scouts, along with the opening of intercepted letters, was commonplace. Locally provided intelligence proved to be both accurate and timely in all of the major rebellions of the Tudor era.[10]

Similarly, the threat from Spain which had manifested itself during the later years of Elizabeth I's reign had led to the continued deployment – and development – of a nationwide intelligence service. Headed by Sir Francis Walsingham, Elizabeth I's

Secretary of State, England's intelligence network had been instrumental in protecting the life of the monarch and preserving the internal stability of the country at a
time when the threat from Spain and fanatical Roman Catholics was substantial.[11]
During his time in office, Walsingham obtained intelligence information from a
wide variety of sources including the interception of mail, the breaking of codes
and the use of spies. Perhaps his most sophisticated intelligence-gathering coup
was the so-called Babington Plot of 1586, which, as it was a major factor in the
decision to execute Mary Queen of Scots, is also his most well-known operation.[12]
However, as the events of Charles I's reign were to show, much of this expertise had
been allowed to waste away during the early years of the Stuart dynasty.

Because there had been no fighting on English soil since the Tudor rebellions,
the fighting that took place on the Continent during the Thirty Years' War provided
an ideal opportunity for both the English (and Scots) to gain experience of current military tactics and to rekindle their knowledge of intelligence-gathering. By
authorising 'unofficial' English forces to fight in Europe, James I devised not just a
cost effective and convenient way of satisfying public expectations and supporting
the Protestant cause, but also a means of allowing the more passionate supporters of
English and European Protestantism to participate in the fighting. The experience
that those English and Scottish soldiers gained during the Thirty Years' War varied
enormously. For the majority, who served as foot soldiers, their experience was
limited to a series of interminable sieges as they became members of Protestant garrisons such as at Mannheim and Frankenthal. Their garrison duties did not appear
to offer the majority of them many opportunities to understand – let alone develop
– the military advantages of obtaining superior intelligence information.

Whilst it is evident that the number and expertise of the veterans returning
from the European wars was used to swell and train the ranks of the newly formed
Parliamentarian and Royalist armies, there is little contemporary evidence that
this fresh expertise was subsequently used to improve the quality of intelligence-
gathering on either side. Even though an estimated 6,000–8,000 Scots served
with the Swedish army (until 1632 trained and organised by their inspirational
monarch, Gustavus Adolphus), and although some 10,000–15,000 Englishmen
and up to 25,000 Scots fought in the Thirty Years' War, very few of them gained
any experience at the senior command level.[13] (Patrick Ruthven – a Scot who
was knighted by Gustavus Adolphus and made a full general in the Swedish
forces – is an obvious exception.[14]) For most young soldiers, their transferable
experience of continental warfare was limited mainly to the training, forming
and deployment of bodies of horse and foot which was not particularly relevant
to military intelligence operations. Although historical accounts of the Battle of
the White Mountain make no references to innovative intelligence-gathering by
either side, as it was the standard reports of sentries and scouts that provided
the intelligence prior to the battle,[15] later battles of the Thirty Years' War, such
as that fought at Lützen (16 November 1632) reveal a greater use of intelligence

information by both sides.[16] Whilst the few British soldiers who served with the regiments of horse would probably have picked up some experience of military intelligence, this would almost certainly have been limited to the duties of scouting.[17] Therefore, despite the relatively large numbers of English and Scottish soldiers who served on the continent in the years prior to the Civil War, few returned home with any significant expertise in intelligence-gathering.

Charles I's attempt to impose religious conformity on the Scots, which led to the outbreak of the so-called Bishops' Wars of 1639–1640, had the unexpected and indirect consequence of offering an opportunity for the English commanders to gain experience of conducting modern warfare. The fighting also served to remind them of the benefits of obtaining superior military intelligence – and the chance to update their intelligence-gathering skills. An evaluation of the conduct of military actions during the conflict therefore supplies us with some clues about the effectiveness of English military intelligence-gathering some two years before the outbreak of the Civil War. Although no major battles were fought, the Bishops' Wars required the deployment of substantial English sea and land forces along the Scottish borders. The complexity of these operations revealed the major difficulties associated with recruiting, training and deploying English soldiers after such a prolonged period of peace.[18] Of particular relevance to this book was the failure of the English intelligence and scouting operations; the ineptitude of the English scouting had become apparent to all when, in the first week of June 1639, the Scottish army was able to deploy, without warning, substantially superior forces against a major English cross-border probe by 4,000 horse and foot. So effective was the Scottish deployment that the English commander decided he had no option but to order an ignominious retreat – a retreat that was witnessed (and mocked) by the whole Scottish army. This humiliation was so keenly felt by both the King and his soldiers that Charles, in harmony with his army on this issue at least, complained that the Scottish forces were able to close within striking distance unnoticed and unreported by the English scouts. 'Have not I good intelligence', lamented the King, 'that the rebels can march with their army and encamp within sight of mine, and I not have a word of it till the Body of their Army give the alarm?'[19]

Although the military inexperience and ineptitude of the commander of the advanced force, Lord Holland, had clearly been a significant factor in this humiliating episode, the scouting and intelligence had also been considered to be much at fault. As the English intelligence-gathering organisation had been led by a man named Roger Widdrington who was appointed as scoutmaster, it was inevitable that the humiliation was believed to have been entirely his fault. The Parliamentarian historian, John Rushworth, was later to summarise the popular view very well when he reported that 'In conclusion this business was hushed up, but great was the murmuring of the Private Souldiers in the Camp.'[20] His view was shared by Sir Edmund Verney, one of the King's captains of foot who was to lose his life carrying the Royal standard at the Battle of Edgehill a few years later, when he wrote 'the truth is we are betrayed in all our intelligence.'[21] These views were also shared and reflected in personal diaries and the accounts presented in the State Papers.[22] Sir Bevil Grenville, another of the English officers (who was later to lead a regiment of Cornish foot soldiers in the Royalist Western Army) reflected the prevailing mood in the English camp when he reported that:

> The Scoutmaster was much exclaimed against, and he complained as much of the Souldiers who were sent out as Scouts, and gave him no timely intelligence. But in the Opinion of the Court and Commanders, the Scoutmaster-General bore the blame; and his Crime was aggravated, because he was a Papist.[23]

Of even greater significance were the comments of the English army's commander, the Earl of Arundel, in his defence of his appointment of Widdrington as scoutmaster. Arundel provided some interesting insights into the sort of skills that were considered to have been most relevant when appointing a Scoutmaster-General. The Earl of Arundel opined that the scoutmaster had been

> ... the fittest Man in England for the Office of Scoutmaster, being born in the County of Northumberland, and one of the best acquainted with all the Highlandmen upon the Borders of Scotland, and who was best able, of any man he knew in England, to gain intelligence from thence; and that it was notoriously known, he was a Gentleman who ever bore a perfect hatred to the Scots, and was a stout active man upon Border-Service in the time of Queen Elizabeth; that he was a person of quality, and he doubted not of his Integrity, and that he would justify himself.[24]

The selection of Widdrington as scoutmaster thus seems a perfectly reasonable choice particularly because he had useful local knowledge as well as relevant and recent experience of operations along the border. It therefore seems rather odd that, despite Widdrington's evident expertise, his claim that the scouts themselves had failed in their duties appears to have been dismissed and set aside as unworthy of further investigation. Indeed Widdrington's claim gains credibility when it is recalled that the failure of the scouting parties to detect the approach of an opposing army was to become a feature of some of the Civil War campaigns conducted between 1642 and 1646.

Despite these humiliating experiences, there is no evidence that any consequent changes were made to improve the effectiveness of English military intelligence-gathering. It is difficult to avoid the conclusion that the evidence of the First Bishops' War provides a pretty damning indictment of the state of military intelligence at the start of the Civil War, leading us to believe that the English intelligence-gathering organisation was largely ineffective and lacked credibility. Although a comparatively limited campaign, the events of the war in Scotland nevertheless provide some historical basis to Clarendon's later claims about the conduct and effectiveness of English military intelligence operations at the beginning of the Civil War just two years later.

The injurious experiences of intelligence-gathering during the Bishops' Wars had demonstrated that, as England had been at peace for so long, few men had any experience of conducting effective military operations – let alone of fighting their own people in their own streets and fields. However, many Englishmen, painfully aware of their lack of military experience and very conscious of the increasing probability of some form of conflict, sought to improve their military knowledge by consulting the wide variety of contemporary military publications which explained the theory and practice of seventeenth-century warfare.[25] The publication that provided most information about the gathering of intelligence was *Militarie Instructions for the Cavallrie* written by the Cambridge graduate, John Cruso.[26] As the collection of intelligence was traditionally a responsibility of the mounted soldiers – the 'cavalry' or 'horse' of the seventeenth-century army – Cruso's work provided a great deal of practical advice for commanders of horse, especially when he advised them that:

> Every good commander must have these two grounds for his actions, 1. The knowledge of his own forces, and wants … [and] 2. The assurance of the condition and estate of the enemy, his commodities, and necessities, his councils and designes; thereby begetting divers occasions, which afterward bring forth victories.[27]

Cruso's elegant and sophisticated work has been well described by one modern writer as being 'so excellent that it held the field undisputed for nearly thirty years'.[28] So it is not surprising that later seventeenth-century works on warfare (for example, Roger Boyle's *A Treatise of the Art of War*, published in 1677, and subsequently Sir James Turner's *Pallas Armata,* published in 1683[29]) merely referred their readers to Cruso's work for advice on the conduct of mounted operations, including intelligence-gathering and scouting.

Even in the final months of peace, the military and political benefits of accurate intelligence began to emerge. As the differences between Charles and his people divided the country at all levels of society, the Parliamentarian leaders had well-placed supporters who had access to the confidences of the members of the Court. Unbeknown to Charles, these Parliamentarian supporters were able to provide Pym with the most useful intelligence about the King's strategies and intentions. Perhaps one of the earliest and most important examples of intelligence-gathering related to Charles' attempt to arrest the 'Five Members' in January 1642. The failure of Charles's plan to nip his troubles in the bud was caused primarily by the timely intelligence reports John Pym received from a Parliamentarian supporter and spy who was not only a member of the Royalist court, but also a confidante of Queen Henrietta Maria. The spy in question was perhaps one of the earlier examples of what we might now call a 'Bond girl', Lucy Percy, the Countess of Carlisle, allegedly the mistress of John Pym, who provided him with intelligence reports describing Charles's most confidential intentions.[30] Her reports not only warned Pym about what the King was planning to do, but also, as her reports were so up-to-date and accurate, enabled him to time his flight from the Commons to perfection. When Charles set out to arrest Pym, he knew that the four MPs were still in the Commons but by the time Charles arrived at the House, his 'birds had flown'. The intelligence that Pym received – and the actions he took in response to that intelligence – ensured that Charles' discomfiture was as complete as was the damage done to the credibility of his cause. Not only did Charles' very public failure to arrest his key opponents lead to a major collapse of public belief in the credibility of his compromise proposals for a peaceful settlement with Parliament; but the public outrage that followed Charles' assault on the privileges of Parliament increased dramatically. Hardly surprisingly, Charles considered that his family's personal safety was now under serious threat from the Roundhead mob – a perceived threat which caused him to gather his family and flee from London. At this critical moment, his flight thus surrendered the capital – with all its political and financial advantages – to his opponents. The next time Charles entered London, he was a prisoner and facing trial for his life.

This was not the only occasion when the Parliamentarian commanders received vital intelligence which enabled them to publicly thwart the King's plans and disrupt his preparations for war. Intelligence information continued to flow into the Parliamentarian camp during the first six months of 1642 as the gulf between the two sides steadily widened. Later in the spring of 1642, the Parliamentarian commanders received intelligence confirming their assessment that the Royalists' shortage of weapons dictated that their immediate priority was to take control of any stockpiles of military stores and ammunition. This intelligence enabled the Committee of Safety, established by Parliament to coordinate measures to ensure their victory, to thwart Charles' plans to seize these arms, which he needed to equip his recruits.[31] Intelligence information, gleaned from the interception of a letter from Lord Digby, one of the King's more hopelessly optimistic and carefree advisers, gave Parliament early warning of Charles' intention to enter Hull and to seize the weapons and munitions which had been stored there since the Bishops' Wars.[32] This intelligence enabled Parliament to pre-empt the King's plan by sending Peregrine Pelham, a supporter of Pym and MP for Hull, with reinforcements to strengthen the resolve of Sir John Hotham, another Parliamentarian supporter and Hull's garrison commander, a few days before the King appeared before the walls of the city. The 'Refusal before Hull' was another intelligence victory for the Parliamentarians that also had a significant nationwide impact because, as well as strengthening the resolve of those opposing the King, it also helped persuade those hitherto uncommitted citizens to take up the Parliamentarian cause. These two events must also have given the Parliamentarian leaders a salutary lesson in the advantages to be gained from accurate and timely military intelligence.

Equally important perhaps was the consequent lesson in the dangers of inadequate or late intelligence-gathering, which was forcefully demonstrated to the members of the Committee of Safety. Without any intelligence warning, the Parliamentarian leadership was caught completely by surprise on 2 August 1642, when Colonel George Goring, the self-professed Parliamentarian supporter whom they had appointed to be the Governor of Portsmouth, had turned coat and seized the city, along with its important magazine, for the King. The declaration of Portsmouth for the King was an embarrassing surprise to Parliament and the subsequent re-capture of the city had required a substantial diversion of both sea and land forces at a time when these resources could have been better used elsewhere.[33]

In conclusion, it seems reasonable to suggest that, although Thomas Cromwell and Sir Francis Walsingham had developed an extensive intelligence services during the reigns of the Tudor monarchs, the experience of the Bishops' Wars had proved that the intelligence-gathering organisation established by the Tudors had been allowed to languish during the reigns of the early Stuart monarchs, James I and his son Charles I.[34] Consequently, when England was engulfed by the turmoil of the Civil War in 1642, the structures for obtaining intelligence had to be resurrected quickly if intelligence-gathering was to make any meaningful contribution to the conduct of the war. From the contemporary evidence, it is hard to avoid the conclusion that the Parliamentarian sympathisers were quicker to appreciate the importance of intelligence-gathering and were thus able to provide some extremely important information from the very early days of Parliament's confrontation with the King. It was this intelligence that enabled them to forestall Charles' attempts to regain the political and military initiative from Parliament. After all this time, it is difficult to envisage just how significant, on the day, were the political consequences of the failures of the King to arrest the Five Members – followed by his rebuff at Hull. The direct consequences not only drove Charles out of his capital and surrendered the seat of government to his opponents, but they also exposed – and exacerbated – his military weakness and political status. It is thus even more surprising perhaps that Charles seems not to have appreciated the impact that this Parliamentarian intelligence information had had upon his military plans and his political credibility. Even before Charles raised the Royal Standard at Nottingham in August 1642, the Roundheads were receiving accurate and up-to-date intelligence information. As there is no evidence that the military advantages this intelligence gave the Roundheads were appreciated by the Cavaliers, they appear to have not seen the need to establish their own intelligence network. This relative weakness made it much easier for Parliament to seize the upper hand.[35]

Notes

1 M. and R. Dodds, *The Pilgrimage of Grace and the Exeter Conspiracy* (two volumes, London, 1915), Volume I, pp.4, 109, 111 and 214; and Volume II, p.190.

2 Ibid, p.169.

3   Ibid, p.256.

4   F. Rose-Troup, *The Western Rebellion of 1549* (London, 1913), p.142.

5   Ibid, pp.245–246.

6   Ibid, pp.296–297. See also, A. Fletcher and D. MacCulloch, *Tudor Rebellions* (fourth edition, London, 1997), pp.55–56.

7   C. Sharp (ed.), *The Rising in the North: The 1569 Rebellion* (Ilkley, 1975), p.24.

8   Ibid, p.63.

9   Ibid, p.64.

10 Rose-Troup, *Western Rebellion*, pp.266–267.

11 R. Hutchinson, *Elizabeth's Spymaster: Francis Walsingham and the Secret War that Saved England* (London, 2006), pp.59–62.

12 Ibid, pp.116–145.

13 S.D.M. Carpenter, *Military Leadership in the British Civil Wars, 1642–1651* (London & New York, 2005), p.54.

14 S. Reid, *Patrick Ruthven, Earl of Forth and Earl of Brentford* (DNB).

15 C.V. Wedgwood, *The Thirty Years' War* (London, 1938), pp.105–107.

16 Ibid, pp.284–287.

17 Ibid, p.239.

18 *CSPD, 1638–9*, pp.566 and 593–594.

19 D. Parsons, *The Diary of Sir Henry Slingsby*, (Longman, London, 1836), pp.34–36. See also J. Rushworth, *Historical Collections* (London, 1659–99), Volume II, Part 2, pp.935–945.

20 Rushworth, *Historical Collections*, Volume II, Part II, p.939.

21 F.P. Verney, *Memoirs of the Verney Family during the Civil War* (London, 1892), p.53.

22 See, for example, Parsons, *Slingsby Diaries*, p.35; and *CSPD, 1639*, pp.272, and 281–283.

23 Rushworth, *Historical Collections*, Vol. II, Part II, p.938; See also J. Stucley, *Sir Bevil Grenville and his times* (Sussex, 1983), p.84. Quite why a Papist would assist the Presbyterian Covenanting Scots army was never satisfactorily explained.

24 Rushworth, *Historical Collections*, p.939. See also *CSPD, 1639*, pp.272 and 281–283. There is no relevant source material for the Second Bishops' War.

25 See, for example, E. Davies, *The Art of War, and Englands Traynings* (London, 1619); Anon, *Instructions for Musters and Armes: and the use thereof* (London, 1631); W. Barriffe, *Military Discipline: or the Yong Artillery Man* (London, 1635); and H. Hexham, *The Principles of the Art Militarie: Practised in the Warres of the United Netherlands* (London, 1637).

26 J. Cruso, *Militarie Instructions for the Cavallrie* (Cambridge, 1632).

27 Cruso, *Militarie Instructions,* Part II, Chapter II, p.57.

28 T. M. Spaulding, 'Militarie Instructions for the Cavallrie', *Journal of the American Military History Foundation* (Vol.2, No.2, 1938), p.106.

29 R. Boyle, Earl of Orrery, *A treatise on the art of war* (London, 1677); and Sir James Turner, *Pallas Armata* (London, 1683).

30 See, for example, T. May, *A Breviary of the History of the Parliament of England* (London, 1655), p.27; J. T. Rutt (ed.) *The Diary of Thomas Burton* (4 volumes, London, 1828), pp.91–102 (which cited a speech of Sir Arthur Haselrig in Parliament, 7 February 1659); E. Ludlow, *Memoirs of Edmund Ludlow* (two volumes, Bern, 1698), Volume 1, pp.24–25; Warburton, *Memoirs*, Volume 1, pp.220, 348; and D. Purkiss, *The English Civil War: A People's History* (London, 2006), pp.123–124.

31 See, for example, Clarendon, *History*, Book V, pp.139–140; and *CSPD, 1641–43*, pp.389–390.

32 T. May, *A History of the Parliament of England* (London, 1647), p.57; and Clarendon, *History*, Book V, pp.53 and 89–91.

33 Clarendon, *History*, Book V, p.442.

34 R. Hutchinson, *Elizabeth's Spy Master* (London, 2006), p.260.

35 Clarendon, *History*, Book IX, p.38.

2

Intelligence Sources and their Military Applications

Before exploring the impact that intelligence information had upon the outcome of the key Civil War battles, it is important to identify and evaluate the very extensive range of intelligence-gathering sources that were available to each side during the conflict. It is also important to appreciate that, unlike a conflict fought overseas where the citizenry was likely to be unfriendly and uncommunicative, during the Civil War there was a greater possibility that the opposing armies would be able to obtain useful intelligence from the local population. Furthermore, the steady improvements in the reliability and speed of the messenger and postal services soon revealed that written reports from sympathisers living around the country were an invaluable source of military intelligence. Accordingly, as the fighting spread and the number of marching armies increased, so too did the demand for – and the supply of – more comprehensive and timely military information. This resulted in the development, not only of a growing number of innovative ways of gathering and communicating intelligence, but also of increasing staff numbers within each military headquarters to verify and promulgate the large number of reports. Nor was the growing demand for information restricted to purely military matters – the growing public desire for news about the conflict led to a dramatic increase in the demand for this information to be included in news pamphlets. At the start of the Civil War, however, when neither side readily seemed to appreciate the advantages of seeking military information from the local people, commanders tended to rely more upon the traditional and readily understood methods for gathering intelligence, such as scouting reports provided by horse patrols.

Scouts and scouting patrols provided the most well-established sources of military information upon which commanders had long relied for the delivery of accurate and timely intelligence about the enemy's position and strength. In his widely read publication about the role of the cavalry, Cruso recommended that these scouts 'must be choice men, valiant, vigilant and discreet' who must 'see that with their own eyes which they inform'. He evidently considered that scouts had an important role to play.

> An expert officer, with 20 or 25 of the best-mounted and hardiest Harquebusiers (or mix of Cuirassiers and Harquebusiers) with two trumpets are to be employed. These are to carry with them some refreshment for themselves and their horses, to that purpose retiring themselves into some wood, or shadie place, placing good Centinells upon trees.[1]

This advice was certainly taken to heart by the Parliamentarians for, when Sir Samuel Luke, the MP for Bedford and captain of horse in Essex's army, was appointed Scoutmaster-General by Essex in January 1643, he was given funding for 'fouer and twenty men and horses who were imploied daily as spies into the enemyes armyes and garrisons'.[2] The size of Luke's scouting team evidently proved to be both practical and successful for it was used as a model throughout the war; later during the conflict, when Mr Samuel Bedford was appointed as scoutmaster to the Committee of Both Kingdoms on 10 June 1645, he was given Parliamentary approval for the establishment of a spying and scouting team of 28 people.[3] The associated requirement to communicate any intelligence information obtained was acknowledged as equally important by the Committee, for they also approved Bedford's accompanying request for '£120 for buying horses, ten men for watching the King's army at 5s a day, one agent for Lincolnshire, one for Oxford and one for the west; each agent to have one spy and 4 messengers at 3s a day.'[4]

The responsibility for scouting was usually assigned to the Lieutenant-General of the Horse.[5] Scouting was recognised as a difficult and dangerous job which required each scout to demonstrate courage, initiative and determination. Apart from being able to ride well, and preferably provide his own mount, the scout also needed to be numerate and literate. The role of the scout – or 'discoverer' as he was also called in some pre-war publications – was described by Cruso in some detail, who wrote that the scout would need to be brave, quick-thinking and intelligent in order to deliver an accurate and well-judged report that would be accepted as reliable by his commander.[6]

Seventeenth-century commanders realised that to find all these characteristics in one person was always going to be difficult, especially as the need to be able to ride narrowed the selection of scouts to the ranks of each side's cavalry; thus the quality of the scout was largely determined by the quality of the cavalry troopers on each side. At the beginning of the Civil War the Royalist horse was probably of superior quality overall, although the Parliamentarian horse did contain some equally good officers and troopers, men such as Edmund Ludlow, Nathaniel Fiennes and Charles Fleetwood who joined as junior ranks and steadily won promotion as the war progressed and their worth was recognised.[7] Later in the war, Parliamentarian commanders appreciated the need to counter the enemy's scouting and deprive their commanders of information; Colonel Massey, the Parliamentarian commander of the garrison at Gloucester, informed the Committee how he had been 'lodging my forces in a thicket of the forest, and so preventing the enemy's discovery of us by their scouts'.[8]

Luke had recruited and led a troop of horse in the early part of the war. He obviously knew and trusted these men as he took them with him as the core of his scouting parties when he was appointed as Essex's Scoutmaster-General. Having to recruit scouts from cavalry of somewhat variable quality was possibly one of the reasons why Parliamentary scouting was not particularly effective in the early campaigns.[9] In the later years, when the training and professionalism of Cromwell's Ironsides had begun to permeate through the ranks of the New Model Army, the quality of Parliamentarian scouting improved significantly and so did the quality of the intelligence being received by the commanders. The improved standard of Parliamentarian scouting was certainly acknowledged by the Royalists; for, in January 1644, a Royalist commander reported to Rupert that the reason for his inactivity was because 'their [Parliamentarian] scouts are so frequent abroad, we might be discovered by them'.[10]

Interestingly, the initially higher quality of the Royalist horse did not necessarily mean that their scouting was any better. Royalist scouting patrols were equally likely to miss detection opportunities, but it is possible that the reasons for any weaknesses reflected social rather than military considerations.[11] Contemporary accounts reveal that, at the beginning of the war, many of the Royalist horse troopers considered themselves to be an elite force of volunteers who were superior to the rest of the army.[12] It may well be that, in the view of these Royalist troopers, recognition of their excellence was more surely to be achieved by charging headlong into battle, where courage would prevail even in the most complex situation. If this was indeed the case, it is unlikely that the perceived tedium of patrolling to gain intelligence information would have inspired them. As the early engagements of the Civil War proved, many young Royalists believed that feats of gallantry far outweighed other military considerations – and the skirmish at Powick Bridge served to justify and reinforce this opinion.[13] Scouting and intelligence-gathering could be seen as a monotonous 'business' and the need to display guile and patience was unlikely to be appreciated by the more impetuous Cavaliers. Thus it is hard to imagine Royalist troopers wishing to become scouts or to have anything to do with the mundane routine of intelligence-gathering.[14]

In the absence of timely and accurate intelligence reports from either their military scouts or other sources, some senior officers were quite prepared to conduct their own intelligence-gathering operations in order to find out what their enemies were up to. Early examples of the scouting and intelligence-gathering operations carried out personally by Prince Rupert are given in a pamphlet which described the various disguises adopted by the prince when he was spying on his opponents.[15] Although these stories may well be apocryphal, Rupert's energy and determination to 'see for himself' attracted comment from friend and foe alike.[16] His activity rate was extraordinarily high as his many responsibilities, coupled with a small staff, required him to supervise or carry out a large number of operations himself.[17] Rupert's successful intelligence-gathering forays were attributed by some Parliamentarians to supernatural powers because his energy and rapidity of movement allowed him to visit so many places that, in their view, no-one could do so much without some form of satanic help.[18]

There were a number of practical implications of providing effective scouting which each commander had to recognise. As intelligence was of little value unless it was received in time to influence the subsequent deployment of troops, Civil War commanders needed early warning of the presence of the enemy so that they could prepare and position their forces prior to any engagement. For example, it took around six hours for the Royalist and Parliamentarian armies to prepare for battle at Edgehill even though both forces were 'in the field' and on the march for London.[19] Failure to provide timely warning normally resulted in one side being caught at a substantial disadvantage. Because such a warning was best provided by a screen of scouts deployed around a force, scouting was seen by Civil War commanders as being the most responsive form of intelligence-gathering – and one under their direct control – even though commanders often had other sources of intelligence available to them.

The main limitation of scouting was that it was difficult for a seventeenth-century army to provide enough scouts to cover the ground effectively. Even a dedicated body of 28 scouts would only be able to offer limited coverage, especially as providing the all-round scouting cover needed to provide reliably adequate warning of the enemy's approach would require the allocation of several hundred troopers. To provide an all round scouting screen (at a distance of 20 miles around the main body with a pair of scouts every half-mile) would require the deployment of over 500 scouts. Deploying that screen of scouts would take at least two hours and recalling them would take over four hours. Few Civil War commanders had that number of horsemen to spare. The reality was that the assignment of scouting forces of hundreds of men was not a feasible option for either Royalist or Parliamentarian Army commanders as they did not have enough horsemen; consequently the assigned scouting forces were invariably inadequate to cover the area they were assigned to patrol. It seems reasonable to assume that, when assigning smaller than ideal scouting forces, commanders were accepting the operational risk that they might be disadvantaged by receiving short notice of the enemy's approach. Although targeting scouting patrols to cover specific areas – or lines of approach – likely to be used by an approaching enemy increased the chances of successful interception, this clearly required the commander to have some reliable intelligence about the direction from which the enemy was believed to be advancing in the first place.

From a commander's point of view, the intelligence reports received from scouts had several advantages over reports received from civilian sources. Because scouts tended to operate reasonably close to their own army, their reports were received relatively quickly and therefore provided the commander with a better idea of the location of his opponent. Equally important was the fact that the reports were often more relevant and reliable as the scout's military experience would have made him aware of what he needed to report and how accurately. As reports from civilians would not necessarily have been perceived to have the same level of reliability, it was likely for this reason that Cruso recommended all intelligence-gatherers should have military experience. The thinking was that scouts would recognise the significance of what they saw, and would thus be able to make informed estimates of the fighting capability of the enemy forces. A good example of this form of intelligence was the locating of the Parliamentarian Army by Rupert's troopers before Edgehill, as their report was accurate enough to allow the effective deployment of the Royalist Army at first light.[20]

In addition to scouts, trumpeters also supplied another traditional form of intelligence-gathering. Like the medieval heralds they replaced, trumpeters provided the official communications between opposing army commanders, and also reported on military activity they observed while doing so. Generals selected their trumpeters carefully for these tasks, again advised by Cruso:

> The trumpeter must be discreet and judicious; not only to be fit to deliver embassies and messages as they ought, but (at his return) to report what he hath observed concerning the enemies works and guards, and what he hath further gathered and espied.[21]

Commanders on either side were well acquainted with the trumpeter's unofficial intelligence-gathering role and sometimes deliberately delayed the return of enemy trumpeters so that any intelligence information they had discovered would be reported too late for it to be of any immediate value.[22] Trumpeters were often sent into the opposing camp under the pretext of negotiating the exchange of prisoners – a pretext for their main task of bringing back the most recent information about the enemy's position and strength. Richard Symonds, the Royalist trooper and diarist, described how Fairfax, the Parliamentarian Northern Army general and later the commander of the New Model Army, used trumpeters in this role just before the Battle of Naseby, when 'a trumpet came from Fairfax for exchange of prisoners from Newport Pagnell'.[23]

Another traditional form of intelligence was provided by deserters, mainly because these deserters were well aware that the warmth of their reception was likely to depend upon the value of the information they could offer. Depending upon the rank of the deserter, these reports could be of major significance; for example, when Sir Richard Grenville, an experienced Cornish general and brother to Sir Bevil Grenville, deserted to the King in 1644, he provided the Royalists with full details of a plot to betray the garrison of Basing House along with Waller's plans for the Roundhead invasion of southwest England in the spring.[24] On one of the occasions when Sir John Hurry (or Urry), an experienced Scottish soldier, changed sides (a fairly regular event during the war), he brought details of a Parliamentarian money shipment which, when Rupert set out to intercept it, led to the skirmish at Chalgrove Field and the mortal wounding of John Hampden, John Pym's deputy and right hand man.[25]

Not all information garnered from deserters was important in and of itself, but an intelligence picture is a jigsaw built up from many pieces of different sizes. The importance of the reports varied considerably; Symonds described how the Royalists were able to monitor the growing weakness of the surrounded Parliamentarian forces when two of Essex's men deserted to the Royalists during the Lostwithiel campaign of 1644 'and told us that provisions were very scarce with Essex'.[26] As the war progressed and the difficulties of recruiting soldiers grew, it became an increasingly popular ruse to gain access to the enemy's plans by posing as a deserter and then joining up with the opposite side. As John Hodgson, a Parliamentarian Captain of Horse, recalled in his *Memoirs*: 'We had spies sent out amongst them into [Sir Marmaduke] Langdale's party, pretending to run away from us, and they were coming in continually with intelligence.'[27] This became a well-established and accepted means of gathering intelligence and continued well into the later phases of the conflict. For example, during the Second Civil War in Cornwall in 1648, a Parliamentarian commander suggested that 'a soldier of the Mount ... may pretend to run away to them [the Royalists], and to stay with them till he can learne their strength and resolucions.'[28] Although deserters were a potentially attractive source of trained manpower as the war went on, commanders became increasingly aware of the danger that enemy spies might be masquerading as deserters in order to gain access to military information.

The interrogation of prisoners revealed much useful information, for the questioning of such men could provide key military intelligence. It was soon realised that the personal papers and letters carried by prisoners when they were captured could also provide intelligence about the enemy's plans and problems. In May 1643, the Parliamentarian Committee of Safety had ordered that all prisoners should be searched and any letters and papers thereby found should be examined for possible military intelligence.[29] In his book, Cruso also emphasised the importance of taking prisoners in order to supplement intelligence sources:

> Because the commodotie of spies cannot always be had, some of the enemy must be assayed to be taken, from whom there may be drawn a relation of the estate of the adverse part, and this exploit is called, taking of intelligence, a dutie of great importance ... and also of much travail and danger. In the night they

must approach the enemies armie, assaying to take some Centinell, or some disbanded souldier in some of the houses there about.[30]

It was this very method of intelligence-gathering that had alerted the Royalists to the presence of Essex on the night before the Battle of Edgehill when Prince Rupert's troopers had captured the Parliamentarian quartermasters seeking billets for their army.[31] Likewise Rupert, the King's nephew and dashing cavalry commander, would have been seeking to obtain intelligence of a similar sort when he was alleged to have asked some Parliamentarian soldiers captured just before Marston Moor in 1644, 'Is Cromwell there'?[32] Again, caution was needed as prisoners – like deserters – were not always what they seemed. Sir William Brereton, the commander of Parliamentarian forces in North West England, inserted a spy into Chester to report on the state of the besieged Royalist garrison. His spy was a soldier who was successfully 'captured' and who had thereby gained entry into the city. Of course, the problem about being a spy masquerading as a captive was that it was difficult to communicate any information securely and regularly – a problem which continued to vex both sides throughout the war.[33]

Prisoners could assist intelligence operations in other ways. When the Royalists decided to remove the threat posed by the Parliamentarian garrison of Marlborough to their lines of communications between Oxford and the west of England, Lord Wilmot, the Cavalier commander, was sent with a force to capture the town in December 1642. When this Royalist force approached Marlborough and the soldiers 'were near the town, they apprehended a fellow who confessed upon examination that he was a spy, and was sent by the Governor to bring intelligence of their strength and motion'. Wilmot's reaction was unusual in that he did not immediately execute the spy. Instead he deployed his whole force for the spy's inspection so that the spy could 'return to the town and tell those that had sent him what he had seen that they should do well to treat with the garrison and give them leave to submit to the King'.[34] It would appear that Wilmot had his own ideas as to how to use captured spies to advance his own military objectives, although this idea had also been used by Jean Parisot de la Valette, the Grand Master of the Knights of St John, during the siege of Malta in 1565,[35] and earlier by Publius Cornelius Scipio the Younger when he had captured some of Hannibal's scouts before the Battle of Zama in 202 BC.[36]

Garrisons also provided commanders with another rich source of intelligence information. In addition to gathering supplies and collecting taxes from the people living inside their area of responsibility, garrison commanders were also responsible for collecting and reporting any military intelligence.[37] The presence of garrison troops extended the area under each side's military control and thus increased the chances of either observing enemy movements or intercepting military messengers. The role of the garrison in the context of intelligence-gathering should not be underestimated, even though the deployment of troops in garrisons, rather than the front line, has often been criticised as being a waste of experienced soldiers.[38] Evidently the value of garrisons was recognised by contemporaries; Clarendon records how the Parliamentarians obtained useful intelligence in this way in 1643, noting that they had established 'many garrisons near all the roads, which the most private messengers travelled with great hazard, three being intercepted for one that escaped'.[39] Clearly there were going to be times when troops would be of more value serving in the field armies, but the merit of maintaining a network of garrisons came to be more clearly appreciated as the conflict continued; the combined number of Royalist and Parliamentarian garrisons in 1645 totalled between 150 and 160.

Not only did those garrisons facilitate the collection of the taxes and other resources that funded the fighting, but the troop of horse that each garrison normally contained proved to be invaluable because it extended the area over which the garrison could gather intelligence and supplies from the local people.[40] Brereton received invaluable information throughout the war from his garrison commanders. In his letter of 26 February 1644, he passed on reports received from Captain Henry Stone, the Parliamentarian garrison commander at Eccleshall, as well as information received from Coventry. 'Captain Stone advertises me that 1,500 horse are come to Litchfield' Brereton wrote, 'and a post from Coventry that there are 2,000 horse and foot on their way from the King.'[41] The need to extend the area of control around the garrison was quickly appreciated by commanders of both sides; in 1643 the Royalist garrison commander of Donnington Castle sought 'an allowance of 6 horses to scout, having none but foot in the castle'.[42] The Royalist garrison at Wallingford was also supplemented by a troop of horse in 1644 for the same reason.[43]

The intelligence reports from garrisons also made an early contribution to the conduct of the fighting for it was the Parliamentarian garrison at Warwick, commanded by Captain Bridges, who, having captured part of the Royalist baggage train in October 1642, was able to inform the Committee of Safety not only that the King had left Shrewsbury, but also that the Royalist Army was within a few miles of Coventry and was marching on London.[44] Therefore the greater the area controlled by their garrisons, the greater the amount of intelligence the relevant commanders received. An obvious additional advantage of stationing a troop of horse within each garrison was that it allowed the garrison commander to make speedy reports of any important or unusual events.

In addition to military reports from scouts, trumpeters, deserters and prisoners, Civil War commanders also received valuable information from other individuals who were generally described in contemporary accounts as spies (or 'intelligencers').[45] As the war spread, the demand for military information – and therefore the sources to provide it – had grown to such an extent that it had become increasingly commonplace to use civilians as well as soldiers for intelligence work.[46] Generally, soldiers had been employed as scouts whilst civilians had largely been employed as spies.[47] But the demand for spies (and the messengers who carried their information) allowed for no social distinctions, and people of all ages and both sexes were recruited.[48] There is evidence that Cruso's advice to infiltrate spies into the 'domesticall service of the chief officers of the enemie' was followed by the Parliamentarian commanders from the very beginning of the war.[49] When the Royalist cavalry captured some of the baggage of the Earl of Essex a few days after the Battle of Edgehill, they discovered a number of intelligence reports written by a certain Mr Blake.[50] As Warburton has observed in his *Memoirs of Prince Rupert*, Blake was well placed to do harm to the Royalist cause as he was Rupert's personal secretary and had thus been acquainted with every movement of the Royalist Army. It was alleged that Blake 'immediately transferred intelligence thereof to Parliament: for this service he received the large sum (for that time) of £50 a-week.'[51] Blake was arrested immediately, and subsequently tried and executed at Oxford. Spies at the most senior levels seem to have presented a number of problems for the Royalists; towards the end of the war, the King's Secretary of State, Sir Edward Nicholas, warned of a 'colonel who is sheriff of some shire that sends intelligence to the rebels'.[52]

For some of the more conservative English commanders – a conservatism shown by a number of both Royalist and Parliamentarian generals – spying was viewed with a disdain bordering on contempt. A fundamental distrust of espionage proved to be deep-rooted in those traditional commanders and this fact had an important effect upon the outcome of the conflict. For example, as Clarendon reported, Falkland, Charles I's Secretary of State, considered that spies 'must be void of all ingenuity and common honesty, before they could be of use; and afterwards they could never be fit to be credited'.[53] As the military historian Peter Gudgin has well observed, it is only comparatively recently that the aversion to something as untrustworthy and unsporting as spying on one's enemies has been overcome for 'intelligence has always been associated with spies, traitors and informers ... [and is seen as] ... something dishonourable, disloyal and dishonest.'[54] Opening somebody else's letters also came into this category and thus made using intelligence information far less palatable to many of the more traditional leaders on either side.[55] Falkland was not alone in holding these reservations for the Earl of Essex also expressed concerns about the reliability of intelligence information. As late as 1644, Essex stated that 'scouts are useful to prepare officers and men for the worst but well grounded intelligence is to be obtained only from a party of the army commander by one whom we may confide in.'[56] This statement suggests that Essex was not entirely persuaded by the intelligence he received, and that he would only believe reports which came from individuals whom he himself personally knew and trusted. It would certainly appear from this remark that both the Parliamentarian Essex and the Royalist Falkland (who was killed at the First Battle of Newbury) shared reservations about the credibility of intelligence from spies – or from sources that were not personally known to them.[57] If this was indeed the case, such reservations would undoubtedly have limited the amount of intelligence information that they were prepared to act upon.

The fact that intelligence-gathering was actively encouraged and engaged in by the young Prince Rupert had not reassured many of the more conservative English officers who considered Rupert's ruthless determination, and the personal attention he was devoting to intelligence-work to be profoundly at odds with their own more traditional approach to warfare.[58] Indeed the military conduct of some of the early Parliamentarian commanders, such as Essex and Manchester, indicates that these sentiments were common to both sides during the first years of the conflict. However, as the war progressed, a new breed of 'amateur' civilian-soldier Parliamentarian commanders – such as Cromwell, Fleetwood, Ireton, Brereton and Pride – emerged as an integral part of the New Model Army.[59] These more pragmatic and businesslike Parliamentarians had few preconceived ideas about how wars should be conducted and were quick to appreciate that the gathering of intelligence was of critical importance to victory. Learning swiftly from their mistakes, and appointed for their military skills rather than for their social standing,[60] this new breed of Parliamentarian leaders soon enjoyed the benefits that superior intelligence brought to their military operations. It is more difficult to discern a change of attitude towards intelligence-gathering among the Royalist commanders. Certainly the appointment of more experienced military officers in place of the land-owning gentry as commanders of the Royalist forces had led to some improvement, but these were relatively isolated cases.[61]

Whatever the social implications of using 'intelligencers' may have been, there were many examples of individual spies being sent into the enemy camps to obtain military information. For example, the Marquis of Winchester (a Royalist commander who seemingly appreciated the merits of intelligence-gathering) 'sent Tobias Beasely to spy in London, where before the war he had been a porter at the Ram Inn, Smithfield'.[62] Age was no barrier for intelligence operations. In his *Memoirs*, Edmund Ludlow, the Parliamentarian commander, described how the Royalist besiegers of Wardour Castle had despatched a twelve-year-old boy to obtain some menial work in the castle kitchens as a cover for his real objectives which was to sabotage the castle's artillery, ascertain the strength of the garrison, poison the water supply and the beer, and blow up the ammunition.[63] And all this for a payment of half a crown!

An important contribution towards our understanding of Civil War intelligence has been made by William Lilley, the astrologer, who claimed to know the extent of the Parliamentarian espionage system in Oxford. Lilley was known to several senior Parliamentarian figures and appears to have contributed his astrological skills to the deliberations of some of the Roundhead commanders during the conflict.[64] When Lilley published his *History of his Life and Times*, his account contained some particularly interesting personal observations on the practical conduct of spying operations in the city. He claimed that 'Parliament had in its continual pay one Colonel of the King's Council of War [along with] another ten other officers and other ranks.'[65] As we shall see later in this chapter, Lilley's detailed description of just how intelligence information was transmitted provides a fascinating insight into the development of intelligence-gathering skills and techniques.

As the war progressed, the need to counter the enemy's intelligence operations became an important military task. Once again, seventeenth-century commanders could well have referred to Cruso for a basic description of counter-espionage responsibilities.

> The best and principal means for a Commander to avoid divers inconveniences, and to effect many worthy designes, are, First to be sure to keep his own deliberations and resolutions secret. Secondly, to penetrate the designes and intentions of the enemie. For which purpose it behoveth him to have good spies, which must be exceeding well rewarded, that so they may be readier to expose themselves to all dangers. The best and most assured spies are ones own soldiers, which (feigning some discontent for want of pay or otherwise) enter into the enemies service, and get themselves into the Cavallrie, as having the best opportunitie (whether in the field or in garrison) to give information.[66]

Such was the fear of communal betrayal aroused by accusations of spying that the reaction of the local populace to anyone suspected of being an intelligencer was often violent. As described above, Tobias Beasely was expected to find out about plans for attacking Basing House, but instead he was caught, condemned as a spy and hanged at Smithfield. Trials were usually conducted under a form of court martial and treatment of suspected spies was harsh; the use of force to extract information was reported with increasing frequency as the war progressed. Indeed, in 1645 the catechism which laid down the rules for the conduct of the Royalist soldiers stated that 'torments were permissible in interrogation'.[67] Parliamentarian news pamphlets contained frequent allegations of the illegal use of torture by Royalists;[68] Bulstrode Whitelocke, the Parliamentarian lawyer, reported how another spy 'taken by the Parliament soldiers at Reading, was tortured into confession by having lighted matches put to his fingers'.[69] Likewise, the Cavalier publication, *Mercurius Rusticus*, also listed examples of Parliamentarian coercion and torture.[70] As reported by the latter, the use of force included threats to females and children. In May 1643, it was reported that during a search of the house of the Royalist supporter, Sir John Lucas, Parliamentarian soldiers had 'put a sword to her [Lady Lucas'] breast, requiring her to tell them where the Armes and Cavaliers were'.[71] Further reports described how troopers of the Earl of Stamford, the Parliamentarian commander, seeking a man in Bridestowe in Devonshire, took his son 'aged about 10 or 11 years old… hanged him up… [and]

pricked him with their swords in the back and thighs' in order to extract information.[72] That particular child survived, but it was reported that Parliamentarian soldiers were prepared to 'seeke after [the hunted man's] children and threaten to kill them if they can find them'.[73]

Both sides were well aware of the dangers posed by spies and were determined to seek them out and prosecute them.[74] The Parliamentary authorities repeatedly demanded the disruption and interception of Royalist intelligence operations by ordering the deployment of boats to patrol the Thames to intercept any Royalist scouting or espionage missions.[75] Scoutmaster-General Luke's agents were either luckier than most, or better prepared, as the contemporary accounts suggest that only one of his spies was executed: one Francis Coles who, in January 1644, was tried and hanged in Oxford. The evidence suggests that Coles had drawn particular attention to himself by travelling in and out of the city on several occasions over the Christmas period in order to report on events.[76] Understandably, the fear of betrayal from within the community was intense and often resulted in harsh and arbitrary punishments. Seventeenth-century publications contained numerous, almost casual, references to the execution and torture of people condemned as spies; for example, in his account of the movements of the Royalist Army, Symons records 'Nothing of any moment done all this day. A spy hanged.'[77] The punishments for captured spies clearly varied – and for no discernible reason. When the Parliamentarian City Council in Gloucester considered the case of one William Garrett, he 'was duly fined forty shillings, in October 1643, he being taken for a spy'.[78] However, most suspected spies met the same fate as Tobias Beasely and were hanged.

Further evidence of the range of counter-intelligence operations which were being conducted during this period is provided by the accounts of the killing of the Roundhead Captain George Bulmer (or Bullman) in the central Thames Valley area in 1643. Variously described as a 'scout' or, by Royalist sources, as 'one of the Scoutmasters of the Rebel army', Bulmer, who led a team of '16 associates', had attracted a reputation as a successful scoutmaster who had 'robbed more passengers, rifled more carriers and intercepted more letters than all the villains in the pack'. On 8 May, the Royalist journal *Mercurius Aulicus* reported that traffic to London was

> ... being continually hindered by one Bullman [sic], one of the enemies [sic] scouts, who doth watch us on all sides, that hardly any intelligence to or from London can escape him, in so much that we have thought sometime to send out a party to take him, or otherwise to prevent him.[79]

Bulmer was clearly considered to pose a significant threat to Royalist operations for it was decided that drastic action was needed. The evidence of the contemporary accounts reveals how Bulmer became the 'target' of a Royalist assassination squad and he was waylaid by a party of scouts led by Lord Taafe.[80] Bulmer was reportedly engaged upon 'a design to give an alarm to His Majesty's quarters' when he was intercepted and shot at Whateley Bridge.[81] A Parliamentary news pamphlet suggested that Taafe had set out to entrap Bulmer by pretending to be 'for the King and Parliament' and that 'Lord Taafe and Bulmer were on a Parley' when Taafe 'very treacherously drew a pistol out of his pocket and shot him.'[82]

The bravery and determination of those who engaged in spying was remarkable. Many were clearly strongly committed to their beliefs and were prepared to act in support of them even though the work was dangerous and the rewards minimal. As has already been explained, spying was generally perceived to be an underhand and ungentlemanly occupation, thought of in terms of treachery towards the opposing side rather than loyalty to the spy's true masters. Potential spies would have had to have a wide range of skills and a great deal of luck. In order to survive, a successful spy would have needed to possess a remarkable combination of imagination, intellect, numeracy, literacy, powers of observation and courage. As if this was not sufficiently demanding, to be successful, the spy would also have required physical mobility, intellectual persistence and loyalty in abundance.

What sort of people became spies during the 1640s? It seems probable that potential agents would have had to have received some sort of education in order to acquire not only the necessary numeracy and literacy skills, but also the expertise needed to assess the military significance of their observations. They would have needed a high level of personal commitment to the cause they supported and this would also have required them to possess a degree of political awareness. Most spies would have expected to benefit in some way if their side were victorious – and the illiterate and penniless poor of English society would certainly have expected financial reward for their information. Clearly the more well-connected spies would have needed to carefully balance personal benefit against the risks they took. The fact that spying was treated with disdain by many members of the gentry would have deterred most of them from becoming intelligencers as they saw the spy's breach of personal and professional honour as an affront to social norms.[83] Indeed when the Royalist soldier, Major Adrian Scrope, was suspected of being a spy in 1644, his defence was that, as a gentleman, he could not possibly have been involved with 'a thing soe contrary to the rule of warre or the profession of a gentleman.'[84] The fact that, even at this stage of the war, Scrope still apparently believed that spying was contrary to the 'profession of a gentleman' tells us much about Royalist attitudes towards intelligence operations.

It would appear, therefore, that the social group most likely to have become actively involved with such covert operations were the members of the 'middle sort' as the historian, Brian Manning, has described them. Manning estimated that 30–40 per cent of the non-gentry fell into this category which included yeoman farmers, substantial tradesmen, land-holding peasants (husbandmen) and self-employed craftsmen.[85] These were the sort of people who acted as spies for both sides as they had not only a reasonable level of education (they could read, write, count and ride), but also often possessed a strong commitment to the cause, whether Royalist or rebel. The increasing suspicion that 'neutral' professional people were somehow involved in spying roused widespread resentment as the Civil War progressed. Even the surgeons who moved between the armies tending to wounded and injured soldiers became prey to suspicion and occasionally they were refused permission to perform their duties because they were suspected of using their trade as a cover for espionage.[86] Thus, in 1644, the Royalist Governor of Pontefract Castle, Richard Lowther, refused an offer of medical support from Lord Fairfax, the commander of the Parliamentarian Northern Army, writing:

> For your chirurgeon I cannot admit of him; but if the medicaments be sent, I shall join my own surgeons with one of your party, a prisoner here, to use the best of their art in the cure of the poor wounded soldiers.[87]

A civil war made it easier for many people to take an active and open role in the conflict as it brought the war to their very doorstep. But if they were in a minority, or if they were a member of a social group not normally expected to take a side in such a conflict, then the options open to them to demonstrate their support became more limited. Women, in particular, did not have many opportunities to participate in an independent role and so it is hardly surprising that some of them seized on whatever chances presented themselves. Nursing the sick and wounded and assisting during sieges were important tasks in which many seventeenth-century women actively participated. But the worlds of espionage and intelligence-gathering were new and offered far more challenging roles – especially if, for whatever reason, an individual was not able to play an overtly active role in the conflict.[88]

As the war expanded across the country, intelligence reports increasingly came in from civilians and it was not just 'professional' intelligencers who provided information. For example, Luke recounted how 'a woman going milking gave intelligence to Sir William Waller [commander of the Parliamentarian forces in the southwest] of the strength of Oxford, and the fittest time to come against it.'[89] Sometimes prominent figures in isolated communities formed *ad hoc* teams which would gather and report intelligence. The work of the local people in the Forest of Dean in Gloucestershire provides a reminder of how blurred the distinction between soldier and civilian could become in the world of Civil War espionage. Here the Royalist 'Edward Clarke of Newent gathered together a team of messengers and spies, including cloth carriers' so that he could 'provide information on the movement of enemy forces and the location of parliamentary sympathisers suitable for plundering.'[90] Sir George Gresley, the Derbyshire landowner and Parliamentarian supporter, similarly provided Brereton with intelligence information, while the Parliamentarian garrison commander of Dartmouth, Colonel Edward Seymour, received regular reports from his friends and neighbours.[91]

In a friendly environment, army commanders could expect intelligence and support from the local people, such as that which Charles I enjoyed when he surrounded Essex at Lostwithiel in Cornwall in 1644. Of course the opposite was more often the case when armies deployed into areas which were unfriendly towards them. Royalist forces encountered problems gathering information from the local people in Berkshire in late 1644, just as the Parliamentarians had encountered problems with the Cornish people during the summer of that year. A letter from Essex, written when his army invaded Cornwall in 1644, revealed the extent to which a hostile populace could effectively isolate intruders: 'Intelligence we have none, the country people being violently against us, if any of our scouts or soldiers fall into their hands, they are more bloody that the enemy.'[92] This sort of pro-Royalist activity by the local populace was not confined to Cornwall. 'Monmouth was retaken by the Royalists in 1644,' according to one observer, 'largely because some of Lord Herbert's tenants kept him informed of the movements of the Parliamentary garrison.'[93] Brereton's letters also contain several similar examples of reports from local people which reveal that, by 1645, Parliamentarian commanders were also being provided with regular reports of intelligence activity which influenced military operations in their area.[94]

As has been shown in the work of the historians Mark Stoyle and others, there were few totally Royalist or Parliamentarian towns or villages.[95] Their research indicates that there are very real dangers in believing that any part of England was completely loyal to either side. Stoyle's detailed analyses show clearly that every area was likely to contain people who supported both factions, and how it was therefore perfectly feasible for commanders on either side to receive intelligence information from the local populace which included supporters of both factions.[96] If the opposing faction was in the ascendancy, the wise man kept his own counsel and waited for the pendulum of fate to bring the faction which he supported back to power. Thus in each and every part of the country there were supporters of either side waiting for the wheel of fortune to allow them to openly declare their true loyalty. It was these people who maintained a correspondence with friends in other parts of the country; and who used this correspondence to pass on any information which they thought might be useful. Even this activity could be dangerous as *agents provocateur* were sometimes used to entrap the unwary. Thus a Parliamentary sympathiser in the Royalist West Country, one Edward Laurence, was trapped by a young boy, Robert Buncombe, who took the letters entrusted to him to deliver, not to the Parliamentary garrison of Plymouth as he had agreed with Laurence, but straight to the Royalist authorities in Exeter.[97]

Much as the loyalties of the common people might ebb and flow with the tide, controlling spies was not without its problems as it was always possible that a spy, however dedicated, might change allegiance if he or she found the grass to be greener on the other side. Bulstrode Whitelocke reported one such example when the Parliamentarian supporter 'the Marquis of Argyll sent into the Army of Montrose [the Royalist commander] some scouts and spies who at first dealt faithfully with him, but afterwards betrayed him, and sent him intelligence that Montrose was distant from him whereas they were near his forces.'[98] Clearly it was possible for Parliamentarian supporters to operate in predominantly Royalist areas, such as Cornwall, just as Royalist supporters could operate in predominantly Parliamentarian areas such as London. These divided loyalties justify the conclusion that there was no lack of potential spies for either side anywhere in the country.

The use of double agents was advocated by Cruso. However, it was evident that the role of the double agent could not be just confined to the ranks of the military.

> There are also spies which are called double, which must be men of great fidelity. These (to gain credit with the enemie) must sometimes give him true information of what passeth to the other side; but of such things, and at such times, as they may do no hurt. But these kinde of spies cannot continue long without being discovered. If it be possible, such spies must be had as are entertained into domesticall service of the chief officers of the enemy, the better to know their intentions and designes.[99]

It is difficult to find any specific evidence of the use of double agents, although Sir John Hurry (see above) changed sides so often that his status in the latter stages of the war came close. The Royalist garrison commander, Colonel Richard Fielding, who was court-martialled by Charles I for surrendering the garrison and town of Reading to Essex in May 1643, employed one of his female spies 'to good effect' as a double agent as he considered 'the advantage he received was greater than she could carry to the enemy.'[100]

The importance of carrying intelligence information quickly, safely and reliably was soon recognised. As commercial, legal and social communications were maintained throughout the war, so carriers, merchants and messengers were able to travel despite the fighting. However, the life of a traveller was not easy as there was no clear boundary between military and civilian enterprise and all messengers were frequently searched. The use of inns for messengers to meet and exchange information was soon recognised; for example in his *Journal*, Luke records how 'the Beard at Newbury is an inne that commonly harbours [those who] receive intelligence and carrye it to Oxford.'[101] The realisation that inns were being used by messengers for this purpose probably led to an incident in July 1643, when a Mr James Butler described how 'the messenger, that carried this letter, having the Prince's pass, was made drunk at Bostal House, this letter was opened, a copy taken, sealed up again and put in his pocket.'[102] As both sides realised the importance of intercepting their opponents' communications, messengers who were unable to establish their *bona fides* were regarded as spies and were often tortured to reveal their messages. Torture was used regardless of sex or occupation, and as the war progressed, the use of force to extract information became more commonplace.[103] Thus the Parliamentary commander, Colonel Birch, described how a woman suspected of carrying messages during the siege of Lathom House

> ... was at length taken and put to the torture [by the Parliamentarians], but she would reveal nothing, and suffered three fingers on both hands to be burnt off before her tormentors, tired out by her invincible fortitude, at length desisted.[104]

Similarly, when Dr William Cox, the Royalist supporter and prebendary of Exeter, was arrested by Parliamentarian forces on suspicion of carrying messages, he was so mistreated that he never fully recovered.[105] The bravery and determination of many of the messengers reflected the passionate commitment that the Civil Wars aroused. For those who could not play an active military or overt supporting role, carrying messages was one of the few alternatives, and the individual courage, particularly of the female participants in this dangerous occupation, proved remarkable. Although their commitment was only occasionally recognised in contemporary accounts, the importance of the contribution they made was reflected by the payment they received. In 1644, messengers were being paid £2 a week which compared favourably with the pay of some army officers.[106] They were clearly worth this level of remuneration, as they often coped with extreme difficulty and danger with great courage and faced the same penalties as the spies themselves. As Richard Symonds noted in his diary on 2 August 1644, 'This day a fellow that was carrying letters for Essex was taken and hanged at the rendezvous.'[107] Often female and alone, with only their wits to protect them from the challenges of hostile sentries, such individuals undertook long and arduous journeys with messages cunningly concealed in their hair or next to their skin.

Some of the methods that were used to conceal messages carried between Raglan and Denbigh Castles included hollow staffs, the heels of shoes and trusses of linen tied next to the body. 'Scotch Nan', who had carried messages between the King and the Marquis of Montrose, used similar devices for hiding missives.[108] Concealing missives was important in case of searches by enemy patrols and one Parliamentarian messenger, Samuel Taylor, had important papers 'sewn into his sleeves' in the hope that they would thereby avoid detection.[109] Royalist messengers employed similar ruses; when Goring was besieged in Portsmouth at the start of the conflict, his messages to the Parliamentarian general, the Marquis of Hertford, were concealed in 'false heels, coat-linings and even the head of a dummy baby'.[110] In September 1642, the Royalist Lord Capel's messenger, 'one Bushell' was found to have 'letters sowed betweene the garter and stocking'.[111] The rich variety and ingenuity of these methods of concealment suggests that the carrying of confidential messages was a major activity during the conflict. Pamphlets and private letters were also carried covertly in addition to purely military communications. It is therefore hardly surprising that both sides tried their utmost to disrupt this means of communication – and to learn as much as they could from any intercepted messages.

Methods of passing messages through the enemy lines became increasingly sophisticated as the war progressed and experience grew. Lilley describes in fascinating detail how letters from Parliamentarian spies in Oxford were passed through the Royalist guards of the city to Luke, the Parliamentarian Scoutmaster-General based at Newport Pagnell. Lilley notes that the spy's message was 'posted' at night through the windows of certain houses in Oxford. The act of 'posting' the letter was masked by the spy urinating against the wall of the house. Once 'posted', these messages were then carried out of Oxford the next morning by messengers 'in the habit of Town-Gardners'. The difficulty of getting the messages past the city guards was overcome by using as messengers people who normally came in and out of the city every day about their lawful business, and who would have therefore been familiar to the guards – and therefore less likely to be searched. These 'Town-Gardner' messengers duly left their missives 'two miles off' in previously agreed places outside the city. Messages were normally placed in holes in ditches from whence they were collected and taken to Luke by troopers from his garrison at Newport Pagnell.[112]

As the significance of intelligence information increased, so more effort was devoted to the interception of intelligence reports. Notwithstanding the precautions which were taken to conceal messages, carrying any letter made the messenger liable to arrest by sentries; thus virtually any documents passed on by messengers were vulnerable to interception and might end up being read by the enemy. Whilst it is not possible to be precise about the number of letters that were read, as most contemporary accounts make frequent mention of the interception of letters, the amount of intelligence that was thereby derived was clearly considerable.[113] Not all of this information was militarily significant of course, but most messages would have contained material that was helpful to the interceptors. Brereton learnt a good deal about the conditions inside Chester from intercepted mail.[114] This was partly due to the fact that important messages were often duplicated and therefore the chances of one copy being intercepted were statistically greater. If the intercepted letter could be read, because it was not protected by a code, then much information could be obtained. The most dramatic example of militarily significant information being obtained in such a way must surely be the interception by the Parliamentarian Scoutmaster-General Watson of the Royalist General Goring's letter to the King just before the Battle of Naseby.[115] Military information vital to the Royalist cause was thus made available to Fairfax at a critical moment in the campaign; the outcome of the subsequent battle effectively won the war for Parliament.

At an early stage of the conflict it was realised that, just as reliable military communications were essential to the efficient management of one's own army, so disrupting the enemy's communications and reading his messages would be equally advantageous. This disruption of the flow of hostile information, would hinder the command and control of the opposing army. In addition, reading intercepted letters would provide useful intelligence about the plans of one's opponents. Capturing enemy correspondence was just as rewarding, as the Parliamentarian commanders found after the Battle of Naseby when the King's cabinet was captured and opened for all to read. But the interception of messages and the capture of mail also allowed the captor to identify (and then capitalise upon) the true allegiance of local worthies. For example, after the skirmish at Sourton Down, when the papers of the Royalist general and commander of the Royalist Western Army, Sir Ralph Hopton, were captured, his opponent, the Parliamentarian commander, the Earl of Stamford, declared that the identification of the Royalist supporters listed therein allowed 'the sequestrations to be levied on such evidence would be worth £40,000 to the Roundhead cause'.[116]

Both sides recognised the need to capture enemy spies and messengers in order to prevent them from passing on their information. This was reflected in the periodic instructions from the Parliamentarian Committee of Safety emphasising the importance of detaining spies and messengers. For example, in January 1643, the Lord Mayor of London was tasked to search water traffic on the Thames bound for Reading in order to ensure that 'no victuals, arms, powder, ammunition or letters of intelligence may be conveyed to the King's army'.[117] Attempts to capture messengers were not always successful. Luke reported how, on 31 May 1644, an order was given to all the sentinels near Newport Pagnell to allow no woman or others to come out of the town, but to interrogate them and send them in again. Yet, as Luke went on ruefully to admit, 'a woman that came to sell provision at the Town, being well horsed, rode full gallop into the City, and the guards shot at her but missed her.'[118]

Nobody was safe from having their letters intercepted and the fact that mail was being tampered with soon became common knowledge; in January 1643, Elizabeth, Queen of Bohemia and sister to the King, wrote to Sir Thomas Roe, the ambassador in the Low Countries, explaining that 'when you think how subject's letters are to be opened, you will not wonder you hear no oftener from me.'[119] A month later, on 23 February 1643, that vacillating nobleman, Lord Saville, wrote a letter to his friend, Lady Temple, in which he said that 'all letters are now opened, so I am glad to disguise my hand, neither with superscription nor subscription. The bearer will know to whom to deliver it and you will easily guess from whom it comes.'[120] Whilst using servants to deliver messages personally may well have provided security for those who could afford the staff, for the majority of people whose only means of communication was the postal services, their letters were increasingly vulnerable to interception and analysis. References

to this form of intelligence-gathering appeared with increasing frequency in contemporary sources; a letter from the Committee to the Earl of Essex described
how the Parliamentarians 'had obtained a packet of intercepted letters from
Exeter to Oxford wherein the condition of Lyme and the state of the West is fully
discovered'.[121] The increasing risk of mail interception led to the use of verbal
messages; Sir John Meldrum, the experienced soldier and Parliamentarian commander, wrote to his general, the Earl of Denbigh, that 'some things concerning
the state of this county not fit to be committed to paper for fear of interception,
I have communicated to the bearer, whom you may credit.'[122] One cannot help
but feel nervous for the personal safety of any messenger apprehended with that
particular message in their possession! The interception of mail was followed by
attempts to decipher the contents; contemporary accounts contain increasing
references to 'intercepted coded letters which shall be sent if they can be got
deciphered,'[123] and to the increasing use of ciphers to protect information.[124] On
19 February, Parliament appointed one George Weckherlin, Secretary for Foreign
Affairs, to be preparer of ciphers and to administer an oath of secrecy to those
with access to intelligence information.[125]

Because frequently all – or at least part – of intelligence reports were protected
by some form of code, breaking the enemy's codes and ciphers rapidly grew in
importance. Thus, intercepting the letter was only the first part of the process of
extracting intelligence. Because both sides used codes and ciphers, these codes
had to be broken if any intelligence was to be obtained from an intercepted
letter. Codes and ciphers had been available since Roman times so their use was
a widely understood process, albeit a lengthy and painstaking one. The codes
used were numerical substitutions for words most often used with individual
alphabetical-numerical substitutions available as a last resort. Examination of surviving codes has revealed that they must have been cumbersome to use as their
vocabulary was surprisingly limited and of little relevance to the average military
commander.[126] It is therefore hardly surprising that they were unpopular to use
because encoding and decoding would have been such a time-consuming and
tedious business. The effective use of codes required a degree of self-discipline
that was not always maintained. The complaint of the Royalist officer, Richard
Cave, to Prince Rupert that 'I have not time to write in cipher, if I had I would
say more,' was a common problem for busy senior commanders and their hard-
pressed staff – if indeed they had a staff at all.[127] Coding (and decoding) was very
rudimentary and this led to delays and frustration. Sometimes messages could
not be deciphered by their intended recipients; moreover some commanders
(most noticeably the Royalist General Goring) considered that the urgency and
importance of such messages should not be delayed by the encoding process. In
1644 Goring was clearly unable to determine what he was required to do when
he received a message from the Royalist commander in the North, the Marquis
(and later Duke) of Newcastle in an unknown code.[128] As Sir William Brereton

also complained that 'the cipher sent by the last express I cannot understand or make any use thereof,' it would appear that these difficulties were experienced by both sides.[129] It is therefore hardly surprising that the encoding of messages was inconsistent.

In the early stages of the war these codes were normally adequate to ensure the protection of sensitive material. However, one evening in late 1642, Dr John Wallis, the chaplain to Lady Vere, a prominent Parliamentarian supporter, was shown a coded letter 'found after the capture of Chichester' from the Royalists. Working on it casually after supper, Wallis managed to decode it within a couple of hours. So began the formation of the Parliamentarian code-breaking team which, by 1643, was being used regularly to decode Royalist letters. In June 1644, the Parliamentarian Committee of Both Kingdoms (which had replaced the Committee of Safety when the Scots entered the war) sent intercepted mail to the code-breaking team to see 'if they can be got deciphered'.[130] Soon afterwards an intercepted letter to Rupert from the Royalist, Sir Fulke Huncks, was successfully 'unciphered'.[131] Understandably Wallis's skill as a code breaker was kept a closely guarded secret, both during and after the conflict. Wallis was a mathematician by inclination and his work *Arithmetica Infinitorum* introduced concepts and ideas that Sir Isaac Newton subsequently developed. Deciphering was used during the Interregnum and, after the Restoration, Wallis was retained as a code breaker by Charles II and later by William and Mary.[132] Yet today the name of John Wallis remains largely unknown.[133] Wallis's talents greatly assisted Parliament from late 1642 onwards and allowed Royalist messages to be decoded and read much more easily. Whilst it is difficult to assess with any degree of precision just how much decoded information was thereby made available to Parliamentarian commanders, the experience gained during the Civil War evidently made its mark on Oliver Cromwell because, when he was Protector, he authorised his Secretary of State, John Thurloe, to systematically open letters placed in the 'Generall Post Office'. In an adjoining office sat Isaac Dorislaus, an advocate to the Parliamentarian Army during the Civil War, of whom it was said that 'scarcely a letter be brought him but he knew the hand that wrote it.'[134] It was the job of Dorislaus to identify the letters of interest so that they might be opened and inspected.

The growing numbers of news pamphlets also provided a new source of potential intelligence information. Public demand for accurate information about the political and military situation grew rapidly as the Civil War spread. In January 1643, Charles decided to establish a Royalist news pamphlet, *Mercurius Aulicus*, to promulgate information from a Cavalier perspective. This decision did indirectly benefit Royalist intelligence-gathering because the pamphlet's 'intelligencers' also provided valuable military information.[135] Consequently the editors of these pamphlets – of whom the Royalist Sir John Berkenhead and the Parliamentarian Nedham Marchmont were probably the best known –

established their own intelligence-gathering organisations to satisfy the public demand for reports on the military situation. Berkenhead was a most successful publisher and his *Mercurius Aulicus* combined the sharpest wit with the latest news to such good effect that it became widely credited by both sides.[136] Luke used to read it and made several references in his letters that showed how valuable an asset *Mercurius Aulicus* was to the King.[137] Parliament soon recognised the need for their own 'official' news pamphlet to counter the popular demand for *Aulicus* and so *Mercurius Britannicus* began to be published from early 1643.

It was quickly appreciated by the Royalists that the information Berkenhead's team of 'intelligencers' had obtained for *Aulicus* was of equal interest to the military intelligence-gatherers. Berkenhead was therefore appointed as a member of the Royalist Council of War in order that his information could be used to best effect by the King's commanders. Both sides had realised that the 'integrity of their reporting was critical to their reputation' and, just as Berkenhead attended the Royalist Council of War, so too were Captain Audley and Nedham Marchmont, the first editors of the Parliamentarian equivalent, *Mercurius Britanicus*, invited to attend meetings of the Parliamentarian equivalent, the Committee of Both Kingdoms, 'where he [Captain Audley] took notes'.[138] To the soldiers and civilians on either side, Marchmont and Berkenhead's 'intelligencers' were indistinguishable from their military counterparts. Similarly no real distinction can be made between the spies who brought Berkenhead and Marchmont their information and the messengers, normally women, who carried copies of either *Mercurius Aulicus* or *Mercurius Britanicus* to London or Oxford for sale. If captured, all were viewed as spies and treated as such.

In order to derive the maximum benefit from any intelligence information that was received, it was essential that all new intelligence reports be evaluated to check their accuracy and their consistency with any other available information before being passed on to other commanders. Initially, there was little evidence that the evaluation of information was carried out thoroughly by either side during the early stages of the Civil War, even though the proven dangers of reacting to deliberately placed misinformation were generally recognised.[139] But, as the war progressed, the evaluation and cross-checking of information became more thorough, at least by the Parliamentarians. The letters of Luke and Brereton reveal that these two senior Parliamentarian commanders not only appreciated the importance of accurate intelligence, but also attempted to analyse and validate the information that they received in order to construct a more comprehensive picture that forecast the Royalists' military plans.[140] Indeed, during 1644 and 1645, Brereton's letters contained some notable examples of well-reasoned and factually sound analysis of Royalist movements and intentions in his area of interest around Cheshire. For example, in 1645 Brereton not only identified the growing threat posed to Chester by the Royalist Army as it moved north, but also coordinated the local Parliamentarian defensive posture. Following the relief of

Chester, Brereton reported the movements of the Royalist Army as it directed its march towards the east – and to the field of Naseby.[141]

Later in the war, there is evidence that the members of the Committee of Both Kingdoms also analysed and correlated the intelligence that they had received; consequently there are numerous intelligence summaries contained in the Calendar of State Papers Domestic,[142] in addition to the reports in Brereton's letters.[143] The Naseby campaign provides a particularly good example of this coordination of intelligence and military operations, as the Parliamentarian intelligence organisation was accurately tracking, reporting and predicting the movements of the Royalist Army for a month before the battle. The accuracy of these reports allowed Fairfax to lead his entire army undetected to within a day's march of the Royalist forces before the latter realised where the Roundhead forces were.[144] The Committee of Both Kingdoms' assessments had the advantage of bringing together intelligence from all local and national sources. Although this provided a large amount of information, the wide scope of these varied reports meant that a great deal of correlation was necessary in order to resolve the inevitable degree of contradiction contained in the reports.

Possessing accurate intelligence was valueless unless that information could be regularly exchanged with the commanders who needed to act upon it. Thus intelligence information was passed upwards to the senior leaders as well as downwards to the relevant subordinate commanders. Parliament's committees appear to have been well supplied by their subordinate commanders for, just as Luke had been thanked for his intelligence support before the Battle of Cropredy Bridge, so Brereton was commended for his weekly reports of intelligence activity to the Committee of Both Kingdoms in 1644.[145] Brereton also wrote regularly to the other Parliamentarian Army commanders and to his subordinates; this was not only to keep them informed of developments, but also to recommend concerted military action of the sort which the available intelligence information suggested might be possible. The Parliamentarian commanders also received regular appraisals of the intelligence situation in their area from London – initially from the Committee of Safety, later from the Committee of Both Kingdoms. These reports came mainly in the form of forecasts of troop movements along with any other information which might be relevant to their decisions.[146]

It seems reasonable to suggest that the evidence of this chapter has indicated that, contrary to the belief of many subsequent historians, there was an abundance of sources of intelligence available to each side during the English Civil War.[147] Whilst intelligence information was being collected from both traditional and new kinds of sources, more secure means of communication were being put in place to ensure a rapid exchange of intelligence between commanders. Considerable imagination and commendable bravery was demonstrated by the seventeenth-century intelligence-gatherers and messengers who faced the severest penalties if caught. Analysis of these sources has indicated that there were a number of significant intelligence operations conducted by each side, with varying degrees of skill and sophistication, throughout the war. A great deal of evidence has also been uncovered which suggests that both sides grew to appreciate the benefits of an effective intelligence organisation and accordingly made increasing use of counter-intelligence operations. The Bullman affair not only reveals that intelligence-gathering could be a ruthless and bloody business, but it also indicates that commanders on both sides were determined to obtain the intelligence information they needed – and protect it from interception. Whilst these intelligence operations may not have been very effective when the conflict began, there is much evidence to show how significantly intelligence-gathering improved during the war. When the intelligence-gathering organisation of one side was less effective than that of the other, the military consequences were immediately damaging for the less well informed party – sometimes seriously so. The next top of discussion is therefore how these intelligence-gathering operations were integrated into the command structure of each side (which must have had an impact on their relative success), and to consider the operational role of the scoutmaster and its development as the war progressed.

Notes

1　J. Cruso, *Militarie Instructions for the Cavallrie* (Cambridge, 1632), Part II, Chapter IV, pp.58–60.
2　The National Archives, Commonwealth Exchequer Papers, SP 28/23, f.8.
3　Bedford had been deputy scoutmaster to Sir Samuel Luke.
4　*CSPD, 1645*, p.583.
5　Cruso, *Militarie Instructions*, Part I, Chapter III, p.6.
6　Cruso, *Militarie Instructions*, Part II, Chapter IV, p.60.
7　See, for example, T. Carlyle, *Oliver Cromwell's Letters and Speeches* (three volumes, London, 1845), Volume 1, p.101.
8　*CSPD, 1644–45*, p.17.
9　E.126 [39], *A True Relation of the skirmish at Worcester* (London, 1642); J. Rushworth, *Historical Collections* (London, 1659–99), Part III, Volume II, p.24.
10　Add. MSS. 18981, f. 9 (J. Cockeran's letter to Prince Rupert dated 16 January 1644).
11　E. Hyde, *The History of the Rebellion and Civil Wars in England, together with an Historical View of the Affairs in Ireland* (sixteen books, London, 1702–4), Book VI, p.80.
12　Ibid, p.82.
13　Ibid, p.46.
14　BL, Add. MSS, 18982, f. 18, document dated 16 January 1645.
15　E.127 [18], *Prince Roberts Disguises* (London, 16 November 1642). Sir Thomas Fairfax provided another example of personal reconnaissance the night before Naseby. See J. Wilson, *Fairfax* (London, 1985), p.70.
16　Clarendon, *History*, Book VI, p.78; and E. 127 [18].
17　C.H. Firth, 'The Journal of Prince Rupert's marches, 5 Sept. 1642 to 4 July 1646', *English Historical Review* (Volume 13, No. 52, 1898), pp.729–741.
18　F. Kitson, *Prince Rupert, Portrait of a Soldier* (London, 1994), p.87.
19　P. Young, *Edgehill 1642* (Moreton-in-Marsh, 1995), p.76.
20　Clarendon, *History*, Book VI, pp.355–360.
21　Cruso, *Military Instructions*, Chapter XI, p.14.

22 For example, Hopton detained Waller's trumpeter during his retreat to Devizes in 1643.
    See C.E.H. Chadwyck-Healey (ed.), *Bellum Civile: Hopton's Narrative of His Campaign in
    the West (1642–44) and Other Papers* (Somerset Record Society, Volume 18, 1902), p.55.

23 C.E. Long (ed.), *Richard Symonds: Diary of the Marches kept by the Royal army during the
    Great Civil War* (Camden Society, 1859), p.190.

24 Clarendon, *History,* Book VIII, p.139.

25 S.R. Gardiner, *History of the Great Civil War 1642–1649* (4 volumes, London, 1893),
    Volume I, p.150.

26 Long, *Symonds Diary*, p.55.

27 J. Hodgson, *Memoirs of Captain John Hodgson* (Pontefract, 1994), p.28.

28 M. J. Stoyle, 'The Gear Rout: The Cornish Rising of 1648 and the Second Civil War',
    Albion. A Quarterly Journal concerned with British Studies (Volume 32, No. 1, 2000), p.45.

29 *CSPD, 1641–43,* p.463.

30 Cruso, *Militarie Instructions*, Part II, Chapter II, p.58.

31 Young, *Edgehill*, pp.75–77.

32 Kitson, *Prince Rupert*, p.191.

33 R.N. Dore (ed.), *The Letter Books of Sir William Brereton* (two volumes, Lancashire and
    Cheshire Record Society, 1984–90), Volume II, p.99.

34 Clarendon, *History,* Book VI, pp.155–157.

35 E. Bradford, *The Great Siege* (London, 1961), pp.145–146.

36 L. Cottrell, *Enemy of Rome* (London, 1960), pp.231–232.

37 C.H. Firth (ed.), *The Memoirs of Edmund Ludlow 1625–1672* (two volumes, London, 1698),
    Volume I, p.52.

38 P. Young and R. Holmes, *The English Civil War, a Military History of the Three Civil Wars
    1642–1651* (London, 1974), p.71.

39 Clarendon, *History,* Volume III, p.23.

40 J. Barratt, *Sieges of the English Civil Wars* (Barnsley, 2009), p.18.

41 Dore, *Letter Books,* Volume I, p.50.

42 BL, Harleian MSS, 6852, f. 197, document dated 2 September 1643.

43 BL, Harleian MSS, 6802, f. 135, document dated 25 April 1644.

44 K. Roberts and J. Tincey, *Edgehill 1642* (Oxford, 2001), p.46.

45 See, for example, Cruso, *Militarie Instructions,* Part III, Chapter IX, p.xv, which discusses
    the role of 'spies'.

46 H.G. Tibbutt (ed.), *The Letter Book of Sir Samuel Luke* (Historical Manuscripts
    Commission JP4, HMSO, 1963), pp.21–22, 42, 45, 53 and 61. These extracts refer to the
    various persons engaged by Luke to carry out his intelligence-gathering operations.

47 Cruso, *Militarie Instructions,* Part III, Chapter XI, p.81.

48 J. Wroughton, *An Unhappy Civil War* (Bath, 1999), p.165.

49 Cruso, *Militarie Instructions,* Part III, Chapter XI, p.82.

50 BL, Add. MSS, 62084B, p.10 (This refers to an entry in Rupert's so-called diary dated 24
    October 1642).

51 E.G.B. Warburton, *Memoirs of Prince Rupert and the Cavaliers* (three volumes, London,
    1849), Volume II, p.5.

52 D. Nicholas, *Mr. Secretary Nicholas (1593–1669) His Life and Letters* (London, 1955), p.209.

53 Clarendon, *History,* Book VII, p.226. Clarendon's description of Falkland's view of the
    employment of spies provides a perfect example of this deep-rooted disdain for spying.

54 P. Gudgin, *Military Intelligence. A History* (Stroud, 1999), p.4.

55 Clarendon, *History,* Book VII, p.226.

56 Ibid, p.15.

57 See Chapter 3.

58 See, for example, Clarendon, *History,* Book VI, p.78; and C.H. Firth (ed.), *The Life of
    William Cavendish, Duke of Newcastle* (London, 1886), pp.59–61.

59 Firth, *Cromwell's Army*, p.49.

60 See, for example, Firth, *Cromwell's Army,* pp.46–47.

61 See, for example, the shrewd use of intelligence-gathering demonstrated by Sir Henry Gage, Governor of Oxford, during his action in September 1644 and Sir Richard Grenville's use of intelligence during the Lostwithiel campaign in August 1644. E. Walsingham, *The Life of the Most Honourable Knight, Sir Henry Gage* (Oxford, 1645), pp.13–14; and M. Coate, *Cornwall in the Great Civil War and Interregnum 1642 – 1660* (Oxford, 1933), p.141.

62 C. Carlton, *Going to the Wars* (London, 1992), p.263.

63 Ludlow, *Memoirs*, Volume I, pp.59–60.

64 W. Lilley, *Special Observations on the Life and Death of King Charles I* (London, 1651).

65 W. Lilley, *The Last of the Astrologers. A History of his Life and Times* (First published 1715, second edition Scolar Press, Yorkshire, 1974), p.77.

66 Cruso, *Militarie Instructions*, Part III, Chapter XI, pp.57 and 81–83.

67 E. 1185 [5], *Soldiers Catechisme* (Oxford, 1645), p.11.

68 See, for example, E. 101 [24], *Certaine Informations* (London, 8–15 May 1643); E. 103 [5], *Certaine Informations* (London, 15–22 May 1643); and E. 104 [6], *A Continuation of Certaine Speciall and Remarkable Passages* (London, 18–25 May 1643).

69 B. Whitelocke, *Memorials of the English Affairs* (London, 1682), p.114.

70 E. 1099 [1], *Mercurius Rusticus* (Oxford, 1645), pp.97–98, and 113.

71 E. 103 [3], *Mercurius Rusticus* (Oxford, 20 May 1643).

72 E. 1099 [1], pp.71–76.

73 E. 106 [12], *Mercurius Rusticus* (Oxford, 10 June 1643).

74 *CSPD, 1641–43*, p.440; and Rushworth, *Historical Collections*, Volume II, Part III, p.314.

75 *CSPD, 1643*, p.314; see also Rushworth, *Historical Collections*, Volume II, Part III, pp.314 and 367.

76 See Philip, *Journal*, Volume 1, p.xv; and E. 30[20], *The Spie* (London, 23–30 January 1644).

77 Long, *Symonds' Diary*, p.24.

78 Wroughton, *Unhappy Civil War*, p.217.

79 E. 102[1], *Mercurius Aulicus* (Oxford, 1– 8 May 1643).

80 E. 249[2], *A Perfect Diurnall of the Passages in Parliament* (London, 30 April-6 May 1643).

81 E. 102[1]. See also, Philip, *Journal*, Volume 1, p.68; E. 101[4], *Speciall Passages and certain Information from Severall places* (London, 2–9 May 1643); and E. 249[2], *A Perfect Diurnall of the Passages in Parliament* (London, 2–9 May 1643).

82 E. 249[2], *A Perfect Diurnall of the Passages in Parliament* (London, 2–9 May 1643).

83 Clarendon, *History,* Book VII, p.226. See also B. Donagan, *War in England 1642–49* (Oxford, 2008), p.94.

84 BL, Add MSS, 18982, f.18, (Letter from Major Adrian Scrope to Prince Rupert, 16 January 1644).

85 B. Manning, *The English People and the English Revolution* (London, 1991), pp.10–11; and B. Manning, 'The Nobles, the People and the Constitution', in T. Ashton (ed.), *Crisis in Europe 1560–1660* (New York, 1967), p.280.

86 W. J. Birken, 'The Royal College of Physicians and its support of the Parliamentary Cause in the English Civil War', *Journal of British Studies* (Volume 23, No. 1, 1983), pp.47–62. See also J. Marshall, *Intelligence and espionage in the reign of Charles II, 1660–1685* (Cambridge, 1994), p.20.

87 R. Bell (ed.), *Memorials of the Civil War: The Fairfax Correspondence* (two volumes, London, 1849), Volume I, pp.185–186.

88 A. Fraser, *The Weaker Vessel* (London, 1984), pp.209–213.

89 Tibbutt, *Letter Books*, p.671.

90 G. A. Harrison, 'Royalist Organisation in Gloucestershire and Bristol' (unpublished MA thesis, Manchester University, 1961), pp.168–171.

91 BL, Add MSS, 11332, f. 112; and Donagan, *War in England,* p.113.

92 *CSPD, 1644,* p.434; and M. Stoyle, *Loyalty and Locality* (Exeter, 1994), p.234.

93 J. R. Phillips, *Memorials of the Civil War in Wales and the Marches 1642–49* (two volumes, London, 1874), Volume II, p.217.

94 Dore, *Letter Books,* Vol. 1, pp.101 and 108–109.

95 Stoyle, *Loyalty,* p.141.

96 M. J. Stoyle, *From Deliverance to Destruction* (Exeter, 1996), p.67.

97 Ibid, pp.103–104.

98 Whitelocke, *Memorials,* p.132.

99 Cruso, *Militarie Instructions,* Part III, Chapter XI, p.81.

100 Clarendon, *History,* Book VII, p.42.

101 Philip, *Journal,* Volume I, p.70.

102 *CSPD, 1641–43,* p.473.

103 See, for example, E. 103[3], *Mercurius Rusticus* (London, 20 May 1643).

104 T.W. and J. Webb (eds.), *Military Memoir of Colonel John Birch* (Camden Society, 1873), p.169.

105 Stoyle, *Deliverance,* pp.189–191.

106 BL, Add MSS, 11331, f.146. A lieutenant's pay at that time was £2 2s and an ensign's pay was £1 1s per week. See also SP28/26, ff. 22, 319, 455, and 486.

107 Long, *Symonds Diary,* p.46.

108 Webb, *Military Memoirs,* p.168.

109 *CSPD, 1644,* p.93.

110 J. Adair, *Roundhead General: The Campaigns of Sir William Waller* (Stroud, 1997), p.34.

111 E.118 [45], *Special Passages* (20 September 1642).

112 Lilley, *Life and Times,* p.77.

113 See *CSPD, 1644,* p.76; Clarendon, *History,* Book VI, p.489; Gardiner, *History,* Volume I, p.64 ; Warburton, *Memoirs,* Volume I, p.492; A. Wicks (ed.), *Bellum Civile: Sir Ralph Hopton's Memoirs of the Campaign in the West, 1642–1644* (Partizan Press, 1988), p.27; Dore, *Letter Books,* Volume II, p.28; I.G. Philip (ed.), *The Journal of Sir Samuel Luke* (three volumes, The Oxfordshire Record Society, 1947), Volume 1, p.27; Wilson, *Fairfax,* p.195; Coate, *Cornwall in the Great Civil War,* p.201; and Tibbutt, *Letter Books,* p.694.

114 BL, Add MSS, 11331, f. 18; and Add MSS, 11332, ff. 80–85. See also Brereton, *Letter Books,* Volume II, p.128.

115 E.262 [10], *Perfect Occurrences of Parliament* (13–20 June 1645).

116 J. Stucley, *Sir Bevill Grenville and his times 1596 – 1643* (Chichester, 1983), p.135.

117 *CSPD, 1641–43,* p.440. A certain John Taylor carried out this task with 11 men, a pinnace and a two-oared wherry at a monthly cost of £27 2s.

118 Tibbutt, *Letter Books,* p.664.

119 *CSPD, 1641–43,* p.436.

120 *CSPD 1642–43,* p.445.

121 *CSPD, 1644,* p.182.

122 Ibid, p.180.

123 Ibid, pp.255 and 333.

124 Ibid, p.106.

125 Ibid, p.19.

126 An example of one such cipher can be found in BL, Harleian MSS. 6802, f. 203 (undated). Manuscript 94 of the Clarendon Papers in the Bodleian Library also contains 16 ciphers that were used by the Royalists. These codes are not 'user-friendly' to operate!

127 BL, Add MSS, 18981, f. 40 (Letter from Richard Cave to Rupert, 15 February 1644).

128 BL, Add MSS, 18891, f. 189. In a letter to Rupert, dated 11 June 1644, Goring recounted his problems with the codes in use observing that it was uncertain 'whether My Lord Marquis's letter can be deciphered or not'.

129 *CSPD, 1644–45,* p.92 (Sir William Brereton's letter dated 2 November 1644 to the
     Committee of Both Kingdoms).

130 *CSPD, 1644,* p.253.

131 Ibid, p.332.

132 D. Kahn, *The Code Breakers* (New York, 1996), pp.166–169.

133 Although a portrait of John Wallis is displayed in the Long Gallery of the Uffizi Palace
     in Florence.

134 C.H. Firth, 'Thomas Scot's Account of his actions as Intelligencer during the
     Commonwealth', *English Historical Review* (Volume 13, No. 51, 1897), p.527. See also
     Rawlinson Mss, A477, f. 10.

135 C.V. Wedgwood, *The Great Rebellion: The King's War 1641–1647* (London, 1958),
     pp.163–164.

136 P.W. Thomas, *Sir John Berkenhead 1617 – 1679* (Oxford, 1969), pp.43–46.

137 Philip, *Journal,* pp.21,158, 505, 696 and 736.

138 A. Macadam, 'Mercurius Britanicus: Journalism and Politics in the English Civil War'
     (unpublished D Phil thesis, University of Sussex, 2005), pp.42–45.

139 BL, Add MSS, 11333, f. 47.

140 BL, Add MSS, 11331–11333. These manuscripts contain numerous examples of the
     intelligence reports and summaries made by, or sent to, Sir William Brereton. Some
     of them are also contained in Dore, *Letter Books,* pp.128–129; Philip, *Journal,* p.81; and
     Tibbutt, *Letter Books,* p.307.

141 BL, Add MSS, 11331–11333, Volume I, ff. 83–89.

142 *CSPD, 1643,* p.30.

143 Dore, *Letter Books,* Volume I, pp.108–109.

144 Clarendon, *History,* Book IX, pp.43–45.

145 *CSPD, 1644,* p.294.

146 BL, Add MSS, 11331–11333; and Dore, *Letter Books,* Volume I, p.50, citing a letter from
     Committee of Both Kingdoms dated 11 March 1645.

147 Clarendon, *History,* Book VI, pp.79–80; and Marshall, *Intelligence and Espionage,* p.18

3

The Strategic Direction and Integration of Military Intelligence

The performance of the English Army during the two Bishops' Wars, fought between 1639 and 1640, revealed that Charles I's military structures had atrophied after years of neglect and that England was not even capable of mustering a militia for effective home defence.[1] From the intelligence-gathering perspective, not only were scouting skills neglected, but even the critical importance of obtaining accurate military intelligence – and passing it along secure and speedy lines of communication – was largely forgotten.[2] Other equally important aspects of intelligence-gathering were overlooked; for example, the Bishops' Wars commanders did not make any attempt to validate their intelligence reports, nor did they shown any aptitude for integrating the intelligence into the planning of military operations.[3] To make best use of military intelligence-gathering, the opposing commanders not only needed to identify the intelligence they required, but also communicate and assess their intelligencers' information quickly so that it could be integrated effectively into their military decision-making processes in a timely manner.[4] As will be revealed, the fighting in 1642 identified a number of significant weaknesses in the management and communication of intelligence, which were steadily corrected as the Civil War continued.

It is important to explore the strategic direction and integration of military intelligence during the Civil War, because any mismanagement of intelligence information would have significantly reduced the contribution made by intelligence-gathering to the outcome of the conflict. Therefore, the aims of this chapter are, firstly, to explore how well each side directed their intelligence-gathering operations and, secondly, to assess how effectively intelligence information was subsequently integrated into the planning processes. It will then move on to describe how each side implemented and developed the role of the scoutmaster before evaluating the importance of this appointment to the strategic direction of intelligence-gathering. The indirect contribution made by intelligence-gathering to other military operations, such as deception and counter-intelligence, will also be considered before finally examining how communication methods were improved in order to satisfy the growing demand for the rapid and secure transmission of information.[5]

How did the High Command on each side manage and use their intelligence-gathering operations? The belief that the political differences between Charles I and his Parliamentarian opponents would be resolved in just one battle dominated the thinking of both sides during the summer of 1642.[6] Accordingly, both parties determined that their most immediate military objectives were to recruit, equip, train and deploy their armies in order to win that deciding battle. However, as relatively few of the political or military leaders had any recent experience of warfare, it was hardly surprising that the need to find out what the other side was up to was not recognised immediately as an equally important priority. Although this attitude changed when the commanders had gained more experience, in the summer of 1642 there is no evidence that the gathering of military intelligence was given any priority at all.[7]

Intelligence-gathering was not the only area neglected; the belief in a 'single-battle' war influenced longer term preparations in other critical areas, such as revenue generation, the gathering and distribution of supplies and the manufacture of weapons and munitions. The requirements to provide consistent longer-term funding, along with the uninterrupted supply of arms and munitions and the creation of a nationwide intelligence-gathering organisation, were not recognised as urgent until it became evident that the Edgehill Campaign had failed to provide the overwhelming victory needed to resolve the political impasse.[8]

Consequently, none of the opposing military commanders gave any specific consideration to establishing a military intelligence structure in 1642. As in the recent Bishops' Wars, intelligence operations continued to be directed by the Lieutenant General of the Horse who was traditionally responsible for directing army scouting patrols.[9] Parliament appointed the Earl of Bedford to be their Lord General of the Horse and his Royalist opposite number was Prince Rupert of the Rhine. Should those officers have required guidance, Cruso's *Militarie Instructions for the Cavallrie* might well have proved helpful. This work stated that the Lieutenant General of Horse

> ... must always have his thoughts busied about the motions of the enemy, discoursing with himself from what part they might shew themselves, with what numbers of men, whether with Infantrie or not, in how many houres they might come upon him ... and whether they might present themselves in a place of advantage; that so it might be prevented. He must also procure to have spies, not only in the enemies army, but also upon their frontiers, to penetrate their designes and intentions, omitting no inventions which may stand him in stead to avoid inconveniences; knowing that diligence is the mother of good fortune.[10]

Similarly, the lack of any maps sufficiently detailed for military use increased the importance of finding reliable guides who could provide intelligence on the local topography, settlements and roads. It was, wrote Cruso, the recognised task of the wagon-master

> ... to provide good guides, of the inhabitants of those places where the march is to be, which may be able to give certain and particular information concerning the high-wayes and cross-wayes, how many there be of them, whether they be even, large, and free or straight, hilly, or impeached with difficult passages.[11]

In the early days of the fighting, army commanders had few officers on their staff to assist them in the ordering of their forces. Initially, therefore, both sides would have been challenged to find the time needed to manage and coordinate their intelligence-gathering organisations.[12]

In theory the Royalist Council of War was given the high command intelligence responsibilities of the Cavaliers. Unsurprisingly, Charles had followed tradition by establishing a Council of War to provide him with strategic advice on military matters, including the direction and integration of intelligence information. This body had the potential to exert an influential role for, when meeting in full session, it was attended by generals of all arms, senior officials, privy councillors and secretaries of state. In theory at least, the Council was therefore able to generate an overall assessment of the military situation and, as originally constituted in August 1642, it should have been able to exercise effective control over the Royalist war effort.[13] Of particular significance is the fact that the full Council of War was intended to be 'a clearing house of information and military intelligence' as it was originally designed to receive 'the information of spies and scouts on the movements of the enemy'.[14]

However, there is little contemporary evidence to show that the Royalist Council of War was ever effective in its intelligence management and coordination role. Whilst few of the minutes of the Council's meetings have survived, Clarendon provides an account of the Royalist deliberations in his *History*.[15] His account shows that the Council's discussions took into account the general intelligence information regarding likely Parliamentarian aims and objectives when establishing Royalist aims and priorities for the forthcoming campaigns.[16] Certainly the Royalist commanders were provided with information about the location and approximate strength of the Parliamentarian Army and, as the war continued, they were always made aware of the general position and probable intentions of the main Parliamentarian field armies.[17] At the beginning of 1645, the Royalists not only knew where their opponent's main forces were, but were also aware of the army reforms which Parliament was in the process of implementing.[18]

However, in practice, the Council of War was not able to realise its theoretical intelligence management potential because Charles I himself was liable to change his mind in order to reflect the latest suggestions made to him. Inevitably this caused confusion and thus the Council never played much of a part in the strategic direction of subsequent military intelligence operations once the Royalist 'grand designe' for each campaigning season had been decided.[19] The execution of these plans then became the responsibility of the individual army commanders, and it was these generals who were expected to provide intelligence of the enemy's movements and intentions using the traditional scouting methods. This delegation to the local military commanders was much favoured by Charles but it had several drawbacks. For example, it did not lend itself to effective central control of military objectives, nor did it facilitate effective cooperation between the armies. Finally, it failed to optimise the experience and expertise of the members of the Council of War.[20] As the war went on, the increasing fragmentation of the Royalists' overall military command structure, coupled with the steady reduction of support as the number of areas under Cavalier control diminished, increasingly undermined the effectiveness of every aspect of Royalist military field operations, not just their military intelligence-gathering.[21]

Contemporary accounts reveal that the Royalist attitude to intelligence-gathering was often somewhat ambivalent. Clarendon's description of the character of Lucius Cary, Viscount Falkland, written after his death at Newbury, provides a revealing insight into some Royalists' perceptions of intelligence-gathering. As Charles' Secretary of State, Falkland was not only one of the King's most senior and closest advisers, but he was also the man with overall responsibility for the direction and coordination of intelligence-gathering for the crown, just as Thomas Cromwell, Cecil and Walsingham had carried out these duties under the Tudors. According to Clarendon, Falkland considered that, whilst the use of military scouts to obtain information was generally reliable and therefore to be encouraged, the use of spies to obtain information through deception and other clandestine methods was inherently dishonourable and therefore to be discouraged. Clarendon recorded that Falkland would not trust people who 'by dissimulation of manners, wound themselves into such trusts and secrets as enabled them to make discoveries for the benefit of the state', because 'such instruments must be void of all ingenuity and common honesty.'[22] Clarendon went on to add that Falkland considered that the 'opening of letters upon a suspicion that they might contain matter of dangerous consequence' was a 'violation of the law of nature, that no qualification by office could justify a single person in the trespass'.[23] Falkland's evident reluctance to employ spies to gather intelligence may help to explain why, at least during his time in office, the Royalist high command took such a hesitant approach to the gathering of intelligence. Whilst intelligence-gathering by military personnel developed as the war progressed, Falkland's reservations regarding duplicitous behaviour can only have served to discourage spying.

On the Roundhead side, the control and direction of intelligence-gathering responsibilities was initially devolved to the Parliamentarian Committee of Safety and, after the alliance with Scotland, to the Committee of Both Kingdoms. The Parliamentarian intelligence-gathering network proved to be much more effective than that of the Royalists, and contributed significantly to the final victory. In many ways, the move to a war footing was easier for the Parliamentarian leaders for they had found it relatively easily to adopt or adapt Parliamentary committees to military purposes, while their control of London had avoided the need for any physical relocation. As soon as war appeared inevitable, Parliament modified its committee structure in order to exercise control over its military forces and the aforementioned Committee of Safety was established on 4 July 1642.[24] While the deliberations of the Royalist Council of War are generally poorly documented, a very substantial amount of material regarding the decisions of the Parliamentary Committee of Safety (and subsequently the Committee of Both Kingdoms) has survived in the Journals of the Houses of Parliament and the Calendar of State Papers.[25] Furthermore, the evidence of the State Papers suggests that, from its very inception, the Committee of Safety appreciated the need for comprehensive intelligence reports. Papers show that the Committee exercised much more positive control over the provision and dissemination of intelligence to Parliamentarian leaders, both military and political, than the Royalist Council of War did.[26] Moreover, as the war progressed, an increasing body of evidence confirms that both the national and local military intelligence situation was being presented considerably more clearly to the Parliamentarian commanders than it was to their Royalist opposite numbers.[27] In the years that followed, the Parliamentarian commanders had access to reliable and timely military intelligence information which they used effectively to counter the Royalists' military operations.[28]

From its inception, the Committee of Safety was receiving reasonably accurate intelligence reports and thus it invariably knew where the King was, and what the Cavaliers were trying to achieve. When they had received accurate and timely intelligence of the King's intentions, the Parliamentarian leaders were able to out-manoeuvre Charles. The minutes of the Parliamentarian Committee of Safety thus reflected a growing appreciation of the benefits of superior intelligence information. The Committee's subsequent instructions to their commanders constantly urged them to exchange intelligence.[29] Indeed, the minutes of both the Committee of Safety and the Committee of Both Kingdoms contain numerous references to the importance of collecting and exchanging intelligence between army commanders and political leaders, particularly after the Scottish Army entered the war and crossed into England in January 1644.[30] The Committee of Both Kingdoms was also careful to disseminate information in order to ensure that each army commander was aware of how the war was progressing; for example, the Parliamentarian commanders at York were promptly told of the outcome of Waller's encounter with Charles at Cropredy Bridge in June 1644.[31] Whilst it is not possible to be certain, there is no evidence to suggest that Charles informed either Rupert or Newcastle of his significant victory at the

Battle of Cropredy Bridge; had the Royalist commanders been made aware of the change in the King's circumstances, it is possible that Rupert would not have forced the engagement at Marston Moor.

The Committee of Safety, therefore, played an active role in Parliament's military planning because, right from the beginning of the conflict, the members of the Committee recognised that they had a key role to play in supporting Essex's army by providing intelligence, money and equipment.[32] As early as May 1642, Parliament appointed 'a Committee of Both Houses to join with the Committee and Commissioners of Scotland ... as a Committee for managing the war, and keeping good intelligence between the forces of the three kingdoms.'[33] In July 1642, the work of this committee was taken on by the Committee of Safety and, in early 1644, by its successor, the Committee of Both Kingdoms.[34] As the committee members gained experience, and as the war expanded, so the intelligence structure was enhanced. For example, in February 1644, a sub-committee was established to consider intelligence matters.[35] On 9 March 1644 the Committee allocated £300 per week to cover the incidental costs of running an intelligence service,[36] and two Parliamentarian civilian staff, Mr Frost and Mr Weckherlin, were appointed as 'intelligence officers' in September 1642 and June 1643 respectively to compile the intelligence reports for the Committee and to assist with coding and decoding.[37] The committee also ensured that Essex received recruits, money, arms, clothes, ammunition, reinforcements and advice.[38]

As the number of Parliamentarian armies increased, so too did the Committee's attempts to provide the same level of support for each army. Given the small size of the Committee and the steady growth of its areas of responsibility, its members inevitably gave priority to what they saw as the most pressing issues. As the conflict expanded, and as their workload increased, the Committee members were criticised for not keeping the House informed of all the details of the military campaign – particularly the intelligence-gathering.[39] This criticism was particularly significant because the Committee provided the chief liaison channel between the legislative, executive, administrative and military bodies of Parliament. Because their initial remit had been to gather information about the position of their own and the enemy's armies, the committee men became increasingly involved in the minute detail of intelligence work. For example, they became immersed in the interception and decoding of Royalist correspondence and even the interrogation of prisoners. The Committee thus assumed responsibility for a large workload and, although it tried hard, the size and complexity of some of the tasks proved too much for its members. Although it later became increasingly vulnerable to accusations of inefficiency, its members did well to identify the importance of intelligence-gathering and provided crucial coordination from the very start of the conflict.

Although Parliament implemented a structure to manage its intelligence-gathering, there is no evidence to show that it established any special central financial arrangements solely to support intelligence operations. As previous historians have discovered, the numerous contemporary references to the financial arrangements which funded Civil War intelligence-gathering operations contain little detail of the intelligence actually provided. The Commonwealth Exchequer Papers and the State Papers contain many examples of payments being made to field commanders for this purpose, but the descriptions of what the money was for are annoyingly vague; for example, on 30 March 1643 the Parliamentarian Sir Vivian Molyneux was paid for the 'provision of intelligence information' – a description that could mean anything.[40] Another typical example is a warrant under the Privy Seal to the Exchequer written at the Court in Oxford on 20 February 1644 simply noted 'Pay George, Lord Digby £300 for secret service.'[41] These entries are typical of many. However, as it was clearly accepted that intelligence-gathering was important and needed funding, there are numerous examples of regular payments being made in order to support the provision of these unspecified intelligence services. The haphazard nature of these substantial payments, and the fact that some of the bills were settled by Parliament's committees, has tended to support the view that, throughout the Civil War, the gathering of military intelligence was considered to be a local responsibility, and thus best managed by the local commanders. Nevertheless, information was handled more centrally by Parliament than it was by the individual regional Royalist commanders.

It is difficult to establish what guidance – if any – the Royalist Council of War offered its regional commanders about how to conduct intelligence-gathering operations. The benefits to be gained from controlling the most territory were recognised and Charles appointed local magnates as military leaders because their status would assist the provision of troops, support, respect and obedience.[42] For similar reasons, the Royalists sought to appoint local gentry as the garrison commanders of Royalist fortresses.[43] These garrison commanders were expected to use their local status to establish their own intelligence structures as part of their military responsibilities, and some important intelligence came from their networks of contacts and informants. Although the Royalist Council of War may have appreciated the need for intelligence information, the actual delivery of that intelligence was hampered by the diffusion of Royalist military responsibilities amongst the regional commanders, and the local magnates' reliance on their tenants and neighbours for intelligence reports.[44]

Thus the success of the regional Royalist intelligence teams was mixed. In the North, the Duke of Newcastle established a sound base of intelligence-gathering in those counties for which he was given responsibility.[45] Reflecting the higher levels of local support for Parliament, the Royalist commander in the South, the Earl of Hertford, was significantly less successful in the predominantly Roundhead counties of Dorset and Devon.[46] Although other regional royalist leaders, such as Lord Herbert in South Wales, Sir Bevil Grenville in Cornwall and Lord Strange in the North West, were successful in raising forces,[47] there is no evidence that any of these men appreciated the need to support their operations with a formal regional intelligence network.[48] Consequently, the responsibility for coordinating Royalist intelligence-gathering appears to have fallen between the Council of War (which had the strategic responsibility but no resources) and the regional commanders (who had access to the resources but no strategic responsibility).

The Parliamentarian situation was fundamentally different as their intelligence management structure was much more centralised; the Committee of Safety remained based in London and received intelligence reports from a wide variety of sources in order to identify what was happening around the country. Having considered this intelligence, the Committee was able to coordinate the military activities of their commanders in the field. Initially this 'central' arrangement worked well, but later in the war, when regional commanders had developed their own intelligence-gathering teams, central control became cumbersome and delayed local military initiative. For example, at the beginning of the Naseby campaign, Fairfax, the New Model Army commander, was ordered around the country as the Committee of Both Kingdoms responded to their latest intelligence information of the movements of the Royalist Army. Eventually the Committee delegated the task of engaging the King to Fairfax and provided Major Leonard Watson, his Scoutmaster-General, with all their intelligence information in order to assist him in that task.[49]

Just as the Committee of Safety found it more practical to delegate the raising of troops to regional level, so too the provision of Parliamentarian intelligence and other military support was delegated to the local county-based management structures using the well-established skills of the MPs and JPs. This practice worked well because, although Parliament's determination to exercise central control through the hands of a few made their system more bureaucratic, it also delegated responsibility within a traditional and proven local structure.[50] As with the Royalists, the most successful Parliamentarian recruiters were the local magnates, such as Hampden and Holles, who were able to adapt their existing personal and business networks to provide military intelligence information. Thus, from the earliest stages of the war, the Parliamentarian central control facilitated the provision of coordinated national military intelligence assessments, and thereby achieved focus and consistency.[51]

Regional Parliamentarian intelligence-gathering operations developed steadily as the conflict expanded and as their local commanders grew more experienced. Perhaps because many of these commanders were businessmen before the war, they were well aware of the importance of obtaining accurate information before making decisions. Certainly key Parliamentarian commanders, like Sir Samuel Luke in Newport Pagnell and Sir William Brereton in Cheshire, proved to be resourceful and determined providers of local intelligence whose accurate information was regularly reported to the Parliamentarian Committees for wider promulgation.[52] As the focus of the fighting spread across the country, Luke and

Brereton's reports from the frontline provided invaluable intelligence. For example, during the months before the Naseby campaign, these two commanders provided a series of accurate reports of the location, size and forecast movements of the Royalist Army which proved to be key factors in the campaign that effectively won the war for Parliament.[53]

As the fighting expanded, both sides soon reintroduced the post of Scoutmaster-General to oversee their intelligence operations – and it is important to appreciate just how this appointment fitted into the emerging Civil War intelligence management structure. The post of Scoutmaster-General had first been introduced in England during the reign of Henry VIII. It was then a new position which was intended to direct the gathering of intelligence information and to integrate that information into the military planning process. In 1518 it was observed that:

> It is the office of the Scoutmaster when he cometh to the field to set and appoint the scourage [scouts], he must appoint some to the high hills to view and see if they can discover anything. Also the said Scoutmaster must appoint one other company of scouragers to search, and view every valley thereabouts, that there be no enemies laid privily for the annoyance of the said camp; and if they discover any, they are to advertise the Scoutmaster; and he must either bring or send word to the high marshal of the advertisement with speed.[54]

In his much later review of seventeenth-century European military organisations, the historian, Sir James Turner, was to observe that the appointment of the Scoutmaster-General was unique to England as he had 'known none of them abroad'.[55] Other contemporary accounts confirm that the Scoutmaster-General was responsible for the provision of scouts who were to 'be directed into crosse wayes and other places of perrill in everie quarter of the campe', and was to ensure that the scouts were 'not to forsake theyr places appointed, till discoverers be put foorth in the morninge to the fielde.'[56] Perhaps reflecting the recent unhappy experiences of scoutmasters appointed during the Bishops' Wars,[57] at the beginning of the Civil War in 1642 no appointments of scoutmasters were made and so scouting and intelligence gathering remained the responsibility of the Lieutenant General of Horse. This situation changed soon after the military experiences of 1642 were absorbed.

As might have been expected, the responsibilities of the scoutmasters developed steadily during the conflict. No doubt reflecting his experiences of the part played by intelligence in the Edgehill Campaign, Essex decided to re-establish the appointment of the scoutmaster – and to make the office-holder responsible for obtaining information about the location, strength and intentions of the Royalist forces. Accordingly, on 14 January 1643, Sir Samuel Luke was appointed by Essex to be Scoutmaster-General to his army with the task of setting up an intelligence-gathering organisation.[58] Paid £7 a day, Luke was allocated funding for

twenty men and horses to undertake this role.[59] Not every Parliamentarian Army
commander appointed a scoutmaster, and the performance of those scoutmasters that were appointed was inconsistent. Whilst Luke had established a useful
intelligence service for Essex, the Major-General of the Parliamentarian Army
in the South West, James Chudleigh, was clearly dissatisfied with his intelligence
service in April 1643 when he condemned the 'intolerable neglect of our Deputy
Scoutmaster' before the skirmish at Sourton Down.[60]

There is no evidence to suggest that the Royalist commanders perceived any
shortcomings in their intelligence structure after the Edgehill Campaign.[61] As
Lieutenant General of the Horse, Prince Rupert had acknowledged the importance of intelligence-gathering and 'took great trouble to gain information about
the enemy'.[62] Contemporary accounts show that he recognised the need to find
out what the enemy was doing, even though the stories of his personal intelligence-gathering exploits probably lost nothing in the telling![63] Nevertheless, a
little later in the same year, there is evidence that Rupert, too, had appointed his
own scoutmaster. In February 1643, an account of the action at Cirencester stated
that the Royalist soldier, Sir William Neale, was acting as Rupert's Scoutmaster-
General.[64] Rupert's enthusiasm for intelligence-gathering does not appear to have
been shared by his fellow commanders as few other Royalist Army commanders
are known to have appointed a scoutmaster at this time. One important exception was Newcastle, commander of the Royalist Northern Army, who appointed
one Mr Smith as scoutmaster in 1643.[65] Although Neale was later described by
the historian, Anthony Wood, as 'the worthy bearer [of information]',[66] no other
records have survived to show that he received the same degree of recognition
from the Royalist commanders for his intelligence-gathering as Luke did from
the Parliamentarian generals.

In marked contrast, Luke's intelligence-gathering operations have been
reported in substantial detail because so many of his reports and letters have survived.[67] Luke was a vigilant and painstaking intelligence chief who, appreciating
the importance of loyalty, recruited his 'intelligencers' initially from soldiers of
his own troop of dragoons.[68] He also used local men as they were more likely
to be accepted as having a legitimate reason to travel if stopped by any Royalist
patrols or sentries. As Luke's reports were comprehensive and generally accurate,
it is easy to see why his intelligence information was so highly regarded by the
Parliamentarian leaders.[69] Luke was later described by Ricraft, the seventeenth-
century writer, as the 'noble commander who watches the enemy so industriously
that they eat, sleep, drink not, whisper not, but he can give us an account of
their darkest proceedings.'[70] Significantly, Luke was appointed as Governor of
Newport Pagnell in October 1643.[71] This garrison was a key link in a protective
chain of strongholds providing defence against Royalist forces moving towards
London, and he was thus ideally situated to provide important information about
local enemy movements. A few of the more far-sighted regional commanders,

such as the Parliamentarian Sir William Brereton in Cheshire, recognised the need to develop and evaluate this local intelligence and to create a more comprehensive intelligence-gathering network.[72] Indeed, Luke's intelligence team at Newport Pagnell provided Essex with important information when he led the Parliamentarian Army to relieve Gloucester later in the year.

The role of the scoutmaster continued to develop as the war progressed. Clarendon makes it clear that, by 1644, the King's Oxford Army possessed a Scoutmaster-General of its own, a man called Sir Charles Blunt.[73] When Rupert was appointed to command Royalist forces in the North West, he had taken his scoutmaster with him, for Neale had been appointed as Governor of Hawarden Castle in Flintshire during March 1644.[74] This appointment of a Royalist scoutmaster to a key border garrison emulated the earlier Parliamentarian appointment of Sir Samuel Luke as the Governor of Newport Pagnell. The appointment of scoutmasters to garrisons in militarily significant areas had some distinct advantages as it allowed the establishment of a stable network of spies and scouts who could monitor military developments with increasing accuracy. Basing intelligence-gathering on garrisons facilitated communications, thereby providing a comprehensive intelligence-gathering network, sensitive to the slightest intrusion. The network of Royalist garrisons was extended during the early months of 1644, as the Royalists fortified Greenland House as part of the defensive network around Oxford. Luke's spies had been monitoring this development and, on 27 February, they reported that the Royalist scoutmaster, Sir Charles Blunt, had been appointed Governor of this 'border' garrison.[75] In May, Blunt was praised by the Earl of Forth for his 'advertisements' of enemy intelligence and had been described as 'a very good hand'.[76] At that time, Blunt was the deputy governor of Donnington Castle – another key frontline garrison. Blunt was not to enjoy his appointment to Greenland House for long. In June he was shot by one of his own officers during a scuffle with a Royalist sentry in Oxford. According to the accounts published in the contemporary news pamphlets, Blunt had objected to being stopped and questioned by this sentry and had physically assaulted him.[77] One of Blunt's own officers, who was supervising the sentries that evening, came upon this scuffle and, not recognising the person assaulting the sentry as his own commander, shot him dead on the spot. As Blunt appeared to have been a capable scoutmaster – and as his successor proved to be nothing like as adept – this incident was to have serious repercussions for Royalist intelligence-gathering in the subsequent campaigns.

The introduction of Parliamentarian intelligence-gathering networks across the whole kingdom was indicative of an increasingly mature intelligence system. Further evidence of the growth of the regional Parliamentarian intelligence networks was provided in March 1644, when *Mercurius Aulicus* reported that 'Herrick the Scoutmaster of Warwicke was taken prisoner.'[78] This report indicated that the Parliamentarian network was being gradually extended to cover individual towns and counties, in addition to the intelligence teams normally associated with the field armies. The number of Parliamentarian scoutmasters steadily increased as the war progressed; for example, in May 1644, a certain Richard Terry was identified as being the Parliamentarian scoutmaster in Coventry.[79] The minutes of the Committee of Both Kingdoms' meeting of 28 October 1644 mention a report being received from the regional Parliamentarian commander, Lord Warriston, 'and the scoutmaster who brought it'.[80] The individual is not named, but the fact that scoutmasters were mentioned with increasing frequency is a firm indication that, on the Parliamentarian side at least, they were becoming progressively more commonplace appointments within a growing intelligence organisation.[81]

As might be expected, the pay of those involved in intelligence-gathering varied according to their role and responsibility; for example, as Parliamentarian Scoutmasters-General, Luke and Watson were paid £7 a day, while a county scoutmaster was paid half that amount. Scouts were paid 5 shillings a day, although they could be paid 'bonuses' for hazardous or arduous duties.[82] By comparison, each day a colonel of a regiment was receiving 13 guineas (£13 and 13 shillings), while a quartermaster received 3 guineas (£3 and 3 shillings).[83]

Some contemporary references to scoutmasters reveal that their intelligence-gathering duties made them vulnerable to capture. For example, when Theodore Jennings, the Scoutmaster-General to the Parliamentarian general, Basil Fielding, Earl of Denbigh, was stopped and searched by a Royalist patrol on 23 August 1644, *Mercurius Aulicus* was delighted to report that the patrol found his scoutmaster's commission in his pocket. Jennings' capture identified one of the practical difficulties of carrying out intelligence-gathering, for, in order to facilitate his duties, he was also carrying a warrant from the Committee of Both Kingdoms which required:

> All Mayors, Justices of the peace, Bailiffs, Captains and all other officers and Corps de Garde ... all Post-masters, and Constables, and other officers whom it doth concern ... to let him pass and repass without any let or molestation.[84]

Jennings's competence must be called into some doubt as it is surprising that he did not take more trouble to conceal – or indeed to destroy – a document which made his identification as an intelligencer so easy!

In 1645, the post of Scoutmaster-General to the New Model Army was keenly contested by two candidates: Samuel Bedford, Sir Samuel Luke's deputy scoutmaster, and Major Leonard Watson, the scoutmaster to the Earl of Manchester's Army of the Eastern Association. It is clear that Fairfax had referred both their names to the Houses of Parliament for a final decision, for, in a letter to Luke, Bedford reported that Fairfax planned to 'leave it to the House to determine'.[85] Clearly the competition was ruthless for, a few days later, Bedford was complaining that 'Watson and his agents deal most unworthily with me, and strive by bribing my scouts to get them to him, or else to give their intelligence first to him as they come through Henley.'[86] The House of Commons duly decided that Watson was to be Scoutmaster-General to the New Model Army, whilst Bedford was appointed scoutmaster to the Committee of Both Kingdoms.[87]

The death of Sir Charles Blunt in 1644 had left the post of Royalist Scoutmaster-General vacant. Although Neale, Rupert's previous scoutmaster, could conceivably have been moved back from Hawarden House to fill the post, in the end a certain Sir Francis Ruce was appointed as Scoutmaster-General of the Royalist Oxford Army.[88] Neale remained in Hawarden House until the end of the war and then vanished into obscurity.[89] We also know that, in 1645, William Cockayne was appointed Scoutmaster-General to the Royalist Western Army.[90] (A list of some of the Civil War scoutmasters may be found in the appendix to this book.) Contemporary references to the intelligence information provided by the two Royalist Secretaries of State, Sir Edward Nicholas in Oxford, and John Culpepper in Bristol, indicate that they had assumed the central headquarters intelligence-gathering duties for the two main Royalist armies.[91] Culpepper's letter of 1 April 1645, which is typical of many, reported that 'Waller [the Parliamentarian general] was quartered last night at Shaftesbury and Cromwell at Stirminster and some of their horse at Wincanton.'[92] Nicholas's position at Oxford enabled him to provide a central point for intelligence reports from Royalist sympathisers; while his co-location with John Birkenhead, the editor of *Mercurius Aulicus*, would also have enabled him to share any information reported by the news pamphleteer's 'intelligencers'. As Oxford was at the centre of the Naseby campaign manoeuvres, Nicholas was well placed to receive timely intelligence reports from all of these Royalist informers. However, contemporary accounts indicate that Royalist scouting was often distinctly ineffective. Of particular interest is the fact that, just before the Battle of Naseby, Rupert was only able to gain any reliable information by carrying out the scouting in person.[93]

The Parliamentarians were especially fortunate that, in the spring of 1645, the Royalist advance was initially towards Chester where Sir William Brereton's well-established intelligence-gathering network provided frequent and accurate reports. After the relief of Chester in May 1645, the Royalists' advance took them towards Newport Pagnell, an area of special interest to Sir Samuel Luke, governor of that garrison and formerly Scoutmaster-General to Essex's army. The intelligence reports of the position of the Royalist Army from these two officers were so accurate that they gave Fairfax and his New Model Army an incalculable advantage over the Royalists. Significantly, although Luke's appointment had theoretically terminated under the Self Denying Ordinance – the Ordinance which precluded Members of Parliament from holding appointments of military command – his contribution towards Parliamentarian intelligence led to his governorship being extended for the duration of the Naseby campaign.[94] It is equally interesting to note that, although Sir William Neale, the former scoutmaster to

Rupert, was governor of Hawarden Castle and was thus well placed to report on the movements of Brereton's army, no intelligence reports from him are mentioned in other contemporary accounts – certainly none appear to have survived. This would suggest that, at a time when Parliamentarian intelligence reports were flowing in, relatively few Royalist intelligence reports were being received by Charles or Rupert.

Military intelligence operations during the English Civil War consisted of more than just the gathering and disseminating of information. The contribution of intelligence to military deception operations increased as commanders developed more confidence in their information. Effective military intelligence not only provided information concerning the position and strength of the enemy, but also provided an insight into the enemy's weaknesses and fears, thereby allowing their exploitation. Throughout history, the chances of military operations being successful have always been markedly increased when they have incorporated tactics designed to deceive or confuse the enemy.[95] Thus Civil War intelligencers set out to identify which confusion and deception measures were most likely to succeed. This important aspect of military intelligence had been recognised by John Cruso when he wrote that each commander must know 'the condition and estate of the enemy, his commodities, and necessities, his councils and designes'.[96] The actions of the Royalist commander, Sir Henry Gage, when he set out to re-supply Basing House with fresh stores and ammunition in September 1644, provide an excellent example of effective confusion and deception tactics. Operating against considerable odds, Gage's strategy of planting false reports, disguising the true identity of his forces and using feints and false reports to conceal his true line of advance so confused his opponents that the Royalists were able to re-supply Basing House and take 100 prisoners at the minimal cost of a loss of some 11 dead and about 50 wounded.[97]

Deception plans were not just used to conceal the movements of armies and land forces; they were also used to conceal the location and movements of individuals. After Rupert's initial success at the skirmish at Powick Bridge, Royalist officers noticed the close attention paid by Parliamentary commanders to the location and movements of Rupert himself,[98] and used the Parliamentarian sensitivity about Rupert's movements in very much the same way that the Second World War Allied leaders used the interest that the German Generals had in the movements of the US General George Patton. Just as the much publicised presence of Patton in East Anglia, coupled with innovative technical deception operations, deceived Hitler as to the true location of the Allied landings in France for some critical weeks,[99] so reports of the presence of Rupert in the Midlands in May 1645 helped to persuade the Parliamentarian commanders that military action against Brereton's forces around Chester was imminent.[100]

A less complicated technique, which was frequently used by both Prince Rupert and the Parliamentarian general, Sir William Waller, incorporated either the cover of darkness, the speed of advance or feints, or a combination of all three intelligence-based strategies, in order to deceive and confuse their opponents. For example, the march of the Royalist Army from Shrewsbury in 1642 was covered by a feint by Prince Rupert towards Worcester,[101] just as Rupert's attack on Newark in April 1644 used a fast speed of advance to deceive the Parliamentary commander, Sir John Meldrum, who simply refused to believe intelligence reports from his scouts that Rupert's forces were advancing so rapidly and were, consequently, much closer to him than he realised.[102] After successfully relieving Gloucester in September 1643, Essex feinted towards the north before doubling back through Cirencester and heading for London.[103] Similarly Sir William Waller's attack on Alton in December 1643 combined a rapid speed of advance, the cover of night and the use of back lanes that were not patrolled, not just to avoid the Royalist scouts, but also to lull Hopton and Crawford, the Royalist generals, into a false state of security.[104] The success of all these military operations depended upon accurate intelligence of the enemy's position, as well as the commander's willingness to exploit any advantage given him by his intelligence information.[105]

The importance of the speedy and safe communication of information was soon realised by the commanders on both sides. The effective integration of intelligence reports into the military planning process was clearly dependent upon the timely receipt of accurate information. Most information was carried by mounted messengers, and letters were normally used because messengers could not always be relied upon to recount long or complicated verbal messages. A messenger on a galloping horse was a surprisingly fast method of transmitting information; using pre-positioned relays of horses, letters could be passed more quickly than might be imagined. Although it must have been more difficult to maintain reliable and fast communications between two forces on the march, the rapidity of the messengers providing the routine postal service between fixed points such as towns or cities was, again, surprisingly fast. As early as 1643, the Committee of Safety was recruiting additional riders to carry its messages and this network was steadily enhanced during the war.[106] In 1645, Sir William Brereton's messages from the Nantwich and Middlewich area were reaching Lord Fairfax in York within two days and Lord Leven with the Scottish Army within three days.[107] When messages were urgent, they were passed very quickly indeed; contemporary accounts show that letters written by Hyde in London 'on Saturday night at twelve o'clock, were answered by the King at York and the reply was ...[back] in Hyde's hands by ten o'clock on Monday morning'.[108]

Parliament showed a keen appreciation of the resources which were needed to support their military intelligence infrastructure, and provided postal services for both official and private letters. As the Parliamentarian sergeant, Nehemiah Wharton, reported from Essex's army on 13 September 1642, 'Every Wensday [sic] you may find a post that serveth our army at the Saracen's Head, in Carter Lane. His name is Thomas Weedon, who is with us once a week constantly.'[109]

Later in the war, in February 1644, the Committee of Both Kingdoms established a new communications and messenger service to maintain a reliable information exchange with Parliament's Scottish allies. With its centre in London, there were links to further stations at Preston, Derby, Nottingham, Manchester and Northampton; from these stations there was a further communications web that covered more remote towns such as Lincoln, Stafford and Nantwich. The relays supported a weekly messenger service, although messengers could be despatched more frequently should the need arise. This network was enhanced still further in November 1644 when a regular timetable for message delivery was established. Riders left London every Saturday morning and travelled via St Albans, Newport Pagnell, Northampton, Leicester, Nottingham, Derby and Manchester to Preston where they arrived at noon on the Thursday. Having collected any messages from the Scots, the messenger left Preston at noon on the Friday and retraced his route arriving back in London on the Thursday night – a round trip of fifteen days.[110] Express riders were used for more urgent personal despatches. This land-based infrastructure was supplemented by a seaborne equivalent which provided communications 'betwixt the province of Munster and this kingdom'. Similar arrangements were made in Weymouth where 'weekly post barks' sailed for the Continent.[111]

A significant advantage of introducing a reliable postal service was that, as more people used it, so it became possible to intercept these postal services and read more of the letters carried therein![112] The Royalists also established messenger services to carry letters and intelligence information within individual counties. Lord Digby and Sir Edward Nicholas, in their roles as Masters and Comptrollers General of His Majesty's posts, were responsible for establishing the equivalent Royalist postal service.[113] However, as the fighting increasingly went against them, the Royalists lost control of more territory to the Parliamentarians and it became more difficult for them to maintain either their intelligence-gathering organisation, or the speed and security of their postal service.[114]

In summary, it appears reasonable to assess the primary evidence as supporting the conclusion that, after the Edgehill Campaign, Essex recognised the urgent need to obtain accurate and timely intelligence. It also reveals that, by 1645, the Parliamentarian commanders were generally much more sensitive than most Royalist commanders to the importance of intelligence information – and that the Parliamentarian intelligence organisation proved to be much more adept at providing such information. Most significantly of all, the Parliamentarians' intelligence was more effectively integrated into their military planning process. As a later chapter of this book will show, the intelligence gained by the Roundheads in June 1645 was immediately acted upon by Fairfax and this led to the decisive Parliamentarian victory at Naseby.[115] Parliamentarian intelligence operations proved their worth all over the country; it was as a result of Brereton's detailed intelligence reports showing that Rupert was gathering forces and planning to break the siege of Chester, that the Committee of Both Kingdoms decided to reinforce and support the Parliamentary forces in Cheshire in 1645. Lord Fairfax's letter to Brereton dated 24 March 1645 concluded with the remark 'By holding intelligence one with another we shall know better how to bend our forces for the annoyance of the enemy and advancing of the service.'[116] Although Rupert succeeded in relieving Chester in 1645, it is evident from this comment that a sound level of intelligence awareness existed among the senior Parliamentary commanders. Leven's letter to Brereton of 17 March 1645 shows the same thing. As the Scottish commander wrote, 'I thank you for your frequent intelligence and desire the continuance thereof.'[117] So, for the Parliamentarians at least, not only is there evidence that the value of military intelligence was appreciated, but also that they were making very effective use of it by the end of the Civil War.

By comparison, the direction of Royalist intelligence operations was inconsistent and appears to have lacked support from certain senior officers, some of whom do not appear to have appreciated the military advantages bestowed by effective intelligence-gathering. With the exception of Charles I's 1644 campaigns and those operations led by Prince Rupert, the Royalist intelligence-gathering operations lacked focus and the information was rarely integrated into the Royalist planning process. Even after Sir Edward Walker, Charles I's Military Secretary, recognised (somewhat belatedly) the significance of intelligence during the Lostwithiel campaign in 1644, no significant improvements were made to the Royalist management of intelligence operations. Consequently their intelligence-gathering organisation rarely provided them with any decisive and battle-winning information. Even when the Royalists did obtain useful intelligence, such as the warning they were given of Essex's break-out from Gloucester in 1643, the Cavalier commanders were not always responsive enough to exploit it.[118]

Of particular significance to the outcome of the fighting was the steady development of the scoutmaster role. The contemporary evidence shows that the main changes to that role were initiated by the Roundhead commanders before being imitated by the Royalists. For example, during 1644, the Royalists would have appeared to have copied the practice, introduced by the Parliamentarians during 1643, of stationing scoutmasters in frontline garrisons. This combination of a peripatetic scoutmaster controlling a fixed intelligence network had several advantages; not only could the scoutmaster establish a more reliable communication system, but he could also bring more consistency to his intelligence reports. It is also interesting to note how, early on in the conflict, the importance of intelligence-gathering was recognised by the Parliamentarians – and, by comparison, how long it took for the Royalist commanders to follow suit. The Parliamentarian network of intelligence operations developed steadily throughout the war. The growth of a county-based intelligence system was confirmed on 24 February 1644, when the Committee of Both Kingdoms established a sub-committee 'for drafting letters to the Scottish army for intelligence, and to those employed to hold intelligence in the several counties'.[119] The fact that the Parliamentarian network was widened – and was supported by an increasingly efficient communication service which linked the Parliamentarian headquarters – is confirmed by a number of contemporary references.[120] Further evidence of the priority which the Parliamentarians gave to the gathering and exchange of information is provided by the numerous exhortations from the Committee of Both Kingdoms to exchange intelligence. The Committee's letter to Lord Fairfax on 5 March was typical of many when it urged him to 'hold a continual intelligence with the Scottish army'.[121]

All the evidence from the contemporary sources indicates that the Parliamentarian commanders had a much better awareness of the military advantages to be gained from integrating intelligence into their decision-making processes than the Royalists did. The Parliamentarian commanders displayed more innovation in developing their intelligence and were prompt to supply the communications and code-breaking support that further improved their intelligence organisations. Finally, and perhaps most significantly of all, the Parliamentarian commanders appreciated their intelligencers as the Royalist commanders apparently did not – and gave them the support they needed throughout.[122] It was a difference in approach which may well have helped the Roundheads to win the Civil War. Having considered how intelligence information was incorporated into the command structures of each side, the succeeding chapters will show how these intelligence-gathering operations developed as the war progressed and how the outcome of these operations influenced, in their turn, the military operations conducted between 1642 and 1646.

Notes

1 C.H. Firth, *Cromwell's Army* (London, 1902), p.11. See also C.V. Wedgwood, *The King's Peace 1637–1641* (London, 1955), pp.229–232.

2 J. Rushworth, *Historical Collections* (London, 1659–99), Volume II, Part II, p.938; and F. Kitson, *Prince Rupert: Portrait of a Soldier* (London, 1994), p.275.

3 See, for example, I. Roy, 'The Royalist Council of War, 1642–6', *Bulletin of the Institute of Historical Research* (Vol.35, 1962), pp.161–162.

4 P. Gudgin, *Military Intelligence: A History* (Stroud, 1999), p.4.

5 See, for example, *CSPD 1644–1645*, p.170 for a detailed description of the schedule of the enhanced Parliamentarian message service.

6 S. R. Gardiner, *History of the Great Civil War 1642–1649* (four volumes, London, 1893), Volume 1, p.34.

7 P. Young and W. Emberton, *The Royalist Army* (Chatham, 1974), pp.19–20, 31–33, and 41–42.

8 E. Hyde, *The History of the Rebellion and Civil Wars in England* (sixteen books, London, 1702–4), Book VI, p.164. See also C.V. Wedgwood, *The King's War 1641 – 1647* (London, 1958), p.146.

9 See, for example, Clarendon, *History*, Book VI, p.44; Rushworth, *Historical Collections,* Part III, Volume II, p.24; and N. Fiennes, *A Most True and Exact Relation of Both the Battels fought by His Excellency and his Forces against the Bloody Cavelliers* (London, 9 November 1642).

10 Cruso, Militarie *Instructions,* Part III, Chapter III p.69.

11 Cruso, Militarie *Instructions,* Part II, Chapter I, p.46.

12 I.G. Philip (ed.), *The Journal of Sir Samuel Luke* (3 volumes, Oxfordshire Record Society, 1950), Volume I, p.ix.

13 BL, Harl. MSS. 6851, ff. 229–30 (Council minutes, 27 November 1643). See also Roy, 'Royalist Council of War', p.161.

14 Roy, 'Royalist Council of War', pp.150–168.

15 Clarendon, *History*, Book VI, p.375.

16 Ibid, pp.295–300.

17 Ibid, pp.355–360; and E. Walker, *Historical Discourses upon Several Occasions* (London, 1705), p.88.

18 Clarendon, *History,* Book IX, pp.5–8.

19 Roy, 'The Royalist Council of War', pp.150–168.

20 Ibid, p.165.

21 Ibid, p.166.

22 Clarendon, *History*, Book VII, p.226.

23 Ibid, p.226.

24 *CSPD, 1641–43*, p.353.

25 *CSPD, 1640–41; 1641–43; 1644, 1644–45; 1645–47; 1648–49; 1649–50; 1650;* and *1651,* passim.

26 L. Glow, 'The Committee of Safety', *English Historical Review* (Volume 80, No. 315, 1965), pp.291–292.

27 See, for example, Sprigg, *Anglia Rediviva,* pp.26–37, and 56–77; R.N. Dore (ed.), *The Letter Books of Sir William Brereton* (two volumes, Lancashire and Cheshire Record Society, 1984–90), Volume I, pp.65–66; H.G. Tibbutt (ed.), *The Letter Books of Sir Samuel Luke: 1644–45* (Historical Manuscripts Commission JP4, HMSO, 1963), pp.287, 293, and 296; Walker, *Historical Discourses,* p.129; and T. Fairfax, *Short Memorials of Thomas, Lord Fairfax* (London, 1699), printed as part of Francis Maseres, *Select Tracts relating to the Civil Wars in England* (London, 1815), p.418.

28 *CSPD, 1644,* p.25; Sprigg, *Anglia Rediviva,* pp.26–37, and 56–77; Dore, *Letter Books,* Vol I, pp.65–66; and Tibbutt, *Letter Books,* pp.287, 293, and 296.

29 *CSPD, 1642–3,* p.454.

30 *CSPD, 1644,* pp.25, 39–40, 75, and 93.

31 Ibid, p.302.

32 Roy, 'The Royalist Council of War', p.168.

33 *CSPD, 1641–43,* p.328.

34 *CSPD, 1644,* p.4.

35 Ibid, p.25.

36 *CSPD, 1644,* p.42.

37 *C.J.* iii, 198. See also, Commonwealth Exchequer Papers, SP. 28/261, paper dated 16 Sept. 1642; and SP 28/264, paper dated 14 June 1643.

38 *C.J.* iii, 59, 102, 108, 189; and SP. 28/261–264.

39 *CSPD, 1641–43,* p.440.

40 The National Archives, *Commonwealth Exchequer Papers,* SP28/7, ff. 21, 55, 140, 302 and 379; SP28/8, ff. 79–81 and 234–235; SP28/9, ff. 158 and 218–219; SP28/23, ff. 40–41 and 44; SP 28/28, ff. 27, 79, 139 and 188; SP2831, ff. 37, 191 and 662: and SP/130, Part II, ff. 26–27 and 81–89, and Part III, ff. 30–33. See also, Young and Emberton, *Cromwell's Army,* pp.116–117.

41 *CSPD 1644,* p.22. See also, *CSPD, 1641–43,* p.87; *CSPD 1644,* pp.44 and 83; P. Young and

W. Emberton, *The Cavalier Army* (London, 1974), p.116–117; Firth, *Cromwell's Army,* p.65; and D. Nicholas, *Mr. Secretary Nicholas (1593–1669) His Life and Letters* (London, 1995), p.206 which reveals how Sir Edward Nicholas was authorised to receive 'divers sums of money disbursed for intelligence and otherwise in the King's service'. D. Nicholas writes that this money was never received.

42 J.R. Phillips, *Memorials of the Civil War in Wales and the Marches 1642–49* (2 volumes, London, 1874), Volume II, p.217.

43 Hutton, 'Structure of the Royalist Party', p.556

44 Roy, 'The Royalist Council of War', p.168.

45 Compare, for example, S.D.M. Carpenter, *Military Leadership in the Civil Wars, 1642–1651* (Abingdon, 2005), pp.72–73; and A. Hopper, *Black Tom: Sir Thomas Fairfax and the English Revolution* (Manchester University Press, 2007), pp.37–43 with F.T.R. Edgar, *Sir Ralph Hopton: The King's Man in the West, 1642–1652* (Oxford University Press, 1968), pp.29–32.

46 See M.J. Stoyle, *Loyalty and Locality* (Exeter, 1994), pp.93–110, 245–246 and 251–255.

47 See E. 102 [17], *A True Relation of The Proceedings of the Cornish Forces under the command of the Lord Mohune and Sir Ralph Hopton; A Famous Victorie obtained by Sir William Waller against the Lord Herbert* (London, 1643); and Clarendon, *History*, Book VI, p.271.

48 R. Hutton, *The Royalist War Effort 1642–1646* (London, 1982), p.83.

49 See, for example, Sprigge, *Anglia Rediviva,* pp.20–21.

50 L. Glow, 'The Committee of Safety', *English Historical Review* (Volume 80, No. 315, 1965), p.290.

51 Ibid, p.291.

52 R.N. Dore (ed.), *The Letter Books of Sir William Brereton* (Record Society of Lancashire and Cheshire, 1990), pp.108–109. See also Add. MSS 11331–11333 for the original letters transcribed by Dore.

53 Dore, *Letter Books,* Volume I, p.488.

54 P. Gudgin, *Military Intelligence. A History* (Stroud, 1999), p.5.

55 J. Turner, *Pallas Armata* (London, 1683), p.265.

56 B. Rich, *A Pathway to Military Practice* (London, 1587), p.40.

57 See Chapter 1, above.

58 TNA, Commonwealth Exchequer Papers, SP 28, f. 127. See also Philip, *Journal of Sir Samuel Luke,* Volume I, p.vi.

59 See, for example, Commonwealth Exchequer Papers, SP 28/7, ff. 8, 55, 140 and 302 for examples of payments made to Luke. See also SP28/31, ff. 37, 191 and 662 for payments to Leonard Watson, Scoutmaster-General to Manchester and then the New Model Army.

60 E. 100[6], *A Most Miraculous and Happy Victory* (London, 1643).

61 Clarendon, *History*, Book VI, pp.99–100.

62 Kitson, *Prince Rupert*, pp.275–276.

63 E. 127[18], *Prince Robert's Disguises* (London, 16 November 1642).

64 Anon, *A Particular relation of the action before Cirencester* (Oxford, 1643), p.8.

65 M. Cavendish, Duchess of Newcastle, *The Lives of William Cavendishe, Duke of Newcastle and of his wife, Margaret, Duchess of Newcastle* (1667, London, 1872 edition), p.39.

66 A.A. Wood, *Athenae Oxonienses* (1721, Oxford, 1813 edition), Vol III, p.902.

67 See H.G. Tibbutt (ed.), *The Letter Books of Sir Samuel Luke 1644–45* (London, 1963); and Philip, *Journal*, which contain numerous examples of these reports to, and from, Luke.

68 Philip, *Journal,* Volume 1, p.xi.

69 See, for example, *CSPD, 1641–43*, pp.473 and 488.

70 J. Ricraft, *The Civil Warres of England* (London, 1649), p.115.

71 See S. Kelsey, *Sir Samuel Luke* (DNB).

72 See, for example, R. Bell, *Fairfax Correspondence,* (two volumes, London, 1849), Volume I, pp.27, 44, 46, and 64; and A. Marshall, *Intelligence and Espionage in the reign of Charles II, 1660–1685* (Cambridge, 1994), pp.18–19.

73 Clarendon, *History*, Book VIII, p.38.

74 See I. Roy, *Sir William Neale* (DNB).

75 Philip, *Journal*, Volume III, p.258.

76 *CSPD, 1644*, p.163.

77 See E. 50[26], *The Kingdomes Weekly Intelligencer* (London, 4–11 June 1644); and E. 50[32], *The Spie* (London, 6–13 June 1644).

78 E. 40[32], *Mercurius Aulicus* (Oxford, 23 March 1644).

79 *CSPD, 1644*, p.149.

80 *CSPD, 1644–1645*, p.76.

81 See Annex 1 for a list of scoutmasters identified during research for the present thesis.

82 See, for example, *CSPD, 1644–45*, p.594. On 15 June 1645, £10 was paid 'to Sir Samuel Luke's man for his pains'.

83 See *Commonwealth Exchequer Papers*, SP28/31, f. 37; and SP28/130, Part II, ff. 26 and 27.

84 E. 9[5], *Mercurius Aulicus* (Oxford, 24 August 1644).

85 Tibbutt, *Letter Books*, p.471.

86 Ibid, p.476.

87 *CSPD, 1645*, p.583.

88 Unfortunately I have been unable to discover any further information about Francis Ruce (Rous).

89 See E. Walker, *Brief Memorials of the Unfortunate Success of His Majesty's Army and Affairs in the Year 1645* (London, 1705), p.130.

90 Cockayne's appointment is listed in the List of Indigent Officers. See Anon, *A List of Officers claiming to the sixty thousand pounds &c. granted by His Sacred Majesty for the relief of his truly loyal and indigent party* (London, 1663), pp.45 and 128.

91 See, for example, Warburton, *Memoirs*, Volume III, pp.91, and 102.

92 Bod. L, Tanner MSS 60, ff. 43, 49 and 50.

93 Walker, *Historical Discourses,* p.130, and Warburton, *Memoirs*, Volume III, p.103.

94 Tibbutt, *Letter Books*, p.549; and G. Foard, *Naseby: The Decisive Campaign* (Barnsley, 1995), p.159.

95 Examples of such deception plans abound throughout history. See for example, Hannibal's deployments before the battles of the Trebbia, Lake Trasimene and Cannae described in J. Peddie, *Hannibal's War* (Stroud, 1995), pp.55, 67–71, and 89–96.

96 Cruso, *Militarie Instructions*, Chapter II, p.57.

97 E. Walsingham, *The Life of the Most Honourable Knight, Sir Henry Gage, Late Governor of Oxford* (Oxford, 1645), pp.15–16.

98 Warburton, *Memoirs*, Volume II, p.275.

99 W. S. Churchill, *The Second World War* (London, 2000), Volume VI, p.11.

100 See, for example, Dore, *Letter Books,* Volume I, pp.110–111, 238 and 261.

101 Clarendon, *History,* Book V, p.76.

102 E. 38 [10], *Prince Rupert's Raising of the Siege of Newark* (London, 1644).

103 Clarendon, *History,* Book VII, pp.205–206.

104 Adair, *Roundhead General,* pp.143–144.

105 Kitson, *Prince Rupert*, pp.275–276.

106 *CSPD, 1644*, pp.28, and 33.

107 R.N. Dore (ed.), *Letter Books of Sir William Brereton* (two volumes, The Record Society of Lancashire and Cheshire, 1990), pp.85–87.

108 *CSPD, 1642*, p.257.

109 S.L. Ede-Borrett (ed.), *The Letters of Nehemiah Wharton* (Wollaston, 1983), p.17.

110 *CSPD, 1644*, p.170.

111 *CSPD, 1643*, pp.28–29.

112 See, for example, D. Kahn, *The Code Breakers: The Story of Secret Writing* (New York, 1996), p.155; and B. Donagan, *War in England, 1642–1649* (Oxford, 2008), pp.3, 94 and 103.

113 See, for example, *CSPD, 1644,* p.6; and G. A. Harrison, *Royalist Organisation in Gloucestershire and Bristol 1642 – 1645* (MA thesis, University of Manchester, 1961), p.171.

114 Marshall, *Intelligence and Espionage,* p.20.

115 Gardiner, *History,* Volume I, p.150; Brereton, *Letter Books,* Volume I, p.36.

116 Dore, *Letter Books,* Volume I, p.126.

117 Dore, *Letter Books,* Volume I, p.87.

118 Bod. L, Clarendon MSS, 1738, f. 5.

119 *CSPD, 1644,* p.25.

120 Ibid, pp.28–29.

121 Ibid, p.35.

122 Dore, *Letter Books,* Volume I, p.87..

4

Establishing the Role of Intelligence-Gathering – the Edgehill Campaign 1642

Historians[1] have frequently cited the gathering of intelligence during the Edgehill Campaign to support their contention that Civil War intelligence operations were so rudimentary and ineffective that military commanders really had 'to walk in the dark'. But just how effective were intelligence-gathering operations during this, the first major campaign of the war? To answer to this question we will begin by setting out the sequence of military events, before considering how subsequent historians have described intelligence during the campaign – and what information they have used to support their conclusions. What do contemporary documents reveal about what really happened, what intelligence was available to the Parliamentarian and Royalist commanders, and how effectively did they use the information? When the available contemporary evidence is considered, it is possible to identify some alternative interpretations of the planning of the Edgehill Campaign that more closely match the established facts contained in the accounts, and to conclude that the judgements of previous historians have been too harsh. The intelligence operations conducted during the campaign, whilst far from perfect, were not as ineffective as has hitherto been suggested.

In order to understand the development of the intelligence-gathering operations, it is useful to understand how the sequence of military events influenced the intelligence operations on both sides. The Civil War developed relatively slowly because the recruitment and deploying of the opposing armies took time. The reversals that the Royalists suffered before Hull in April and July 1642 so weakened Charles' credibility that few men join his army when he raised his standard at Nottingham on 22 August. However, when the King moved west towards Wales and the Marches, Royalist recruitment rapidly improved and Charles' forces grew in both size and capability.

The Royalist Army reached Shrewsbury on 20 September and Charles decided to establish his administrative as well as his military headquarters in that town whilst he continued to recruit and train his army. With the Royalist forces gathering at Shrewsbury, Essex moved his army from Northampton to Worcester, which he reached on 24 September. The one significant military action which occurred during the Royalist redeployment to the west was when Prince Rupert skirmished with the advancing Parliamentarian horse at Powick Bridge outside Worcester on 23 September. This short action, which resulted in a decisive victory for the Royalist horse, had a psychological impact out of all proportion to its military significance. Whilst it established the reputation of Prince Rupert as an intuitive and daring cavalry commander, it also seriously weakened the Parliamentarians' confidence in the operational performance of their own cavalry. As the city of Worcester covered the direct approaches to the possible Royalist reinforcements forming up in the South West and was close to the road to London, the city was garrisoned by Essex and became his head-quarters. In addition to settling his forces around Worcester, Essex also garrisoned Hereford, Coventry, Northampton, Banbury and Warwick Castle. This ring of fortified settlements covered all the possible routes to London, thereby allowing the Parliamentarian troops stationed in those places to provide intelligence of any Royalist move towards London.

The Edgehill Campaign effectively began when the Royalist Army left Shrewsbury on 12 October and marched south along the River Severn to Bridgnorth which it eventually left on 15 October. Between 12 and 14 October, Essex issued a series of instructions to Lord Wharton, one of his brigade com-manders, to deploy a force (which eventually totalled up to 6,000 men) to the north of Worcester to reinforce the Parliamentarian forces at Kidderminster and Bewdley. When the Royalist Army left Bridgnorth, it changed direction to the southeast and marched by way of Wolverhampton and Birmingham towards London. The Royalists paused again for a review by Charles I on Meriden Heath near Coventry on 18 October where it was joined by regiments from Lancashire. The review completed, the army continued its march via Kenilworth, Chesford and Southam before reaching the Edgeworth/Edgecote area on the afternoon of 22 October. Essex, however, did not leave Worcester until 19 October at which time Charles was reported to be about 25 miles away at Meriden.[2] Following instructions from Parliament to respond to the reported movements of the Royalist Army,[3] Essex had led the Parliamentarian Army out of Worcester and marched eastwards through Stratford-upon-Avon. On 21 October, a scouting party from the Warwick garrison intercepted part of the Royalist baggage train, thereby providing useful intelligence that the King was on the march to London. The Parliamentarian Army reached Kineton on 22 October. When the Royalist Army arrived at Edgecote, the King decided to rest the army the next day, except for one of the Royalist brigades, commanded by Sir Nicholas Byron, and 4,000

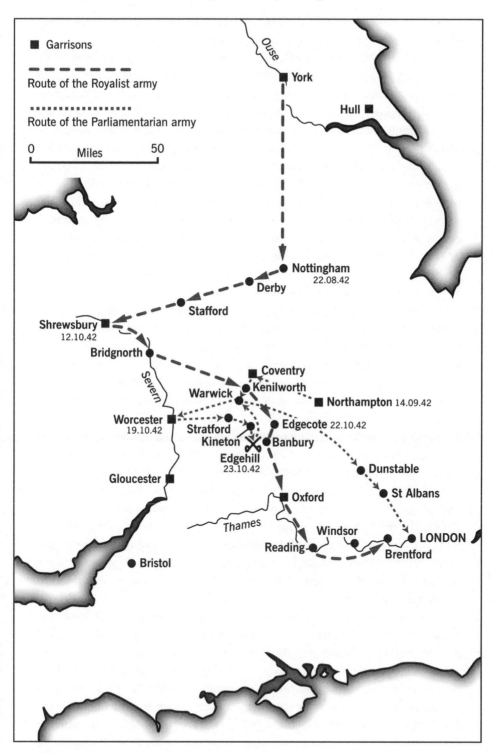

The Edgehill Campaign, 1642.

men of that brigade who were to take four guns and assault the Parliamentarian garrison at the nearby Banbury Castle on Sunday, 23 October.

At some time on 22 October, Rupert despatched a party of 400 troopers under Lord George Digby, now serving the King as a Royalist horse commander, to scout the surrounding area. The scouting party returned having found no sign of the Parliamentarian Army. However, that evening, a party of Rupert's horse captured a group of Parliamentarian quartermasters at the village of Wormleighton. Having questioned the captives, Rupert sent a patrol of 24 troopers under a certain Lieutenant Martin to Kineton to confirm the prisoners' report that the Parliamentarian Army was in that area. When Martin confirmed the location of the Parliamentarian forces, Rupert sent a message to the King suggesting that, in view of the immediate proximity of Essex's forces, the Royalist Army should cancel their previous plans and concentrate without delay along the ridgeline of Edgehill as this was seen as a safe assembly point for regiments quartered in twenty square miles of country and a place from which Essex's movements could be observed and his progress blocked.

Charles accepted his nephew's recommendation and, without calling a Council of War, issued orders to this effect at about 3am in the morning of Sunday 23 October. The Royalist Army concentrated between 12 pm and 1pm that same afternoon. The Parliamentarian commanders were first informed of the presence of the Royalist Army mustering on the top of Edgehill at about 8am on 23 October. A Parliamentarian cleric reported that Essex and his commanders were on their way to church when they received this information.[4] The best estimate of the strength of the Royalist Army is that it numbered 14,300 men in all: 2,800 horse, 1,000 dragoons, 10,500 foot and 20 guns.[5] The best estimate of the strength of the Parliamentarian Army at Edgehill is that it numbered 14,870 men: 2,150 horse, 720 dragoons, 12,000 foot and 30 guns.[6] The numbers of the Parliamentarian Army present at Kineton on that Sunday morning had been reduced by the number of garrison forces as well as delays in finding sufficient transport and horses to move all the artillery pieces. Consequently several guns of their artillery train, escorted by two regiments of foot and a regiment of horse, were about a day's march behind the main body and did not join Essex until the evening after the battle.

Before battle was joined on the morning of 23 October 1642, a Parliamentarian regiment of horse, recruited by the somewhat misleadingly named Colonel Faithful Fortescue, deserted to the Royalists just before Rupert led his troopers in a charge against the enemy. The contemporary accounts do not make it clear when the Royalist commanders were informed that this Parliamentarian cavalry force was intending to change their allegiance. Certainly the news was not widely known amongst their new allies – the Royalist soldiers – for many of Fortescue's troopers, not having discarded the orange sashes which distinguished them as Roundheads, were killed by Royalist soldiers who do not appear to have been informed of Fortescue's change of allegiance. The Royalists' dashing cavalry charge swept away many of the Parliamentarian horse and foot, but was carried too far and for too long. By the time the Royalist horse had returned to the battlefield, the remaining Parliamentarian horse and foot had brought the isolated and unsupported Royalist infantry to the very edge of defeat. The return of the Royalist horse brought the battle to a close. It was a bloody and savage affair but, as neither side was decisively defeated and driven from the field, the battle ended inconclusively. Although both armies deployed again the next day, there was no full-scale engagement. Towards the end of the day, Essex withdrew his army to Warwick. His withdrawal was harassed by Prince Rupert's cavalry who captured the bulk of the Parliamentarian baggage train – including Essex's own baggage which contained his personal papers.

Once Essex had withdrawn towards Warwick, the Royalist Army captured Banbury before regrouping around Oxford. Charles was reluctant to move until he had received definite intelligence of the Parliamentarian Army's position and intentions. As Essex was also waiting for the same information about the Royalist Army, there was a period of mutual indecision before the intelligence reports from Prince Rupert's scouts describing the weakness of the garrison of Reading proved too tempting for the Royalists to ignore and the King was persuaded to continue his advance.[7] Once Essex received intelligence that the Royalist Army had left Oxford and was marching towards Reading, he moved swiftly towards London which he reached on 8 November. The Royalist advance was eventually countered and reversed at Turnham Green by the combined strength of Essex's army and the London Trained Bands which had been deployed to block the western approaches to London. As Essex's plan of campaign had apparently forecast, the Royalists realised that they were too heavily outnumbered to risk a battle. Accordingly, a day later, the Edgehill Campaign ended when Charles withdrew his army to Oxford.

To what extent has our understanding of the role of military intelligence in the Edgehill Campaign been influenced by the accounts of the subsequent historians? When the evidence contained in the contemporary accounts of the campaign is compared with the current historical perceptions of what happened, it is clear that there is a substantial difference of opinion which needs to be explored and explained. As the earliest historical accounts of the Battle of Edgehill only provided a brief and incomplete chronological description of the military action, any contribution made by intelligence information upon the conduct and the eventual outcome of the battle has, perhaps inevitably, received little or no attention. A great deal of contemporary evidence has now been assessed and it suggests that intelligence-gathering played a significant role in the campaign, although few subsequent historical publications considered any – let alone all – of this evidence in their accounts. It is therefore most illuminating to establish just which contemporary sources describing intelligence-gathering have been considered by historians in their accounts of the campaign and the Battle of Edgehill.

The first histories of the conflict were those written by the Parliamentarian historians May and Rushworth during the Interregnum.[8] Both of these men set the pattern for subsequent seventeenth-century and eighteenth-century accounts as they provided only a brief description of the Edgehill Campaign. The impact of any intelligence-gathering was not mentioned in any of the seventeenth-century accounts of the campaign, although May's description did include an important insight into the strategic plan of the Roundhead commander when he wrote that Essex intended to 'follow his [the King's] March neere at hand, and by the help of those forces which the City of London would pour forth upon him, utterly ruine his inclosed army.'[9] The relevance of this evidence will be considered in more detail later in this chapter.

Clarendon's *History* was the first near-contemporary Royalist account that explored the Edgehill Campaign in any detail. It is in this account that we are told that the King did receive intelligence reporting the movements of the Parliamentarian Army, although Clarendon played down the significance of these reports as he considered them to be contradictory, and therefore of limited value. For example, he noted that 'some reported that [Essex's army] remained still at Worcester; others, that they were marched the direct way from thence towards London'; he also described how intelligence reports about the disposition of Essex's army led to 'some difference of opinion which way he [the King] should take'. Clarendon's *History* described the support that the Royalist Army expected to receive from local people along their proposed route of march and the Royalist perception that Essex was bound to move his army to 'put himself in their way'.[10] Clarendon also included the only account of the intelligence about the movements of the Parliamentarian Army which had been received before the battle by the Royalist commanders. In view of the number of references Clarendon made to intelligence reports, it is all the more surprising that he evidently did not consider this intelligence-gathering to have been effective, for his summary of the Edgehill intelligence operations was particularly dismissive. He observed, as we have seen, that:

> The two armies, though they were but twenty miles asunder when they first set forth, and both marched the same way … gave not the least disquiet in ten days march to each other; and in truth, as it appeared afterwards, neither army knew where the other was.[11]

Hardly surprisingly, it is this negative comment on the conduct of intelligence-gathering by both sides which has been most often quoted by later historians. Notwithstanding the discovery – and wider availability – of increasing amounts of contradictory contemporary evidence, Clarendon's dismissive assessment of the impact that intelligence-gathering operations had had upon the Edgehill Campaign has been simply accepted by scholars for many years. In the absence of any comprehensive evaluation of all of the contemporary accounts to counter this conclusion, his words remained largely unchallenged. Furthermore, because subsequent historians were more interested in exploring the politico-economic and social aspects of the conflict, Clarendon's description does not appear to have been made the subject of further study and thus gained further credibility due to its sheer longevity.

It was not until the mid-nineteenth century that historians began to clarify the military details of the Battle of Edgehill; exploring such questions as where exactly it was fought, how many soldiers took part and what actually happened. Because contemporary accounts of the size and deployment of the armies were inevitably contradictory, the immediate priority for the nineteenth-century historians was to compile a comprehensive and clear description of events. Warburton's *Memoirs* provided one of the first reconstructions of the battle,[12] which relied principally upon Clarendon's account, albeit an account supplemented by some other con-temporary accounts, such as the memoirs of the Royalist, Sir Richard Bulstrode.[13] It is of interest that Warburton's version contained one important new source as it referred to a manuscript which he had discovered whilst working on the papers of Prince Rupert, and which is now referred to as 'Prince Rupert's Diary'.[14] This manuscript, which was probably written just after the war by one of Rupert's personal staff, showed that Essex had been receiving regular intelligence reports of the Royalist plans before the battle. As we have seen, the day after the Battle of Edgehill, Rupert's horsemen captured Essex's 'cabinet of letters', amongst which were a number of letters from a certain Mr Blake, who was Rupert's secretary (or 'privy chamberlain').[15] These letters showed that Blake had 'betrayed all his Majesty's Counsells' and had given Essex high level intelligence information about the Royalist intentions and plans. Gardiner's reconstruction of the Edgehill Campaign in his great *History* of 1893 also referred to the contemporary accounts written by Clarendon and Bulstrode, but it did not examine the role played by intelligence during the campaign, and did not mention Blake at all.[16]

Thus Clarendon's seemingly substantially flawed depiction of the Edgehill Campaign intelligence operations as ineffectual continued to be widely accepted for about 200 years until 1904 when the distinguished Victorian historian, Sir Charles Firth, published an article in which he began to question the accuracy of Clarendon's assessments.[17] Despite Firth's warnings about Clarendon's objectivity, which were reiterated by Ronald Hutton in January 1982,[18] no further research was conducted into the role played by intelligence in the campaign until the 1970s when Peter Young became the first military historian to study the events leading up to the battle in any detail. Although Young paid comparatively less attention to intelligence-gathering itself, he did draw attention to the apparent lack of Parliamentarian scouting when he wrote that 'the news of the King's advance does not seem to have reached Essex very quickly', and commented that Essex was 'so ill-served by his intelligence that it was not until 18 October that he could make the decision to move'.[19] Young also identified those aspects of Essex's manoeuvres that remained puzzling when he wrote that 'commentators have failed to discern any reasonable motive for [Essex] placing himself at Worcester.'[20]

Although Young extended substantially the exploration of contemporary accounts as part of his research, he did not complete a full analysis of all the available evidence. In particular, he did not appear to have considered May's *History of the Parliament* (which suggested that Essex wished to entrap the Royalists before the walls of London) when accounting for the fact that Essex did not immediately move out of Worcester to intercept the Royalist Army. Young explored Clarendon's account of the Royalist Council of War's deliberations prior to their decision to march on London, and repeated Clarendon's comments about the alleged inefficiency of the Royalist scouting, and about the impact that inaccurate intelligence had allegedly had upon the Royalist decisions the day before the battle. Young drew attention to Clarendon's statement that the King had had 'no intelligence that the Earl of Essex was within any distance' before ordering the army to rest while Sir Nicholas Byron took a brigade to capture Banbury.[21] More interestingly, he reintroduced the so-called 'Prince Rupert's Diary' to the debate, initially brought in by Warburton in his *Memoirs*; Young located the papers in the Wiltshire Record Office after they were thought lost since Warburton consulted them during the 1840s. As Young observed, the 'Diary' not only described the role played by Mr Blake, the Parliamentarian spy, but also described how Lord Digby had led a Royalist scouting patrol to locate Essex's army the day before the battle.[22] His evaluation of a larger number of contemporary sources (in addition to Clarendon's account) enabled him to establish that intelligence reports had played a part in the movements of both armies prior to the battle itself.[23] However, although Young's research identified many of the contributions which intelligence-gathering operations made to the campaign, his book did not include any analysis of – or draw any conclusions about – the impact these intelligence operations had upon the outcome of the campaign.

Since Young's book on Edgehill indicated how intelligence information had influenced the conduct – if not the outcome – of the campaign, historians have begun to pay more attention to the part played by intelligence-gathering. However, these studies are generally not consistent with each other as they do not include all the evidence found in the contemporary sources. For example, the study by military historians, Young and Holmes, first published in 1974, continued to quote Clarendon's statement that 'neither army knew where the other was', ascribing this ignorance to 'poor intelligence and insufficient cavalry reconnaissance'. They attributed the 'poor intelligence' to the fact that 'Essex had no scoutmaster', and 'the insufficient cavalry reconnaissance' to the inadequate training and ill-defined role of the Parliamentarian horse.[24] Blake's intelligence reports were not mentioned, even though his reports provide the rationale for their conclusion that Essex 'appears to have thought that the King was still intending to attack Banbury'.[25]

Another account of the Edgehill Campaign – the detailed study by the historians, Alan Turton and others, published in 2004 – does include comments on the contemporary evidence of the intelligence information which was available to each side.[26] However, this study makes no reference to the reports of Mr Blake, although it does mention Lord Digby's patrol the day before the battle. Despite Hutton's suggestion that Clarendon's *History* 'ought to be the last, not the first, source to be consulted on a question, after all the contemporary evidence has been reviewed',[27] Turton and his co-authors appear to have continued to cite Clarendon's *History* as their principle contemporary source for their assessment of the contribution made by intelligence. Thus their conclusion that intelligence-gathering on both sides was ineffective inevitably reflected Clarendon's perception that Essex 'had no idea where his enemy actually was', and that the King was 'lacking any intelligence of the route of Essex's march'.[28]

A more recent account of the Edgehill Campaign can be found in Malcolm Wanklyn and Frank Jones' *Military History of the English Civil War*, published in 2005.[29] Reflecting the reports of troop movements published in the contemporary news pamphlets, Wanklyn and Jones acknowledged that the Royalist feint towards Worcester described in the pamphlets would have served several purposes. Not only would it have confused Essex about London being the Royalists' true objective, but it would also have delayed the departure of Essex's army from Worcester, and increased the chances of the Royalist Army avoiding the Parliamentarians altogether. Theirs was therefore the first historical study since May to note that Essex intended to follow (rather than to intercept) the Royalist Army as it marched towards London and to trap it before the fortifications of the capital and the Parliamentarian forces drawn together under the command of the Earl of Warwick (who was normally in command of the Parliamentarian fleet). In the latest study of the Edgehill Campaign, contained in Wanklyn's *The Warrior Generals* published in 2010, the contemporary account of the 'excellent intelligence' provided by Blake is described, as is the contemporary evidence of Prince Rupert's feint towards Bridgnorth as Charles led his army towards London, and Digby's patrol the day before the battle.[30]

Having considered how subsequent historians have described the Edgehill Campaign, it is now appropriate to compare their studies with the contemporary evidence of how military intelligence influenced the campaign. But, before exploring the evidence of intelligence-gathering that was reported in the contemporary accounts, it is prudent to examine and comment on the reliability of these primary sources. Clearly any letters or memoirs written by eyewitnesses of the events leading up to the battle will reflect the political views and personal experiences of the writer, and due allowance must be made for this when weighing the accuracy of such accounts. However, the accounts written by the military commanders are particularly relevant to this book as they provide an insight into how intelligence information influenced their subsequent decisions.[31] Interestingly, even junior officers' accounts of the campaign contain references to intelligence operations; for example, one of the few to emerge from the skirmish at Powick Bridge with his reputation enhanced was the up-and-coming Parliamentarian commander, Captain Nathaniel Fiennes, who described how the Royalists advanced to take up position on Edgehill 'having, no doubt, got Intelligence ... of our army'.[32]

In addition to the eyewitness accounts, a number of documents describing events relating to the campaign were printed either during or shortly after the campaign. As many of these accounts were partisan news pamphlets, their content again needs to be treated with caution. Clearly most had propagandist intent, and this may have dissuaded previous historians from relying on the information they contain. However, a comparison of the pamphlets' version of events with that found in the journals of both the House of Commons and the House of Lords shows that the information printed in the pamphlets was generally accurate.[33] Independent confirmation of the fact that letters from Essex were received on a number of occasions during this period (as stated in the pamphlets) is provided by the journals of both the House of Commons and the House of Lords, although, because these letters were referred unopened to the Committee of Safety, the journals do not reveal their precise content.[34]

It is interesting to note that, from September 1642, weeks before the King led his forces away from Shrewsbury, the London pamphlets contained a substantial amount of detailed intelligence information about the stationing of both forces.[35] The pamphleteers were quick to report that Essex had placed a number of garrisons in towns covering the possible approach roads to London, such as Coventry, Warwick and Banbury, in order to obtain intelligence of any Royalist movement towards the capital. In early October, further reports were published about the garrisoning of Hereford with '1,000 foot, 400 horse and 2 guns'.[36] Other reports stated that, whilst Essex was stationed at Worcester, he 'had placed Garrisons in severall townes of consequence, as Bewdley and Kitterminster [Kidderminster]'.[37] The subsequent increases in the size of the Kidderminster garrison in response to Rupert's cavalry deployment were also reported promptly.[38] This information was also confirmed by another report, published on 13 October, which stated that Essex 'had made strong Fortifications about Worcester, and had placed garrisons in ... Bewdly and Kidderminster'. This article also amplified the earlier report that the Earl of Stamford was in Hereford with 'a regiment of foot and 500 horse'.[39] It seems reasonable to conclude that, if the Royalists had read them, these pamphlets could have provided Charles and his military commanders with a pretty good idea about where Essex had deployed his army.

During September and October 1642, hardly a day went by without the London news pamphlets also reporting the composition and strength of the Royalist Army. For example, at the beginning of October, it was reported that 'Prince Robert [Rupert] with about ten Troops of horse was at Bridgenorth, the Kings Majesty being for the most part at Shrewsbury.'[40] The pamphleteers claimed that their reports were accurate and to be trusted as they were quoting information contained in letters that Essex had sent to Parliament. As early as 3 October, one writer claimed that the Royalist Army had grown to such a size that a move on Worcester was imminent.[41] On 10 October it was reported that the Royalist Army was '12,000 foot and 4,000 horse' strong'.[42] On 11 October it was reported that the Royalist Army was '9,000 foot, 2,500 horse and 1,500 dragoons'.[43] Clearly some of these reports were contradictory for, on 12 October, a London pamphleteer had made a substantially smaller estimate reporting that the Royalist Army comprised '6,000 foot, 3,000 horse and 1,500 dragoons'.[44] These inconsistencies reflected Parliamentarian uncertainty about the actual size of the Royalist Army. Essex knew that Royalist recruiting had been slow and that the King was seeking to 'make an addition to his ... army'.[45] Essex was also aware of the forces being recruited by the Royalist magnate, Lord Herbert, in Wales.[46]

In addition to reporting the size of the Royalist Army, the news pamphlets also printed letters from Essex which had informed Parliament of the senior appointments within the enemy forces. For example, on 11 October it was reported that 'Lord Ruthven [who subsequently was appointed to be the Royalist Captain-General] is come out of Scotland' to join the King's army.[47] Later reports outlined how the Royalist Army was organised; on 15 October both editions of the *Perfect Diurnall* reported that Parliament knew that the King 'hath divided [his army] into two parts, one part which Prince Robert [Rupert] hath the command of, and in the nature of a flying army marceth [sic] before, the King with the other part marceth after'.[48]

The news pamphlet reports also reflected the contemporary speculation about the Royalists' 'grand designe' to regain London; on 8 October, it was reported that 'the King is yet at Shrewsbury, but an honest man of that Towne saith some of the prime Officers of the Army gave out confidently that the King will go towards London next Wednesday.'[49] This report predicted that the Royalists would leave Shrewsbury for London on 12 October which was in fact the very date that Charles did lead his army into the field. This was the first report of several to appear in the London press announcing the imminent departure of the Royalist Army for the capital.[50] Subsequently, the pamphlets reported the King's movements after the Royalist Army had left Shrewsbury, as predicted, on 12 October.[51] The evidence of the news pamphlet reports – and of a number of other contemporary sources – shows that Essex knew within a few days that the Royalist Army had left Shrewsbury and was marching towards Kidderminster.[52] Thus, when the Parliamentarian Army eventually left Worcester, it is hard to avoid the conclusion that Essex knew the King was marching on London with an army of some 14,000–15,000 men. Essex also knew that Rupert was sweeping ahead of the main body of the Royalist Army with a force of mounted troops.

As these initial reports did not reveal the immediate destination of the Royalist Army, Essex needed more information before he could order his army to move.

On 11 October, it was reported in London that 'forty troops' of Rupert's cavalry had moved south towards Worcester 'to plunder and pillage'.[53] As it was perfectly reasonable for Essex to have thought that this deployment of Rupert's cavalry might have presaged the move of Royalist Army to the southwest to collect more reinforcements, Essex moved to counter Rupert and to reduce the extent and damage of the Royalist foraging parties. He therefore ordered the progressive deployment of Lord Wharton, one of his brigade commanders, and about 6,000 men north to Kidderminster between 12 and 14 October 'to discover the state of the King's Army'.[54] This deployment was immediately reported by the pamphleteers who published Essex's letter to Parliament in which he stated that he had 'sent Lord Wharton with 7 troops of horse to Kidderminster to discover the state of the King's army and to prevent the Cavaliers in their plundering of the country'.[55] At this stage of the campaign, it is evident from the contemporary sources that Essex was deploying his forces to counter a Royalist advance southwards towards Worcester.

Whilst Wharton's force deployed against Rupert's cavalry, Essex appears to have needed more reports of the main Royalist Army before he could form a clear idea of Charles' intentions. Although the pamphleteers were quick to report that the Royalists had 'departed on Tuesday last [11 October] from Shrewsbury to Bridgnorth',[56] a few more days elapsed before Essex reported his initial interpretation of Charles' movements to Parliament on 14 October.[57] Essex does not seem to have been satisfied with his grasp of the Royalist intentions until 15 October, when a further pamphlet report included a letter from Essex in which he appeared to appreciate, for the first time, the purpose of the Royalist manoeuvres. In this letter, Essex reported the withdrawal of Rupert's cavalry force to rejoin the Royalist Army near Birmingham, stating that

> ... intelligence was brought that they [Rupert's cavalry] were retreated back another way, and were marched to Wolverhampton, and that the Kings army being divided into two parts, Prince Robert [Rupert] with about 8 troops of horse, at the same time when the other army appeared, marched to Birmingham.[58]

In a later edition, the *Perfect Diurnall* reported that Essex had informed Parliament that 'he intendeth to advance with his army and follow close after his Majestie.' Perhaps in an attempt to reassure Members of Parliament that their army was reacting to the Royalist manoeuvres, Essex reported that, whilst the King was at Wolverhampton, some elements of the Parliamentarian Army were 'within seven miles of His Majesty's Army'.[59] As Essex did not leave Worcester until 19 October, any suggestion that his entire army was within seven miles of the King was certainly not accurate as, at that time, the bulk of the Parliamentarian Army was still in camp some 25 miles away from the Royalists' reported position. Roundhead pamphleteers predicted an early confrontation when they reported that 'Essex with his main army are now upon their march to Bridgenorth ... it is very probable they will have another battle very shortly.'[60] News of the skirmish between a Royalist force led by Lord Digby and a Parliamentarian force commanded by the MP, Denzil Holles, just outside Wolverhampton also provided Essex with the intelligence that the Royalist Army was on the move.[61] All the news pamphlets cited Essex's reports to Parliament as the basis of their reports about his movements and those of his Royalist opponents.

Essex was clearly uncertain about the immediate destination of the Royalist Army and his perplexity continued until the enemy had left Bridgnorth. Evidence of this is provided by the Parliamentarian Army commanders, who, in their subsequent account of the Battle of Edgehill published on 28 October, stated that 'we marched from Worcester, Wednesday the 19, upon intelligence that their [the Royalists'] army was moved from Shrewsbury and Bridgnorth.'[62] Because Bridgnorth lay on both the route to London as well as on the route to the southwest, the reference to 'Shrewsbury *and Bridgnorth* [author's emphasis]' confirms that the destination of the Royalist Army was not known for certain until the Royalists had left Bridgnorth. Only then could Essex be sure that the Royalist Army was heading for London, and thus order his own army to march from Worcester. Thus, on 19 October, Essex recalled Lord Wharton's force from marking Rupert and covering the northern approaches to Worcester and led his army out of that city. Another pamphlet reported that, on the same day that Wharton's reinforced force was ordered to rejoin Essex and the main army, Rupert 'having information that more Forces were coming to aid the Lord Wharton ... immediately marched away with all his forces'.[63] By now, the pamphleteers were reporting that MPs had received a letter from Essex informing them that the King's army had reached Wolverhampton, whilst Rupert was approaching Birmingham and was twelve miles from Coventry.[64] It appears reasonable to conclude from the pamphlet reports of Essex's letters to Parliament that he now knew the approximate location of the Royalist Army, and that he now had a degree of confidence in his intelligence assessments.[65] The fact that the MPs had ordered Essex to leave Worcester probably reflected their increasing concerns that Charles was marching on London.[66]

So, if Essex knew the King was on the march, why did the Parliamentarian Army not leave Worcester at once? A number of the London news pamphlets refer to the Parliamentarian Army 'following' the Royalist Army.[67] These reports thus support May's contention that Essex was planning to 'follow his [the King's] March neere at hand, and by the help of those forces which the City of London would pour forth upon him, utterly ruine his inclosed army'.[68] Therefore a deliberate decision to delay deployment of the Parliamentarian Army from Worcester was perfectly consistent with Essex's strategy to trap the Royalist Army between the hammer of his army and the anvil of the strengthened defences of London.

Coordinating his attack on the Royalist Army with other Parliamentarian forces would have given Essex an overwhelming numerical advantage. This would explain, not only why Essex delayed his departure from Worcester, but also why he urged Parliament to reinforce the Trained Bands of London with those from Middlesex and Essex under the command of the Earl of Warwick. A news pamphlet report, published in mid October, confirms that the Committee of Safety ordered that the Earl of Warwick be removed temporarily from the command of the fleet so that he could take charge of the defences of London, and lead the Trained Bands of Essex, Hereford, London and Middlesex against the Royalist Army.[69] Subsequent news pamphlets also reported that the Earl of Warwick was reinforcing the garrison of London.[70] Meanwhile, the Common Council of London had met on 18 October to discuss the defence of the city.[71] Some contemporary reports suggested that Essex hoped Charles would attack one of his garrisons while on his march to London as this would also have allowed the Roundheads an earlier opportunity to trap the Royalists between that garrison and their own pursuing Parliamentarian Army.[72] Accordingly, on 5 October, when intelligence reports suggested that Charles might attack Coventry, Essex ordered that city to prepare for a possible Royalist assault.[73] Thus the contemporary evidence supports the conclusion that Essex's allegedly dilatory reactions were not due to poor intelligence information but a deliberate action in accordance with his overall strategic plan to confront the King with combined Roundhead forces of overwhelming strength.

Although the Parliamentarian pamphleteers were reasonably discreet when discussing the strength of their own forces, they certainly disclosed enough information to provide any Royalist commanders reading their reports with some reasonable intelligence about the strength of the army opposing them. In addition, the Royalist commanders were receiving information from local sympathisers. As Rupert was despatching scouting patrols the day before the battle specifically to find Essex's army, it is reasonable to conclude that he knew there was a strong possibility that Essex was nearby as he had left Worcester in pursuit of the Royalists.[74] All in all, it does not seem fanciful to conclude that the regular bulletins which appeared in the London news pamphlets could well have provided a rich source of military intelligence for the commanders of both sides.

It is clear that the Parliamentarians were also receiving intelligence from another source.[75] There is good contemporary evidence to suggest that Essex was kept well informed of the Royalist Army's plans whilst he was on the march. For example, the intelligence that, on the afternoon of 22 October, the Royalist Council of War had decided to send Sir Nicholas Byron's brigade and four guns to attack Banbury[76] was known by the Parliamentarian commanders that same evening,[77] and was published in a London news pamphlet on 23 October.[78] This was indeed rapid dissemination of intelligence because it shows that Essex knew of the Royalist plans to attack Banbury within a few hours of that decision being taken. The Royalist attack was only cancelled when definite intelligence of the location of Essex's army was provided either very late on 22 October or very early in the morning of 23 October. The source of this intelligence of the attack on Banbury has never been confirmed but it must have come from someone who knew all about the deliberations of the Royalist Council of War. Whilst it is impossible to be certain, it does seem most likely that the spy, Blake, was the source of this intelligence as not only was he privy to the deliberations of the Council, but he had also been regularly communicating intelligence to Essex. Thus it seems that Essex was receiving intelligence on the intentions of the Royalist Army right up to a few hours before the battle.

What is not so clear from the contemporary accounts of the battle is at what point the Royalists first heard of the intended desertion of the troop of Sir Faithful Fortescue, part of Sir William Waller's regiment of horse. The fact that several of the deserting Roundheads did not discard their identifying orange sashes – and the fact that several were thus killed by uninformed Royalist troopers – would serve to indicate that this decision was not planned in advance and was only communicated on the field of battle just before the Royalists charged. The contemporary records describe how Quartermaster John van der Grish, one of officers from the deserting Roundhead troop, rode up to Prince Rupert just before the order for the Royalist horse to charge.[79] Although Rupert endeavoured to inform all his troop commanders of this last-minute defection, there was evidently not enough time for this news to get to all of the Royalist forces.

In conclusion, it appears that a detailed analysis of the primary sources reveals that, in fact, a substantial amount of intelligence-gathering was conducted during the Edgehill Campaign. Furthermore, there is strong contemporary evidence of a great deal of intelligence information circulating about the position and size of the two armies. Even Clarendon's account confirms that the Royalist commanders were aware of the position of Essex's field army and of the main Parliamentarian garrisons. The Royalists' plan to march on London also capitalised on the military concerns that dominated Essex's planning and showed that Royalist intelligence reports had, in fact, provided them with accurate information of the Parliamentarian Army's weaknesses. The Royalist scouts were the first to establish the position of their enemy, and they were able to do so in such a timely manner as to allow the deployment of their full force onto an unassailable position unhindered by their opponents. The regular accounts of army movements and troop numbers which appeared in the news pamphlets were broadly accurate and their accounts were consistent with other contemporary sources, such as the journals of the Houses of Commons and Lords.

Contemporary evidence shows that Essex deliberately held back from marching to intercept the Royalists after he had received intelligence reports that they had left Shrewsbury. Far from condemning Essex for not immediately pursuing the King, the evidence which supports the conclusion that

Essex always intended that the Parliamentarian Army should *follow* the Royalist forces, and entrap them against the fortifications of London where they would be heavily outnumbered and deep inside 'hostile' territory. Previous accounts have not acknowledged the fact that Essex could not have ordered his army to move until he was certain of the Royalist Army's true destination. This destination was not clear until after Charles had left Bridgnorth. The contemporary evidence also indicates that Essex was well aware of the Royalists' movements and intentions, while Wharton's actions to contain the movements of Prince Rupert's horse show that Essex had, in fact, responded promptly to intelligence of the Royalist cavalry probes. Notwithstanding all of these contemporary intelligence reports, it has frequently been claimed by subsequent historians that Parliamentarian intelligencers failed to provide Essex with accurate information that the Royalist Army had left Shrewsbury.[80] This suggestion was repeated in Young's account of the Edgehill Campaign when he stated that Essex was 'so ill-served by his intelligence that it was not until 18 October that he could make the decision to move.'[81] However, the contemporary sources suggest that, not only was Essex fully aware of the movements of the Royalist Army, but also that he delayed the deployment of his army in order to follow his 'grand designe' – a plan which reflected the intelligence he was receiving about the movements of the Royalist Army.

Interestingly, contemporary sources also contain circumstantial evidence of another reason for Essex's delayed departure from Worcester. The reported movements of the Parliamentarian Army indicate that Essex may have been misled by a Royalist deception plan based on their intelligence of the uncertainties facing Essex. According to Clarendon's *History*, the Royalist commanders knew that Essex could not be sure of the destination of Charles' army until it had left Bridgnorth.[82] The news pamphlet reports of the movements of both armies provide a *prima facie* case that the Royalist Army feinted to the southwest to draw Essex in that direction before they headed for London. However, although Clarendon's account shows that intelligence reports had alerted the Royalist commanders to the advantages of such a manoeuvre, and although the primary evidence suggests that Rupert and his horse were deployed to wrong-foot the Parliamentarian Army by provoking them into an incorrect reaction, there is no definite contemporary evidence that proves beyond all doubt that the Royalists had in fact planned a deception. However, even if it is not possible to prove that such a feint was planned, the Royalist deployment of Rupert's cavalry certainly caused the Parliamentarian commanders to react as if it had been.

The contemporary evidence just does not support the perception of some subsequent historians that the two armies met 'by accident'.[83] Nor do the reports of the contemporary news pamphlets support Clarendon's comment that 'neither army knew where the other was'.[84] Clarendon's long-standing criticism of the Royalists' failure to establish the exact position of the Parliamentarian Army is not supported by any evidence. Indeed, the contemporary accounts that are available reveal that Rupert had sent out scouts to detect the approach of the Parliamentarian Army. This action was of such a routine nature that it was usually neither recorded nor reported. Most unusually, Rupert's so-called 'Diary' records that, on the afternoon or evening of 22 October, the day before the Battle of Edgehill, and some hours before the advanced quartermasters of Essex's army were captured, Digby was despatched 'with a party of 400 horse to have found the enemy'.[85] In the event, the scouting patrol found nothing. The undulating and wooded nature of the local terrain around Edgehill may well explain the Royalist patrol's failure to detect the approaching Parliamentarian Army. Yet the fact that such a large patrol was despatched – and that a contemporary note recorded the results – is unusual and therefore of interest. The very fact that this patrol was ordered indicates that the Royalist commanders were shortly expecting to come into contact with the Parliamentarian Army. Indeed the size of the patrol, and the seniority of the officer leading it, provide definite indications that Rupert was not only expecting the patrol to find the main body of the enemy during this mission, but also that he was anxious that the patrol would be strong enough to be able to return safely with important information. It is probably fair to conclude that the recording of the despatch of this patrol in Rupert's Diary also indicates a degree of subsequent justification by Rupert of the effectiveness of his conduct of the Royalist pre-battle intelligence-gathering. On the Parliamentarian side, as Lord Wharton's speech to Parliament on 27 October 1642 reveals, there is evidence that Essex was constantly receiving accurate and timely intelligence information about the Royalist movements from Blake, his spy in the Royalist Council of War.[86] The contemporary accounts reveal that all the intelligence information available to either side was being taken into account when the movements of both the rival armies were being planned and that Clarendon's judgement of intelligence-gathering during the Edgehill Campaign was neither fair nor accurate.

The contemporary evidence reveals a clear possibility that Essex did not plan to engage the Royalist Army until it had reached London. Essex's 'designe' to follow the Royalist Army and trap it before London was jeopardised when the Parliamentarian quartermasters were captured by Rupert's troops and the close proximity of the Parliamentarian Army thereby revealed to the Royalist commanders. Essex might yet have redeemed the situation had his scouts detected the Royalist patrol sent to verify this intelligence information, and he was also let down when his patrols failed to detect the redeployment of the Royalist Army during the early hours of 23 October. As Captain Fiennes wrote to his father (a member of the Committee of Safety) 'his Excellency [Essex] had not timely intelligence of their [the Royalists] designe' because Essex's scouts did not inform him of the Royalist Army's concentration on Edgehill.[87] As we have seen, Essex was being kept informed of the deliberations of the Royalist Council of War and therefore knew that the Cavaliers had been planning to attack Banbury. What Essex was *not* aware of was that, as Rupert's scouts had found his army, the Royalist plans to attack Banbury were changed overnight. As no Council of War was summoned, Blake may well have been unaware of any change to the Royalist previously agreed plans – or, more likely, did not have enough time to inform Essex of the change. In this respect, Wanklyn is correct – albeit a little harsh – to criticise Essex for being 'less well informed' of this last minute change to the Royalist plans. Essex was indeed surprised to find the Royalist Army lining up on Edgehill – not because he had no idea where the Royalists were, but because the last – and usually accurate – information he had received (only a few hours before) had informed him that at least part of the Royalist Army should have been miles away attacking Banbury!

Clarendon's uneasy relationship with military commanders – and Prince Rupert in particular – goes some way to explain why his account of the Edgehill Campaign is so misleading and at such odds with the verifiable facts as reported in the contemporary accounts. These accounts reveal that a more accurate assessment of the Edgehill Campaign would be that both sides received generally accurate intelligence assessments, and that any intelligence failures were largely the result of inexperienced scouts, as scouting had failed to detect enemy movements at key moments during the campaign – a failure consistent with the experiences of the earlier Bishops' Wars. The subsequent historian's description that 'intelligence activities were on a primitive level and that most civil war battles were more often the result of armies meeting accidentally' is not supported by the evidence contained in the contemporary accounts of the Battle of Edgehill.[88]

It seems, therefore, that the perception left by Clarendon's *History* that intelligence-gathering was ineffective was itself inaccurate and did not reflect the evidence contained in other contemporary accounts. It is thus all the more unfortunate that so many subsequent historians should have cited his *History* as evidence in their studies of intelligence operations during the Edgehill Campaign. As has been shown by some of the more recent accounts, which have drilled deeper into the contemporary records, both armies made use of intelligence information during the campaign and used their intelligence to inform their strategic – as well as their tactical – decisions and plans. Useful intelligence was obtained from spies, news pamphlets and scouts. Admittedly there were some mistakes made by both sides but the Edgehill Campaign provided some invaluable experience of intelligence operations for both sides – it will be interesting to explore in the subsequent chapters of this book just what each side decided to do to enhance their intelligence-gathering capabilities as a result of their experiences of the Edgehill Campaign.

Notes

1 See, for example, Edward, Earl of Clarendon, *The History of the Rebellion and Civil Wars in England, together with an Historical View of the Affairs in Ireland* (sixteen books, London, 1702–4), Book VI, p.79; E.G.B. Warburton, *Memoirs of Prince Rupert and the Cavaliers* (three volumes, London, 1849), Volume II, p.10; A. Marshall, *Intelligence and Espionage in the reign of Charles II, 1660–1685* (Cambridge, 1994), p.18; P. Young, *Edgehill 1642* (first printed 1967, first reprinted, Moreton-in-Marsh, 1995), p.70; and C. L. Scott, A. Turton and E. G. von Arni, *Edgehill The Battle Revisited* (Barnsley, 2004), p.5.

2 E. 240 [45], *England's Memorable Accidents* (17–24 October 1642).

3 T. May, *History of the Parliament of England* (London, 1647), Volume II, p.70.

4 E. 124 [26], *An Exact and True Relation of the Dangerous and bloody Fight, Between His Majesties Army, and the Parliaments Forces, neer Kineton in the County of Warwick, the 23 of this instant October* (London, 1642).

5 Young, *Edgehill*, pp.82–90.

6 Ibid, pp.92–102.

7 Clarendon, *History*, Book VI, pp.97–98.

8 T. May, *The History of the Parliament of England* (London, 1647), Book III, pp.10–18; and J. Rushworth, *Historical Collections* (London, 1659–99), Part III, Volume II, pp.33–36.

9 May, *History*, Book III, p.15. May repeated this suggestion in his *Breviary*, p.55 which was published in 1655. See also Wanklyn and Jones, *Military History*, p.47.

10 Clarendon, *History*, Book VI, pp.75–76.

11 Ibid, p.79.

12 Warburton, *Memoirs*, Volume II, pp.4–36.

13 Ibid, pp.12– 30; and R. Bulstrode, *Memoirs and Reflections* (London, 1721), p.79.

14 BL, Add MSS, 62084B. I am grateful to Professor Wanklyn for pointing out that the 'Diary' was compiled by Bennet, the prince's secretary, in the year or so before Rupert's death which helps explain why it is no more than a rough draft.

15 Warburton, *Memoirs*, Volume II, p.4.

16 S. R. Gardiner, *History of the Great Civil War 1642–1649* (four volumes, London, 1893), Vol. I, pp.38–51.

17 C.H. Firth, 'Clarendon's History of the Rebellion', *English Historical Review* (Volume 19, 1904).

18 R. Hutton, 'Clarendon's History of the Rebellion', *English Historical Review* (Volume 97, No. 382, 1982).

19 P. Young, *Edgehill 1642: the Campaign and the Battle* (Kineton, 1967), p.70.

20 Ibid, p.71.

21 Clarendon, *History*, Book VI, p.80; and Young, *Edgehill*, p.74.

22 Young, *Edgehill*, p.76.

23 Young, *Edgehill*, pp.74–76.

24 Clarendon, *History*, Book VI, p.79; and Young and Holmes, *Civil War*, p.72.

25 Young and Holmes, *English Civil War*, p.73.

26 Scott, Turton and von Arni, *Edgehill*, pp.5–8.

27 R. Hutton, 'Clarendon's History of the Rebellion', *English Historical Review* (Volume 97, 1982), pp.70–88.

28 Scott, Turton and von Arni, *Edgehill*, p.5.

29 M. Wanklyn and F. Jones, *A Military History of the English Civil War, 1642–1646* (London, 2005).

30 M. Wanklyn, *The Warrior Generals: Winning the British Civil Wars 1642–1652* (New Haven and London, 2010), pp.21–24.

31 See, for example, E. 124[26], *An Exact and True Relation of the Dangerous and Bloody Fight, Between His Majesties Army and the Parliaments forces.* Published on 28 October, this account was written by six of the Parliamentarian commanders - Hollis, Stapleton, Ballard, Balfour, Meldrum and Charles Pym.

32 E. 126[38], *A Most True and an Exact Relation of both the Battels fought by His Excellency and His Forces against the bloudy Cavaliers* (London, 9 November 1642).

33 For example, the report of the escape of Captain Legge contained in the *Journal of the House of Lords 1642–43*, p.400 is accurately recounted in the news pamphlets *Speciall Passages* (E. 240[38] and E. 123[5]) and *England's Memorable Accidents* (E. 240[45]).

34 See, for example, *Journal of the House of Commons 1640–42*, 15 October 1642, p.811. The same letter duly appeared in *The Journal of the House of Lords 1642–43*, Volume 5, p.401 on 18 October 1642.

35 See, for example, *CSPD, 1641–43*, p.389; E.121 [31], *Special Passages, A Continuation of Certaine Special and Remarkable Passages* (London, 1642); and E.121 [14], *Special and Remarkable Passages* (London, 6 October 1642).

36 E. 240[37], *Memorable Accidents* (London, 3–10 October 1642).

37 E. 121[41], *A Continuation of Certain Speciall and Remarkable Passages* (London, 8–13 October 1642).

38 E. 240[40], *A Perfect Diurnal of the Passages in Parliament* (London, 10–17 October 1642).

39 E. 121[41].

40 E. 121[24], *A Continuation of Certaine Speciall and Remarkable Passages from both Houses of Parliament* (London, 3–8 October 1642).

41 E. 240[37], *England's Memorable Accidents* (London, 3–10 October 1642).

42 E. 240[42], *England's Memorable Accidents* (London, 10–17 October 1642).

43 E. 240[40], *A Perfect Diurnal of the Passages in Parliament* (London, 10–17 October 1642).

44 E. 122[15], *A Continuation of certain Special and Remarkable Passages* (London, 10–14 October 1642).

45 E. 121[31].

46 E. 124[26], *An Exact and True Relation of the Dangerous and Bloody Fight* (London, 1642).

47 E. 121[41].

48 E. 240[40], *Perfect Diurnall* (Editor S. Pecke) and E. 240[41], *Perfect Diurnall* (Editor J. Grismond).

49 E. 121[41].

50 See also E. 122[15], *A Continuation of Certaine special and Remarkable Passages from both Houses of Parliament* (London, 10–14 October 1642); and E. 123[5], *Speciall Passages and Certain Informations collected from Severall Places* (London, 11–18 October 1642). E. 240[40] included a report dated 11 October – a similar report of the same date was printed in E. 240[41].

51 See, for example, E.121 [24], *A Continuation of Certaine special and Remarkable Passages from both Houses of Parliament* (London, 3–8 October 1642); E. 121[41]; E. 123[5], *Special Passages* (London, 11–18 October 1642); E.240 [40]; and E. 240[42].

52 See, for example, a report dated 11 October 1642 in E. 123[5].

53 E. 124[4], *Exceeding Joyfull Newes from the Earl of Stamford, the Lord Wharton, and the Lord Kymbolton* (London, 21 October 1642).

54 See, for example, reports of this deployment in the news pamphlets E. 123[5]; E. 240[42]; and E. 240[41].

55 E. 240[40].

56 E. 240[42]. See also E. 240[40].

57 E. 240[45], *England's Memorable Accidents* (London, 17–24 October 1642).

58 E. 240[41], *A Perfect Diurnall of the Passages in Parliament* (London, 10–17 October 1642). See also E. 240[40].

59 E. 240[40].

60 See, for example, E.121 [24]; BL, E. 240[41]; and E. 240[46].

61 Warburton, *Memoirs,* Vol. II, p.9.

62 E. 124[26].

63 E. 124[4].

64 E. 240[46], *A Perfect Diurnall of the Passages in Parliament* (London, 17–24 October 1642).

65 E. 123[5].

66 See, for example, May, *History,* p.70; and Bulstrode Whitelocke, *Memorials of the English Affairs* (London, 1682), p.61.

67 See, for example, E. 240[40]; and E. 240 [42]. Wanklyn and Jones, *Military History,* p.47 also states that it was Essex's intention 'to follow the Royalist Army, not to intercept it'.

68 May, *History,* Book III, p.15. May repeated this suggestion in his *Breviary,* p.55, published in 1655. See also Wanklyn and Jones, *Military History,* p.47.

69 E. 123[5].

70 Ibid.

71 E. 240[45]. Clarendon also reported the work undertaken to improve the defences of London in his *History,* Volume II, p.7.

72 E. 240[45].

73 E. 240[37].

74 Clarendon, *History,* Book VI, p.76.

75 BL, Add MSS, 62084B.

76 Clarendon, *Memoirs,* Volume II, p.379.

77 See E. 124[26]; and E. 124[32].

78 E. 240[46], *A Perfect Diurnall of the passages in Parliament* (London, 17–24 October 1642).

79 Clarendon, *History,* Volume II, p.360. See also BL, Add MSS, 62084B (Prince Rupert's Diary).

80 See, for example, Clarendon, *History,* Book VI, p.79; Warburton, *Memoirs,* Volume II, p.5; Young, *Edgehill,* p.70; F. Kitson, *Prince Rupert,* (London, 1994), pp.94–95; and Turton, *Edgehill,* p.5.

81 Young, *Edgehill,* p.70.

82 Clarendon, *History,* Book VI, pp.75–76.

83 Marshall, *Intelligence and Espionage,* p.18.

84 Clarendon, *History,* p.80.

85 BL, Add. MSS, 62084B, *Prince Rupert's Diary,* p.9. This text was later quoted in Warburton, *Memoirs,* Vol II, p.10; and Young, *Edgehill,* p.273.

86 E. 124[32].

87 E. 126[38].

88 Marshall, *Intelligence and Espionage,* p.18.

5

The War Expands – Intelligence Operations in 1643

As the Battle of Edgehill had failed to provide the expected military resolution of the political impasse, both sides used the winter months of 1642–43 to prepare for the resumption of the conflict.[1] An immediate consequence of the indecisive battle was a marked expansion of the fighting throughout England during 1643, as regional commanders sought to raise more men to reinforce their field armies. But what was the impact of the expansion of the conflict upon the conduct of intelligence operations? This chapter will evaluate the impact that the development of intelligence-gathering operations around the country had upon the principal military campaigns of 1643. In order to set the scope of this evaluation, this exploration will start with a summary of those main military events of 1643 which will be included in this evaluation, before moving on to consider what subsequent historians have said about the intelligence-gathering activities which were conducted in support of those events. The key question which will then be addressed is what the contemporary sources reveal about intelligence operations during the principal campaigns of 1643. In conclusion, the overall contribution which was made by intelligence-gathering to the conduct of the war during 1643 will be assessed. For the sake of clarity and easier understanding, we will explore the conduct of military intelligence operations by considering the actions in three main theatres of action: the North, the central Thames Valley area and the South and South West of England.

Turning first to the North. The agreed historical accounts of the principal military events of the 1643 northern campaigns indicate that the Royalist armies achieved considerable success during the first quarter of 1643 as they heavily outnumbered their Parliamentarian opponents. Sir Thomas Fairfax, the son of Ferdinando, Lord Fairfax, the senior commander of Parliamentarian forces in the North, had led a successful attack on Leeds on 23 January. Lord Goring had recently been ennobled and appointed as Lieutenant-General of Horse to the

Earl of Newcastle (who was to become a Marquis and then a Duke). Promoted since he briefly held Portsmouth for the King in 1642, Goring soon showed his mettle by defeating Sir Thomas Fairfax at the Battle of Seacroft Moor on 30 March. Demonstrating the resilience that was to become the hallmark of the northern Parliamentarians, Fairfax recovered swiftly and successfully stormed Wakefield. However, this victory did not overturn the Royalists' numerical superiority and, shortly afterwards, the Earl of Newcastle defeated the Fairfaxes comprehensively at Adwalton Moor on 30 June. Taking advantage of his opponents' disarray, Newcastle advanced into Lincolnshire before demands from the local Yorkshire Royalists required him to return north and eradicate the remaining Parliamentarian threat by capturing the besieged city of Hull. Hull, sustained by the ships of the Parliamentarian navy, was to remain in Parliamentarian hands throughout the war. Despite Charles' subsequent demands for Newcastle to march south to assist his move on London,[2] the Royalist Northern Army remained besieging Hull until October when the threat from Scotland required Newcastle to break off the siege and head north to contain the Scots invasion.

Moving further south, the accepted history of the principal military events of the 1643 central Thames Valley campaign reveals that the main Parliamentarian campaigning in this area began in the spring, with an attack on the Royalist garrison at Reading. As Royalist scouting failed to provide any timely intelligence of the Parliamentarian movements, Essex achieved a degree of surprise when he laid siege to the city on 15 April. In the absence of Rupert (who was besieging Lichfield), the Royalist response was ill-coordinated, hesitant and confused. Consequently, despite some last minute Royalist attempts to re-supply the town, Reading surrendered on 27 April. Although the Royalists feared a further Parliamentarian advance towards Oxford, the Roundheads' plans were thrown into disarray by an outbreak of fever in Essex's army. After capturing Lichfield on 21 April, Rupert took full advantage of the Parliamentarian inertia and mounted a series of raids on the largely immobile Parliamentarian Army. These raids led to the skirmish at Chalgrove Field on 18 June where John Hampden, Pym's right-hand man, was mortally wounded. Later in the year, the capture of Bristol by the Royalists marked the nadir of the Parliamentarian cause. However, as the Duke of Newcastle was embroiled in the siege of Hull, he was unable to march his army south – a decision which led the Royalist Council of War to decide not to advance on London. Instead they chose to consolidate their recent territorial gains in the South West by besieging Gloucester, a city which they believed would fall quickly.[3] Faced with the potential loss of the entire South West to the King, Parliament responded decisively. Reinforced by the London Train Bands, Essex marched his army and relieved Gloucester on 6 September, before managing to evade the Royalist Army and head back towards London. The pursuing Royalists forced Essex to fight at Newbury, but Charles was worsted in the ensuing (first) battle fought there on 20 September. The Royalists were successful, however, in subsequently reoccupying Reading.[4]

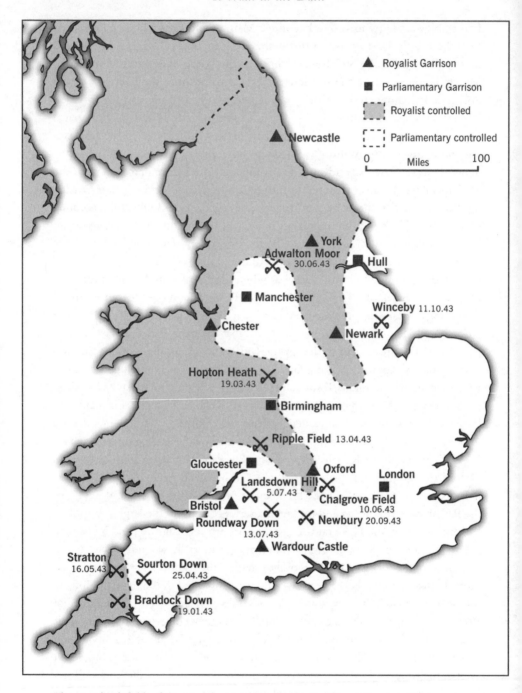

The main battlefields of 1643 and the area controlled by the King at the start of that year.

Finally, the accepted history of the principal military events of the 1643 campaign in the South shows that the year began well for the Royalists in the South West when their general, Sir Ralph Hopton, defeated the Parliamentarian forces of his then opposite number, General Ruthin, at Braddock Down on 19 January. However, elsewhere Sir William Waller inflicted several defeats on the Royalists in the Severn Valley, most notably in March when he captured the Welsh army raised by the rich Royalist magnate, Lord Herbert, at Highnam, near Gloucester. Recovering from a reverse at Sourton Down outside Okehampton in Devon on 25 April, the western Royalists, who were well supplied with local intelligence about the Parliamentarians' movements and strength, won a decisive victory at Stratton, near Bude, on 16 May – a battle which cleared all of their enemies from Cornwall.[5] Soon afterwards, Hopton's Cornishmen of the Western Army joined up with Royalist reinforcements from Oxford, led by the Marquis of Hertford and Prince Maurice, and advanced into Somerset and Wiltshire. This combined Royalist Army subsequently defeated Waller at the Battle of Lansdown, outside Bath (5 July) and, a few days later, at Roundway Down outside Devizes (13 July). The Royalist Western Army then combined with Charles' Oxford Army, under the command of Prince Rupert, and captured Bristol on 26 July. Once Bristol had fallen, Prince Maurice was appointed to command the Western Army and led it against Exeter – which surrendered on 4 September – before marching further west to besiege Plymouth. In the meantime, as has been already described, in August Charles advanced to besiege Gloucester. In December, Waller defeated Hopton's forces at Alton in Hampshire before marching into Sussex and recapturing Chichester and Arundel Castle. Thus the year ended with the Royalist advance upon London from the South West effectively checked.

Having summarised briefly the key points of the military campaigns of 1643, it will now be interesting to establish just what subsequent historians wrote about the use of intelligence in those campaigns before comparing and contrasting their accounts with the evidence of the contemporary and primary sources which are now available for examination. Just as the northern military campaigns of 1643 have attracted relatively little attention from historians, so even less has been written about the intelligence-gathering operations conducted in support of them. The first contemporary historian, the Parliamentarian Thomas May, made only one reference to intelligence-gathering, when his report of the northern campaigns stating that Parliamentarian intelligence had estimated the size of Newcastle's army to be 'about eight thousand horse and foot'.[6] Writing later in 1659, another Parliamentarian, John Rushworth, left more relevant information as he provided several illuminating references to the use of intelligence by both Lord Fairfax and his son, Sir Thomas. Rushworth described how both Royalist and Parliamentarian intelligence reports were used to inform the military actions of the Parliamentarian commanders when they attacked Wakefield,[7] and how intelligence allowed the smaller Parliamentarian forces to target the weakest

Royalist garrisons for their attacks.[8] The later Royalist accounts of the fighting in the north were much thinner on detail as Clarendon did not personally witness any of the northern fighting and could not persuade William Cavendish (by then the Duke of Newcastle) to contribute to this part of his *History*.[9] Although he received some assistance from Sir Hugh Cholmley, who had been the Royalist Governor of Scarborough, Clarendon's *History* did not comment on the impact intelligence operations had had upon the Royalists' northern campaigns of 1643. Clarendon made few references to Newcastle's victories and did not mention the Battle of Adwalton Moor at all. Indeed, he wrote little about the siege of Hull except when describing the reasons why Newcastle was unable to march south to join the King later that year.[10]

This absence of detailed contemporary evidence describing intelligence-gathering in the 1643 northern campaign was reflected in the subsequent historical accounts written during the following 300 years,[11] such as Gardiner's *History* which contains comprehensive and detailed summaries of the chief military actions, but follows the example set by Clarendon and does not mention the impact of intelligence operations.[12] Apart from meeting the Queen and her munitions convoy, Prince Rupert played little part in the northern campaigns of 1643 and so Warburton only made a passing reference to those campaigns in his *Memoirs*.[13] Even Markham's detailed biography of Sir Thomas Fairfax contained no account of any significant contribution made by intelligence to his military success during the year.[14] Finally, in his edition of the Duchess of Newcastle's autobiography,[15] Sir Charles Firth made no substantial reference to intelligence-gathering activities in the north during 1643.

However, since the Second World War, historians have begun to explore the northern campaigns of 1643 in much more detail.[16] Disappointingly, although their accounts provide a much clearer insight into the various battles, few of them have described the part played by intelligence-gathering. Indeed, the contemporary evidence that described intelligence operations during that year appears to have been hardly explored at all until 2004, when David Cooke cited references to the intelligence information which appeared in Sir Thomas Fairfax's letters describing his campaigns.[17] Only the more recently published biographies of the northern commanders have included a few more references to intelligence operations. For example, in his biography of Fairfax, John Wilson described the action at Wakefield and cited the contemporary accounts which acknowledged the impact that intelligence had had upon the outcome of the Parliamentarian campaigns in the north.[18] Similarly, Stanley Carpenter's later account of Civil War generalship described how the Fairfax's 'grand designe' had relied upon receiving accurate intelligence about the position and strength of Royalist forces. Interestingly, on several occasions Carpenter's *Leadership* implicitly (but never explicitly) acknowledged the impact that intelligence-gathering had had upon the conduct of the 1643 campaign.[19] For example, Carpenter argued that it was the interception

Although courageous in battle, King Charles' political vacillations and indecisiveness left confusion in his wake and did much to lose him the war, his crown and his life.

Sir Edward Hyde was an experienced statesman whose biased reporting of the English Civil War did much to initiate the 360-year-old perception that intelligence-gathering was ineffective. (National Portrait Gallery, D 19011)

Although brave, dashing and charismatic, Prince Rupert was not tolerant or a team player and made as many enemies as friends. Paradoxically his active support of intelligence-gathering was not widely shared by his fellow Royalist commanders.

Much in the shade of his brother Rupert, Prince Maurice was a professional soldier and a more capable commander than many of the Royalist Grandees appointed in command of Charles' forces. (National Portrait Gallery, D 841)

Above: The Skirmish at Powick Bridge (23 September 1642). Although only a skirmish, this decisive victory for the Royalist cavalry made Prince Rupert a hero and provided early proof of the intelligence obtained from effective scouting. It was along this lane that the Roundhead cavalry advanced to cross the bridge and engage Prince Rupert's cavalry.

Middle: The Battle of Edgehill (23 October 1642). In contradiction of Clarendon's account, contemporary sources provide compelling evidence that intelligence played a significant part in the decisions leading up to this battle. Facing Edgehill and with Radway village on the left, this photograph shows the battlefield from the right flank of the Roundhead position.

Bottom: The Battle of Highnam (24 March 1643). The excellence of the Parliamentarian intelligence led to an overwhelming defeat of the Royalist forces at Highnam and deprived Charles of forces he would soon sorely need. This photograph shows the grounds around Highnam Court where the Royalist army was bivouacked.

Whilst a sensitive and reliable Secretary of State, Viscount Falkland's intellectual reservations about the integrity and trustworthiness of espionage exerted a baleful influence on the development of Royalist intelligence-gathering.

Lord George Digby, an erratic and often irresponsible councillor whose advice as Secretary of State was invariably wildly over-optimistic and ill-considered. (National Portrait Gallery, D 28787)

As Charles' Secretary of State, Sir Edward Nicholas had no real understanding of the advantages that could be gained from intelligence information until he witnessed the potential benefits during the Lostwithiel Campaign. (National Portrait Gallery, D 28915) London

Sir Edward Walker was Charles I's Military Secretary whose written records have provided invaluable insights into the Royalists' conduct of intelligence operations. (National Portrait Gallery, D 27860)

The Battle of Sourton Down (25 April 1643). Advancing towards Okehampton, Hopton's Royalist Western Army was ambushed and ignominiously driven back across Sourton Down by a smaller Roundhead force which enjoyed timely intelligence of Hopton's advance.

The Battle of Stratton (16 May 1643). Provided with crucial intelligence from Royalist supporters, the Cavalier commanders were able to inflict a crushing defeat on a divided Roundhead force and subsequently drive the Parliamentarians out of Cornwall. It was up these slopes that the Cornish forces advanced to defeat the Roundhead army.

The Battle of Lansdown (5 July 1643). Although Waller, the Parliamentarian Commander, used intelligence information to take up a strong position, he was unable to resist the charge of the Cornish regiments who snatched victory from the jaws of defeat when, under heavy fire, they stormed up this hill and drove the Roundheads from their positions.

The Bevil Grenville monument.

WILLIAM CAVENDISH
Duke of Newcastle.

RALPH Lᵈ Hopton, His Majesties General of the Western Army.
This is from a Painting in Sʳ Tabot Ashleys hands. M.Vᵗ Gucht sculp.

Well supported by professional soldiers, the Duke of Newcastle became one of the most successful Royalist Grandee generals. Unfortunately, his decision to flee to the Continent after losing the Battle of Marston Moor effectively passed control of the North to Parliament. (National Portrait Gallery, D 28178)

Sir Ralph Hopton was an experienced and determined general who led the Royalist Western (and Cornish) army to victory during 1643. Injured after the Battle of Lansdown, Hopton was appointed to join the Royalist Council in the West after his defeat at Cheriton in 1644. (National Portrait Gallery, D 26991)

Sir Bevil Grenville was the charismatic commander of Cornish forces who was well supplied with local intelligence information. His death at Lansdown was a blow to the morale of the Royalist Western army.

George Monck was initially a Royalist commander who was captured by Sir Thomas Fairfax at Nantwich. Monck subsequently joined the forces of the Protectorate and, as commander in Scotland, became a strong supporter of military intelligence-gathering.

The Battle of Roundway Down (13 July 1643). Warned of the approach of the Royalist relieving force, Waller drew up his army along the edge of this plain. The dramatic charge of the Royalist cavalry drove Waller's horse from the field and over the skyline on the right. Hopton's foot deployed from Devizes and completed the destruction of Waller's army.

The First Battle of Newbury (20 September 1643). Although beaten by the Cavaliers in the race to Newbury, effective scouting enabled Essex to seize Round Hill – a key feature of the battlefield and turn an initial Cavalier advantage into a hard-fought Roundhead victory. This photograph shows how Round Hill dominates the site of the battlefield around it. IMG 9795.

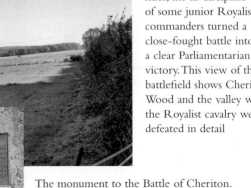

The monument to Lord Falkland who was killed during the First Battle of Newbury.

The Battle of Cheriton (29 March 1644). Despite good intelligence information being obtained by both sides, the ill-discipline of some junior Royalist commanders turned a close-fought battle into a clear Parliamentarian victory. This view of the battlefield shows Cheriton Wood and the valley where the Royalist cavalry were defeated in detail

The monument to the Battle of Cheriton.

Iohn PYM Efquire,
Burges for Tauiftocke in Deuon
fhire.

Determined to restrict the political powers of
the monarchy, John Pym's shrewd management
of the factions of Parliament – and his alliance
with the Scots – brought about the defeat
of Charles and the Royalist cause. (National
Portrait Gallery, D 33401)

John Hampden's loyal support of Pym was
important in the early stages of the war and his
death at Chalgrove Field dramatically increased the
political pressures on Pym as he struggled to keep
the factions of Parliament united against the king.
(National Portrait Gallery, D 26919)

Although popular with his soldiers, the Earl of
Essex proved to be an indecisive commander
whose commitment to defeating the King in
battle has long been doubted.

Early successes earned Sir William Waller the
title 'William the Conqueror' and showed him
to be a shrewd user of all aspects of all forms of
intelligence, Waller's over-confidence led to the
loss of his army at the Battle of Roundway Down.

MERCVRIVS AULICUS,

A DIVRNALL,

Communicating the intelli-gence, and affaires of the Court to the reft of the KINGDOME, begin-ning the firft day of *January*.

By Ir *John Birkenhead*

Verdi. Athens Sep. p. 639.

OXFORD,

Printed by H. Hall, *for* W. Webb Book-feller, neere to Queenes Colledge. 1642.

Mercurius Aulicus, a Royalist news pamphlet – like its Parliamentarian equivalents – often contained useful intelligence information about the movements and sizes of the opposing armies.

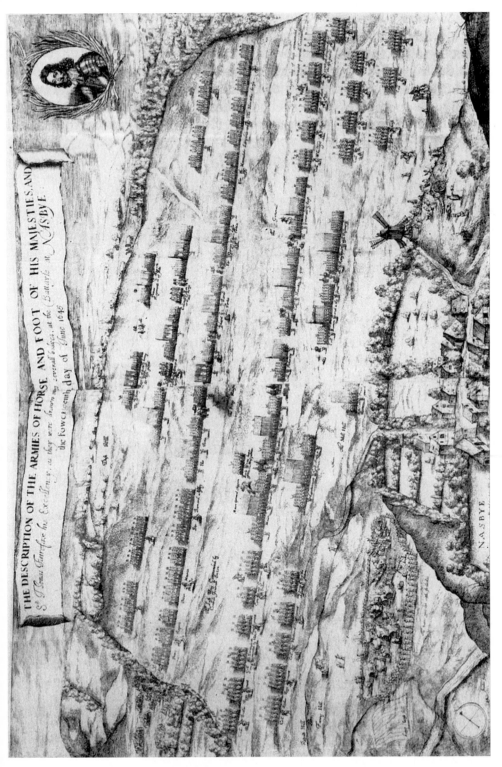

The Battle of Naseby. This map provides an indication of the deployment of the opposing forces before this decisive battle which led to the end of the fighting.

The Battle of Cropredy Bridge (29 June 1644). Both sides benefited from good intelligence during this battle. This photograph is taken from Cropredy Bridge itself and shows where the Royalist forces counter-attacked Waller's assault across the River Cherwell (shown in the foreground).

The Battle of Marston Moor (2 July 1644). Although good use of his intelligence information enabled Rupert to relieve York with hardly a blow being exchanged, Rupert's subsequent rejection of local intelligence led to his defeat and the subsequent loss of the North to the Royalists. Cromwell's Plump marks the line of the Parliamentarian position along the ridge that dominates the battlefield.

The Battle of Lostwithiel (31 August 1644). Excellent Royalist intelligence-gathering by the Cornish population led to the capitulation of the Parliamentarian army. Essex fled by boat to avoid capture. The undulating land around Lostwithiel shows how local intelligence enabled the Royalist army to surround the Parliamentarian forces.

Sir Thomas Fairfax was taciturn, yet fearless and inspiring on the battlefield. He was appointed to command the New Model Army. His experiences in the north made him recognise the value of intelligence and his shrewd use of intelligence information proved decisive during the 1645 campaign.

A natural trainer and leader, Oliver Cromwell's rise through the ranks of the Parliamentarian forces owes as much to his military prowess as his political connections. By the end of the First Civil War, Cromwell had become a significant military and political figure and a force to be reckoned with. (National Portrait Gallery, D 16572)

Although Sir William Brereton had no previous military experience, he soon appreciated the value of accurate military intelligence information and he became a successful military commander for Parliament in the North West.

A strong supporter of Cromwell and his future son-in-law, General Henry Ireton played an important role in the use of intelligence information in the campaign that preceded the Battle of Naseby. (National Portrait Gallery, D 28762)

The Second Battle of Newbury (27 October 1644). Although the Royalist forces were outnumbered, the combination of intelligence failures and a lack of Parliamentarian leadership and determination allowed Charles and his army to avoid a decisive defeat. Charles later recovered his artillery from where he had left it in Donnington Castle.

The Battle of Naseby (14 June 1645). During this campaign, the intelligence-gathering of the New Model Army proved to be vastly superior to that of the Royalists and played a decisive part in the stunning Parliamentarian victory. This photograph shows the position of the Royalist forces on Dust Hill from the monument on the Parliamentarian position.

The Naseby monument.

The Battle of Langport (10 July 1645). For this final major engagement of the First English Civil War, superior Parliamentarian intelligence led to a further – and final – defeat being inflicted on the last remaining Cavalier army despite the terrain (as shown in this photograph) greatly favouring the defence.

Intelligence-gathering in the field – A hidden scout counts the number of advancing enemy forces before making his report.

Breaking the enemy's codes – Using a coded letter captured at Chichester, the Parliamentarian mathematician John Wallis de-cyphers the Royalist codes.

The Battle of Torrington (16 February 1646). Cornish Royalist resistance was brought to an end after the Roundhead scouting led to a surprise attack being made on the strong Royalist position at Torrington.

Wardour Castle. The Royalist besiegers of Wardour Castle infiltrated a twelve-year-old boy to work in the kitchens of Wardour Castle. He was tasked to sabotage the artillery, ascertain the strength of the garrison, poison the water and the beer, and blow up the ammunition – and all of this for a payment of half a crown!

Lucy Hay, Countess of Carlisle, who was Pym's spy in the court of the Queen, probably became one of the first 'Bond girls' when she provided Pym with the intelligence of Charles I's attempt to arrest the Five Members in January 1642. (National Portrait Gallery, D 19033)

John Wallis's mathematical genius was instrumental in his success at decoding Royalist cyphers from 1643 onwards. Wallis continued his code-breaking work throughout the Interregnum and into the subsequent reigns of Charles II and William III. (National Portrait Gallery, D 22976)

Working in conjunction with John Wallis, Isaac Dorislaus would identify those Royalist messages being passed through the post office and pass them on to Wallis for de-cyphering and copying. (National Portrait Gallery, D 26985)

Appointed by Cromwell to be his Secretary of State, John Thurloe co-ordinated and enhanced the intelligence-gathering expertise that had begun to be developed during the First English Civil War. (National Portrait Gallery, D 4248)

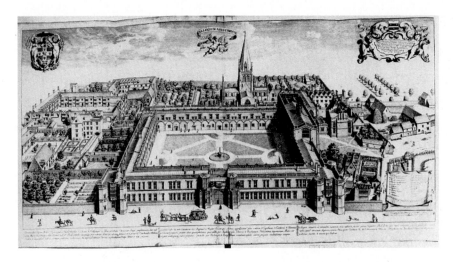

Above: Christ Church College was the headquarters of Charles, the Cavalier court and his Royalist councillors during the conflict, and the place from which Royalist intelligence-gathering operations were managed.

Left: The commander of the Roundhead garrison at Gloucester, Edward Massey led the resistance to the siege by Charles I's army in 1643 which proved to be a turning point in the war.

Below: The scornful rejection of the King's demand that Gloucester should surrender to him proved to be a major error of Royalist intelligence, and one which had serious repercussions upon the Royalist cause.

of letters from Sir Thomas Fairfax to his father that had given the Royalists a decisive intelligence advantage in the opening months of the campaign because these letters had described the Parliamentarians' military plans.[20] The question of implicit references to intelligence information, rather than explicit examples of intelligence-gathering, will be considered later in this book.[21]

Although historians have had relatively little to say about intelligence-gathering operations in the northern campaigns of 1643, the position is rather better when it comes to their treatment of intelligence-gathering operations in the central Thames Valley during the same year. As this campaign was the one which involved the largest armies, and was the campaign fought closest to London, it was understandably the one that attracted most comment from contemporary – and subsequent – historians. For example, in May's account, the actions of Essex's army are described in some detail, as are the fall of Reading and the subsequent fever that debilitated the Parliamentarian Army.[22] However, apart from an occasional reference to Rupert's movements, he made no significant mention of any intelligence operations. Nonetheless, May did provide a contemporary account of intelligence operations in his later description of the Gloucester and Newbury campaign. For example, the use that Essex had made of intelligence information during his march to lift the siege of Gloucester was covered in detail. May's account then went on to describe how Essex had used his intelligence about the Royalist dispositions to break away cleanly from the Royalist forces around Gloucester and start his march back to London.[23] Subsequently, Rushworth's *Historical Collections* also described the capture of Reading and the Chalgrove Field skirmish, but then made no mention of the contemporary evidence that it was intelligence obtained by Rupert that had informed the conduct of his raids on Essex's forces. In contrast, Rushworth's account of the part played by intelligence-gathering in the relief of Gloucester and Battle of Newbury was much more detailed. After describing the relief of Gloucester, Rushworth also described how the intelligence which Essex had received about the Royalist dispositions had allowed him to evade Charles' army and to gain an initial advantage on the race back to London.[24]

Because he was based at Oxford in 1643, Clarendon was especially well placed to include the contemporary accounts of the intelligence operations that had influenced the conduct of military operations in the central Thames Valley area. For example, his account of the loss of Reading included a description of one particular intelligence-gathering technique which had involved the Royalist garrison commander, Colonel Fielding, knowingly using a double agent in an attempt to obtain accurate information about the Roundheads' intentions – whilst planting false information about his own plans. Clarendon described some interesting contemporary reports of how Royalist intelligence was obtained during this period, not only from the Royalist scouts who penetrated far behind the enemy lines, but also from Roundhead deserters, such as Colonel John Hurry (or Urry), who 'acquainted [the Royalist commanders] where the parliament horse lay, and how loose they were in their quarters'.[25] Similarly, Clarendon's account of the Gloucester and Newbury campaign described several examples of the intelligence information which the Royalists had possessed about the garrison commander at Gloucester, and the position of Essex's relief force during that campaign.[26] Clarendon cited the contemporary evidence of a key Royalist intelligence report which had declared that Colonel Massey, the Parliamentarian Governor of Gloucester, would surrender the city 'if the King himself came with his army and summoned it'.[27]

As Clarendon reported that this intelligence had 'turned the scale' during the Council of War's debate about what to do next, it was clearly a major reverse to the Royalist plans when representatives of the city subsequently gave an 'insolent and seditious' response to the King's demand that they surrender to him. Clarendon recorded that, when the intelligence had been considered by the Royalist Council of War, it had led them to believe that the city would fall within ten days. Clarendon went on to observe that this estimate was over-optimistic, as had been the Royalist assessment of the chances of Parliament being able to mount a rescue operation. Clarendon stated that Royalist intelligence had alleged

> ... that the enemy had no army; nor, by all intelligence, was like to form any
> soon enough to be able to relieve it [Gloucester]; and if they had an army, that
> it were much better for his majesty to force them to that distance from London,
> and to fight there where he could ... choose his own ground.[28]

Having described intelligence operations in some detail, it is disappointing that Clarendon's *History* did not explain why the Royalists failed to respond to the intelligence of Essex's withdrawal from Gloucester. Indeed, as Clarendon wrote that the Royalists believed the Parliamentarian Army would take the northerly route back to London, he blamed the cavalry for being 'less vigilant towards the motion of the enemy' and the garrison at Cirencester for 'the negligence of the officers'.[29]

Clarendon's *History* went on to describe the impact that intelligence-gathering had had upon the outcome of the First Battle of Newbury in some detail. For example, he recounted how the Parliamentarian scouts had recovered the initiative for Essex during the hours before the battle by carrying out a more effective reconnaissance of the ground and of the Royalists' overnight deployments. By enabling Essex to deploy relatively advantageously, Clarendon considered that the intelligence provided by the Parliamentarian scouts had given Essex a potentially decisive advantage in the forthcoming battle. Clarendon also recorded how, because the reconnaissance by the Parliamentarian scouts had provided the Roundhead commanders with useful intelligence on the topography of the likely battlefield, Essex was able to secure the high ground on the western edge of the site. Having occupied Biggs Hill and Trundle Hill – and Round Hill a little further to the east – the Parliamentarians were able to dominate the enclosed land from which the Royalist attack would be launched.[30]

Although Clarendon's account of the 1643 Thames Valley campaign made several references to intelligence-gathering, these do not appear to have caused him to revise his negative perception of it. Later historians also had a good deal to say about intelligence operations during the campaign; Warburton's *Memoirs* described the campaign in some detail and included several examples of Royalist commanders reporting intelligence of enemy movements to Rupert.[31] Of particular interest to this evaluation are Warburton's descriptions of how Rupert used his intelligence information during the raids on Essex's army after the fall of Reading, and of how Essex used the scouting reports of the Royalist dispositions to evade Charles' army around Gloucester.[32] Warburton's account also described how Hurry had 'proved his sincerity ... by giving important information and furnishing a chart of the enemy's country'.[33] Gardiner's *History* also made two specific references to intelligence-gathering. Firstly, he described the information provided by Hurry that had led to the Chalgrove Field skirmish,[34] and secondly he described how the Royalist scouts reported Essex's manoeuvres as he doubled back towards Cirencester, noting that the Royalist commanders had not reacted in time.[35] Once again, these historical accounts did not explore the wider impact of these intelligence operations on the campaign as a whole.

The most recent historical accounts of the central Thames Valley campaigns of 1643 have presented a more comprehensive description of the intelligence-gathering operations than hitherto. Whilst descriptions of the campaigns to relieve Gloucester and the First Battle of Newbury have often been published,[36] it was not until Young and Holmes' account of the skirmish at Chalgrove, and of Rupert's subsequent raids upon Essex's fever-ridden forces, that the immediate benefits of superior intelligence were identified.[37] Of all the accounts of the Gloucester and Newbury campaigns, Jon Day's 2007 publication is perhaps the first to provide contemporary evidence of the full extent of intelligence information being provided to the commanders on both sides.[38] Day reveals that, whilst Essex had been receiving intelligence from the spies run by Luke, the Parliamentarian Scoutmaster-General, the Royalists had been getting reports from their spies operating with the besiegers of Gloucester.[39] Day also described how Essex's withdrawal from Gloucester had been made possible by the intelligence he had received about the dispositions of the Royalist forces. He argued, not only that this intelligence had allowed Essex to march swiftly away from the main Royalist Army, but also that it had enabled him to capture an important supply column at Cirencester. Thus, Day concluded, partly as a result of the superior Parliamentarian intelligence, the Royalists lost the opportunity to attack Essex when he was isolated and miles from London.[40] It thus appears reasonable to suggest that the historical accounts of the central Thames Valley campaigns of 1643, unlike those of the campaigns in the North, have made more use of the contemporary references to intelligence-gathering. In the last twenty years, scholars have begun to review the full extent of the intelligence operations which were conducted in 1643 and to show that they provided key information to the commanders on both sides.[41] With this in mind, we now turn to explore how historians have treated the role of military intelligence in the campaigns which were conducted in the South and South West of England during that same year.

Interestingly, the historical accounts of the impact of intelligence operations in the southern campaigns contain more detail than the accounts of the campaigns which were fought further north. For example, May's *History* reported how intelligence operations had several times influenced Parliamentarian planning in the area. He stated that intelligence was not only used to counter the Royalist plot to capture Bristol, but it was also used to provide information about the disposition of the Royalist Army around Highnam, the scene of Waller's destruction of the so-called 'mushroom' army.[42] Later on, Rushworth's *Historical Collections* made a number of similar contemporary references to the contribution made by intelligence and, in particular, to the reports of Parliamentarian scouts in the actions at Highnam, Sourton Down and Lansdown.[43] Even Clarendon contributed a very full account of the war in the South West, mainly because he received substantial information from Hopton and Colonel Walter Slingsby, one of the Royalist officers who had fought under Hopton's command.[44] In his accounts of the fighting, Clarendon included a significant number of references to intelligence information which had been obtained by both Hopton and Waller during their confrontation, and of how scouting reports had influenced the outcome of the battles at Stratton, Lansdown and Roundway Down.[45] He also described how intelligence gathered about the position of Royalist patrols had been used by Waller to defeat Hopton's forces at Alton later that year.[46]

Disappointingly, later historical accounts did not mention these intelligence-gathering operations in anything like the same amount of detail and it was not until the twentieth and twenty-first centuries that local histories of the Civil War began to re-evaluate their impact upon military operations. The Somerset Record Society had published Charles Chadwyck Healey's edition of the Hopton and Slingsby's manuscripts in 1902,[47] but it was not until 1933 that the local historian, Mary Coate, made reference to the primary evidence which described the impact that local intelligence-gathering had had upon the outcome of the fighting in the South West. In her account of the Cornish involvement in the Civil War, Coate described how the Parliamentarian commander, John Chudleigh, had cursed his inefficient scoutmaster before the skirmish at Sourton Down,[48] and how the local people had provided useful information to the Royalist commanders about Parliamentarian dispositions before the Battle of Stratton.[49] Coate's research into the engagement at Sourton Down revealed the advantages that had been gained by those Civil War commanders who obtained accurate military intelligence, and her conclusions were developed by other historians in their subsequent accounts of the 1643 South West campaign. For example, in his biography of Hopton, published in 1968, F.T.R. Edgar referred to intelligence operations when he stated that Hopton had assumed the scoutmaster's intelligence duties and claimed that much intelligence information about the position and size of the Parliamentarian Army had come from his Royalist Cornish regimental commanders, such as Sir Bevill Grenville.[50]

Later, John Adair's biography of Sir William Waller contained a great deal more contemporary information on intelligence-gathering and its impact on the campaign. Adair noted that Waller was recognised by his opponents to be a skilful general who had achieved a number of military successes for Parliament. Adair acknowledged that Waller's achievements reflected his skilful use of the ground and his awareness of his opponents' intentions – advantages that he derived from the intelligence provided by his scouts. For example, Adair described how Waller used the intelligence information of his opponents' dispositions at Highnam to destroy the Royalist Army raised by Lord Herbert.[51]

More recently, local historians have continued to acknowledge the part played by intelligence in their accounts of regional campaigns. For example, in his studies of the Civil War in Wiltshire and Hampshire, Tony MacLachlan has referred to the use of intelligence-gathering by both sides and has described how Waller's extensive use of scouts provided him with the timely intelligence which allowed him to gain a significant advantage in the run up to the Battles of Lansdown and Roundway Down and, towards the end of 1643, at the capture of Alton.[52] Further primary evidence of intelligence-gathering is contained in MacLachlan's account of the siege of Wardour Castle.[53] Mark Stoyle's more recent publications have also provided revealing insights into the contribution made towards the gathering of intelligence by local people.[54] It can be seen, therefore, that the latest historical accounts of the military campaigns of 1643 have begun to acknowledge the impact of intelligence-gathering upon the outcome of the battles. How then, do these historical accounts compare with the evidence contained in the primary sources?

Returning to the North, we find that the evidence of the primary sources reveals that, despite the comparative lack of recognition from many subsequent historians, a great deal of important intelligence information was provided to the commanders. The reports of eyewitnesses and the contemporary news pamphlets contain detailed evidence that the majority of northern military actions were informed by intelligence information. As the aim of this part of the present chapter is to explore the impact of intelligence-gathering on all of the main actions of the northern campaigns, it therefore seems sensible to start by considering the primary evidence provided by the two leading military antagonists in the northern campaigns of 1643, the Duke of Newcastle and Sir Thomas Fairfax.[55] The correspondence of the Fairfax family contains numerous references to the problems caused by the intelligence about their movements which was obtained by the Royalists from both intercepted letters and local supporters.[56] Sir Thomas criticised the standards of his own intelligence providers writing that 'our scouts could get no notice of them.'[57] Nonetheless, Parliamentarian commanders did acquire intelligence of some Royalist movements, once receiving an accurate report that 'the Earl of Newcastle, with his whole force, intended to fall upon our quarter at Tadcaster.'[58] The Fairfaxes were not alone in expressing early concerns about the state of Parliamentarian intelligence; Sir John Hotham, the Parliamentarian Governor of Hull, had written to Fairfax that 'our misery is we know not where his force lies, nor in what condition he is.'[59]

Fairfax's account of the Parliamentarian intelligence operations was written just after the war. It contained not only eyewitness descriptions of some of the northern actions, but also numerous references to the ways in which intelligence information had informed Parliamentarian decisions. For example, Fairfax described how the Parliamentarian operations around Bradford had been determined by intelligence reports when 'upon better intelligence of how the enemy lay, I marched in the night by several towns where they lay.'[60] Fairfax went on to describe how his scouts had harassed the Royalists 'till at last our few men grew so bold, and theirs so disheartened, that they durst not stir a mile from their garrisons.'[61] Consequently, Fairfax drew his opponent into the West Riding and the woollen industry towns such as Leeds, Halifax and Bradford where the Parliamentarians enjoyed the support of the majority of the local people and 'from whence our chief supplies came'.[62] Once the Royalists had entered this comparatively 'unfriendly' territory, Fairfax was able to obtain the intelligence he needed so that his smaller forces could determine where they might attack at an advantage, or when to avoid an engagement if at a disadvantage. The primary evidence of Fairfax's account shows that his opponents had also been obtaining intelligence from local sources, as the Royalists had had 'friends enough to direct them, and give them intelligence'.[63]

Fairfax conceded that Parliamentarian intelligence reports had not always been accurate and that they had sometimes 'made us doubt our intelligence', as when he had attacked Wakefield and found the Royalist garrison larger than he had expected.[64] Nevertheless, as his *Memorials* contained so many contemporary references to the intelligence information he received, it is surely reasonable to draw the conclusion that intelligence-gathering had played a significant role in the conduct of the 1643 Parliamentarian northern campaign. Fairfax was clearly aware of the impact that intelligence had had on the operations of both sides for he acknowledged that the Royalists had also benefited from accurate reports about their enemies. For example, Fairfax described how the Royalists had had 'present intelligence of our march' before the Battle of Seacroft Moor, and how 'they had notice of our coming' before his attack on Wakefield.[65] Fairfax also recounted how the initial Parliamentarian operations had been impeded by his own inefficient scouts who had 'had no effect or notice of them, and no alarm was given'.[66] Fairfax was not the only one to comment on the inefficiency of the

Parliamentarian scouting in the North during the early days of 1643. In February a Roundhead pamphleteer reported how 'the enemy approached ... within a mile of Bolton ... before there was any certain intelligence brought into those within ... for the enemy was in view before they were aware.'[67]

The fact that Fairfax realised the importance – and achievability – of accurate intelligence was shown when he specifically sought local information when he led the Parliamentarian cavalry forces into Lincolnshire following the Parliamentarian defeat at Adwalton Moor and the consequent Royalist siege of Hull. In the event, the Roundhead intelligence organisation in that county was unreliable and their information about the Royalist movements was erratic, although Fairfax did receive some useful reports. For example, when the local Parliamentarians were given the 'intelligence the [Royalist] army would march the next day to Bolingbroke for the relief of the castle', this information enabled a Parliamentarian force to engage – and defeat – the Royalists at the Battle of Winceby on 11 October.[68] Similarly in December 1643, when Fairfax was ordered by the Committee of Both Kingdoms to move to the west and assist Brereton, the Parliamentarian commander in Cheshire, to defeat the recently reinforced Royalist forces at Nantwich, Fairfax sought further information when he asked Brereton 'what your intelligence is concerning the interposition of the enemy's forces?'[69]

On the other hand, the significance of intelligence to the northern operations of the Royalist Army is reflected in the Duchess of Newcastle's contemporary description of the information that had been received by her husband. For example, she recognised that the flow of intelligence was dependant upon the sympathies of the local people noting that 'By reason the whole county was of their [Parliamentarian] party ... my Lord could not possibly have any constant intelligence of their designes and motions.'[70] Notwithstanding this somewhat gloomy view, the Duchess later described how intelligence from friendly sources had led to the Royalist success at the Battle of Seacroft Moor on 30 March when she recounted how 'My Lord received intelligence that the enemies General of the Horse had designed to march with a party from Cawood Castle' which prompted Newcastle to order Goring 'to attend the enemy in their march' – a clear example of a battle initiated by an intelligence report.[71] Her account reveals that Newcastle's decision had been further informed and influenced by another report that the main Parliamentarian Army 'was still at Tadcaster, and had fortified that place'.[72] These corroborated intelligence reports led to Goring's successful interception of the Roundhead force and the subsequent Royalist victory. Later, the Duchess reported how Newcastle had also received 'intelligence that the enemy in the garrisons near Wakefield had united themselves' for a surprise attack on the town. Subsequently, Fairfax found the Royalist fortifications manned and the hedges along his line of approach lined by musketeers.[73] But, as we indicated earlier, intelligence-gathering was more difficult when the Royalist forces entered those parts of Yorkshire that favoured Parliament.

There is clear primary evidence that both sides in the North derived much intelligence from reading their opponents' letters. For example, in May 1643, the Royalist commander, Sir John Belasis, noted that 'from the intercepting of some letters, the Earl of Newcastle … had discovered a plan for the surprising of the Queen as she travelled through Yorkshire.'[74] Letters from Sir Thomas Fairfax describing the Parliamentarian 'designe for Yorkshire' were also intercepted by Belasis and passed on to Prince Rupert.[75] The contemporary accounts of the interception of Parliamentarian letters reveal that Newcastle was informed 'that the Lord Fairfax by quitting Selby, Cawood and other places on the river, had put himself out of all possibility of being supplied with forces, arms or ammunition by the way of Hull'.[76]

More examples of the primary evidence of intelligence-gathering by both sides in the North are provided in the printed reports of military activity that appeared in both Royalist and Parliamentarian news pamphlets. For example, in January and February various publications reported the return of the Queen from Europe, where she had been seeking arms, munitions and support from the principal European governments, 'with an incredible quantity of powder and other ammunition'.[77] Throughout the year, the intelligence obtained from the interception of letters was regularly reported in London. During the last week of January 1643, there were accounts in several pamphlets of the interception of mail. For example, it was noted on one occasion that 'there was intercepted this week letters going to the Lord Newcastle from His Majesty and Secretary Nicholas.'[78] These reports covered a wide range of issues; one Roundhead pamphleteer raised doubts about the loyalty of Hull's Parliamentarian governor, Sir John Hotham, when he reported that he 'had intelligence of the danger the town [Hull] was in by Sir John Hotham's unfaithfulness'.[79] Other reports gave details of changes to the Royalist command structure and descriptions of senior Royalist prisoners after the storming of Wakefield.[80] These printed reports gave some interesting insights into the breadth of the intelligence information which was available to each side. For example, they reported a plot to betray Lincoln to the Royalists, as well as news of 'papist plots' which was based on intercepted 'letters from the King to the Queen … to acquaint her that he would make some new officers of state'.[81]

Thus the contemporary accounts provide very strong evidence indeed that intelligence-gathering made a substantial contribution to the outcome of the 1643 northern campaigns. It shows not only that both Royalist and Parliamentarian operations relied upon intelligence reports of the enemy's position and strength, but also that their information came from a wide variety of different sources. Although both sides received intelligence from their local supporters, the fact that, initially at least, Royalist supporters were in the majority gave Newcastle the advantage upon which Fairfax had commented.[82] The territorial and numerical advantages enjoyed by the Royalists also enabled them to intercept Parliamentarian messengers more easily.[83] Do contemporary accounts of the more southerly campaigns provide similar evidence of effective intelligence-gathering operations?

The evidence of the primary sources describing the role of military intelligence in the central Thames Valley campaigns of 1643 reveals that a great deal of intelligence was being reported and that the actions of the commanders in the area were frequently guided by this information. Kept well informed by Pym of the progress of the peace discussions which had been conducted during the winter months, Essex prepared his forces to march against Oxford. He was therefore well placed to move quickly once the talks had concluded and, on 16 April 1643, he took advantage of the King's vacillations and besieged Reading. As Essex's prompt advance had caught the Royalists by surprise, their response was slow and hesitant. Evidence of Parliamentarian intelligence-gathering is provided by a printed report which notes that Essex's troops 'intercepted a servant of Sir Lewis Dyves' who informed them of the Reading garrison's shortage of powder and of how 'the supply was prevented by some [Parliamentarian] troops of horse.'[84] Although a relief force was on the way, the Royalist commander of Reading surrendered the town on 27 April.

Later in the year, the London news pamphlets contained intelligence reports that relief forces were being sent to assist the beleaguered Parliamentarian forces in the west. Even before Bristol fell, one writer claimed that there was 'a considerable party forthwith designed to march into the west to relieve the siege before Bristol.'[85] The next week, the same pamphleteer reported that:

> Sir William Waller is to be speedily sent forth towards the west and to relieve Gloucester, from whence we have intelligence this day that they are in good condition ... there is no doubt but Gloucester will endure a longer siege than Bristol did.[86]

The belief that Gloucester would hold out if besieged was widespread; during the week that Gloucester was invested, a London news pamphlet reported that 'On Sunday last the Cavaliers began to besiege the City of Gloucester, with an army of 6000 men, but the inhabitants thereof are so well provided ... they can hold out this three months.'[87] A further report that '5000 horse [are] to be sent down to the city of Gloucester for the strengthening of that city in case Prince Rupert ... should come against it to besiege it' was published at the same time.[88] Parliament was clearly being kept well informed by Colonel Massey, the Gloucester commander, of the state of his garrison and of the reported intentions of the Royalist Army after the fall of Bristol.[89] The evidence of the pamphlets was confirmed by similar reports from Sir Samuel Luke's agents. On 29 July, Luke reported that 'the King's forces have taken Bristol and that Prince Rupert is now before Gloucester', and this was followed two days later by a report that the Royalists 'intend to go speedily against Gloucester'. Finally, on 2 August, Luke reported that 'the King went to Bristol and intends to stay there till Gloucester be taken and afterwards they resolve to go against London.'[90] Clearly, Parliamentarian intelligence about the Royalists' intentions and capabilities was broadly correct.

The Royalists were so confident of their intelligence that the battles of the preceding three months had left the Parliamentarian forces in some disarray, that, at the end of July, *Mercurius Aulicus* reported that 'the Rebel Army under the command of the Earl of Essex is growne very weake, and able to do nothing to the hindrance of His Majesty's Service.'[91] Contemporary evidence of their intelligence-gathering shows that the Royalists were also well aware of the tensions between Essex and Waller and of the 'designe on foot of raising a new armie under the command of Sir William Waller'.[92] The Royalists reported that the Parliamentarians had 'given up Exeter for as good as lost', and they also boasted that:

> Unless supplies be sent [to Gloucester] of Men, Armes and Money (neither of which the pretended Houses can afford … at the present time) they are not able to hold out against His Majesty's forces but of necessity must give up the towne on the first assault.[93]

More evidence of the intelligence reaching the Royalist commanders came from the same report in *Aulicus* which described the tensions between the two Houses and claimed that there was 'a Civil Warre between them'. Clearly there was a difference of opinion between the Royalist and Parliamentarian pamphleteers about the determination of the Gloucester garrison to resist a Royalist assault – and of the ability of the Parliamentarian commanders to provide a relief force. The Royalist decision to besiege rather than storm Gloucester thus appears to have been partly influenced by flawed intelligence about the preparedness of the garrison and the commitment of the garrison commander.

Royalist intelligencers seem to have been slow to discern the formation of a relief force for Gloucester. But, as the relief force marched westwards, some reports of its progress were published; for example, *Mercurius Aulicus* reported that 'Essex was at Aylesbury on Monday night, last night at Bicester.'[94] This report reflected the intelligence being provided by General Wilmot, the victorious Royalist general at Roundway Down, who had been tasked to protect Oxford and monitor Parliamentarian movements in the Thames Valley corridor. On 3 August 1643, Wilmot informed Rupert that Essex '[has] his foot at Chilton and his horse at Wotton; this day, I am informed, his rendezvous is near Bicester'.[95] Despite the intelligence that forecast a weak and short-lived resistance from the Gloucester garrison, and the reports of the approach of the Parliamentarian relief force, the Royalist plan to capture Gloucester was not altered or advanced. Contemporary evidence confirms that the Parliamentarian commanders were receiving regular intelligence from Luke about the increasing mood of frustration within the Royalist camp. As early as 11 August, Luke's agent reported that:

> Because they [the Royalists] have small hope of taking it [Gloucester] he hears they intend to leave the siege and go presently against London for they say themselves that the Roundheads will die every man before they yield it up.[96]

Similar reports continued to be received by the advancing Parliamentarians; on 17 August, for example, Luke was reporting that 'there was a small probability of taking the city', and, on 20 August, he reported that the Royalists 'wish they had never set [their forces] upon Gloucester'.[97] Meanwhile, Parliamentarian pamphlets were reporting the advance of Essex's army to relieve Gloucester. In mid August, the author of *Certain Informations* observed 'it is hoped that the Lord General of the Parliamentarian Army will send some aid to them [the Gloucester garrison] because he yesterday [14 August] mustered his horse at Kingston upon Thames and found them to amount to the number of 4000.'[98] Later pamphlets gave details of the Parliamentarian advance on a day-by-day basis, reporting 'how farre his Excellency the Parliament's Lord General was advanced to the relief of Gloucester,' the report concluding that 'news was brought to London that ... the siege was raised from below Gloucester.'[99]

Although the relief of Gloucester was an important success for the Parliamentarians, Essex was acutely aware that, as well as being isolated and far from his base in London, he was now also vulnerable to attack from a Royalist Army which was back under the dynamic command of Prince Rupert. Essex appreciated that he had two options for his return to London: he could either move to the north and return via the Midlands, or he could march back along the Thames Valley corridor. Essex elected initially to move north to Tewkesbury as this allowed him to concentrate his army and move clear of Gloucester. Tewkesbury was an ideal location for it offered a choice of either a northerly or a more southerly route for the march back to London. It was at this moment that Essex reaped an enormous benefit from the Parliamentarian intelligence-gathering organisation. Luke's journal shows that, on 13 September, Essex was sent vital intelligence reports that 'the King and his army were this morning at Pershore and marching towards Worcester.'[100] Luke's agent also reported that there was a large Royalist food convoy in 'Cirencester and thereabouts, 40 carts ... laden with beer, bread, cheese and other provisions'.[101] These reports of the latest Royalist positions allowed Essex to side-step the Royalist Army during the night of 14/15 September, ordering the rapid counter-march of the Parliamentarian Army towards Cirencester. As was reported at the time by a Parliamentarian soldier, 'we caused a bridge to be made over the Severn, and sent some forces to Upton Bridge, as if we intended to march to Worcester, and caused the enemy to draw all his forces together for the defence of that place.'[102] This rapid march, 'when we went cleane another way marcht all day and the greatest part of the night from Tewkesbury to Cirencester', not only allowed Essex to escape the encircling Royalist forces, but also allowed him to capture the Royalists' keenly-awaited provisions – provisions which were also urgently needed by the Roundheads for their return march to London.[103] On 16 September, Luke's men provided useful corroboration of their earlier intelligence when they reported from Evesham that 'the King was there and intended not to stir all this day.'[104]

The Royalist scouts detected the Roundhead manoeuvres towards Cirencester and Sir John Byron, one of Charles' military commanders, reported the change of direction of Essex's army to Prince Rupert. Later on, when Byron was pointing the finger at Rupert for failing to 'credit my intelligence', and adding that, if the Prince had heeded him, 'the advantage Essex gained might have been prevented',[105] Rupert was quick to claim that he had told the King of the change but the King 'believed himself better informed' and did not act upon the reports.[106] As this was the night when Rupert had lost contact with the King (who he eventually found playing cards with Lord Percy and watched by the Earl of Forth) it appears that delays in communication of this important intelligence were much to blame for the lack of Royalist response. Although both Byron's and Rupert's accounts indicate that the information was received in time for action to have been taken, Digby's later account claimed that the intelligence was received too late:

> We were quickly hurried by the newes that Essex had faced about, and had in the night, with great silence secrecy, and strange diligence, almost gained Cirencester, and surprised two new raised Regiments of ours there, before we could get any certain notice of this.[107]

To his credit, Charles recognised the magnitude of this mistake and did his best to redeem the situation by personally urging on the flagging Royalist foot during the rain-swept pursuit that followed.[108]

Once the two armies were on the move, the task of reporting their position was a relatively straightforward scouting task for both sides. As one of the Parliamentarian scouts reported, 'the enemy was coming upon us with a great body of horse, which caused the Lord General [Essex] to make a stand.'[109] This stand allowed the Royalist Army to get to Newbury before Essex, but it did not prevent the Parliamentarian scouts from advising Essex about the position of the Royalist forces that night, and the best positions to occupy. As Digby reported:

> [B]y break of day, (instead of the flight which upon all their former proceedings, we had reason to expect) we discovered them settled in the most advantageous way imaginable of receiving us … there we found them, their foot, their horse and their cannon planted with much skill.[110]

Superior intelligence about the local topography – and the Royalist disposition – had allowed the Parliamentarian forces to seize the advantage in this critically important battle, and this reflected the contribution made by intelligence information throughout the central Thames Valley campaigns during 1643. The evidence of the contemporary accounts shows that both sides had obtained advantages from a full range of intelligence sources, ranging from scouting reports to information from deserters.

Lastly, the evidence of the primary sources describing the role of military intelligence in the campaigns in the South and South West also reveals that, as in the North and Thames Valley campaigns, the decisions taken during the chief military actions were also informed by accurate and timely intelligence. One of the main sources of contemporary evidence about the South West campaigns is provided by Sir Ralph Hopton's manuscript account.[111] Hopton made numerous references to the intelligence information that he, as the principal Royalist commander, constantly received whilst his army was deployed in Cornwall. For example, Hopton's advance on Okehampton just before the skirmish at Sourton Down had been encouraged by intelligence from 'a friend in [that town] who assured [him] that the enemy in Okehampton were in very great disquiet and fear'.[112] Hopton's evidence is supplemented by that of Walter Slingsby, an officer in Hopton's army, and further contemporary evidence is provided by a Royalist captain of horse, Richard Atkins, who was attached to the army of Prince Maurice as the adjutant-general.[113] A Parliamentarian perspective is given by Sir William Waller in his *Vindication*, which was written as an explanation of his actions just after the war, although not published until 1793.[114]

Although Slingsby wrote that 'meale and intelligence were two necessary things for an army', there is no evidence that Hopton ever appointed a scoutmaster.[115] Nevertheless, it is clear that Hopton received accurate and timely intelligence from the local population who reported news of Parliamentarian movements to their 'local' regimental commanders, such as Sir Bevil Grenville. For example, when the Earl of Stamford's Parliamentarian forces marched onto land owned by the Grenvilles, the Royalists immediately received intelligence from Grenville's tenants of the Roundheads' position.[116]. On one occasion, Hopton 'retreated into Cornwall' having received intelligence 'that the enemy was advanced as far as Okehampton, and that their numbers far exceeded those of the Cornish army'.[117] Subsequently, 'intelligence was brought of the Enemyes advancing into the north part of Cornwall, and that they had made their head quarter att Stratton.'[118] In addition to receiving information from his scouts and local sympathisers, Hopton also obtained intelligence from intercepted letters; 'in the first days of March they intercepted a letter from [the Parliamentarian] General Ruthven to the Mayor of Barnstable.'[119]

There is little evidence that Hopton made specific use of spies, although some contemporary accounts record that men were apparently appointed by Hopton to act as 'intelligencers' – a description that embraced spies, messengers and scouts.[120] Hopton certainly used clergymen as messengers, hoping that their clerical status would protect them. However, this did not prevent one of his messengers, Dr Cox, from being subjected to a savage interrogation as an alleged spy by the defeated Parliamentarians after Stratton.[121] Hopton's scouts provided him with intelligence of the Parliamentarian positions which he used to defeat Ruthven at Braddock Down.[122] But Royalist scouts were not always effective for they did not detect Chudleigh's ambush at Sourton Down. On the eve of that engagement, Hopton wrote that the Royalist Army was 'never … in better order … nor ever … in lesser apprehension of the enemy.'[123] Had Hopton been able to obtain any of the London news pamphlets, he might have gained useful intelligence, as these publications contained much information of military significance. The movements of Roundhead commanders were regularly reported,[124] as were Roundhead accounts of the outcome of various battles and skirmishes.[125]

The contemporary accounts show that, like Hopton, Sir William Waller was keenly aware of the importance of being well informed. Waller's adroit use of intelligence showed that he had not only learnt the importance of finding the enemy's position, but also that he recognised the considerable tactical advantages to be gained from denying his opponent any intelligence about his own movements. Following his earlier engagements with Royalist forces, Waller quickly established a reputation for carrying out key manoeuvres under the cover of darkness in order to deny his opponents' scouts any useful intelligence. Even some of the Royalist commanders acknowledged that Waller employed 'good intelligence' to gain positions of military advantage;[126] Colonel Walter Slingsby stated that Waller was 'the best shifter and chooser of ground when he was not master of the field that I ever saw.'[127] Contemporary accounts of Waller's defeat of Lord Herbert's Royalist Welsh forces at Highnam on 24 March provide excellent contemporary evidence of how superior intelligence enabled Waller to eliminate a large Royalist force before it had even had a chance to influence military events.[128] While marching on Gloucester, Herbert's army occupied Highnam House, owned by Sir Robert Cooke, a Parliamentarian sympathiser. As a result Waller soon received accurate intelligence of the strengths and weaknesses of the Royalist position. Using the cover of darkness to conceal his movements from any Royalist scouts, Waller was able to launch a coordinated attack on the rear of the Royalists. He crossed the Severn on a bridge of boats floated down from Gloucester, and was guided into position at Highnam by Cooke himself. Whilst his forces were moving into position around Highnam, Waller's intelligence was so accurate that he had enough time to personally intercept a financial contribution of some 'seven hundred pounds' raised for the Royalist cause, by impersonating the Royalist officer sent to collect it.[129]

For any of his military manoeuvres to succeed, it was essential that Waller had precise intelligence of his opponent's positions and intended movements. Scouting was therefore a key element of his generalship and evidence of the effectiveness of his intelligence organisation was provided by Hopton in his account of the campaign in the South West. For example, he notes that 'Waller, having intelligence of the blowing up of the ammunition' after the Battle of Lansdown, 'lost noe time' in pursuing the withdrawing Royalist forces.[130] After the Royalist reverse at Sourton Down, a letter from the King to Hopton was captured. As this letter ordered Hopton to 'use your best diligence to horse all your foot, both musketeers and pikes, as dragoons that they may march to us with the more ease, speed and safety', it shows how intercepted mail was being used to provide Waller with intelligence of the movements and strategic intentions of the Royalist Army.[131] During the Royalists' advance towards Bath, the contemporary accounts show how Waller used his knowledge of their movements, and that of the local topography, to anticipate and forestall them. Unnoticed by Hopton's scouts, Waller was able to deploy his army in an almost unassailable position on Lansdown Hill and he would have been confident of victory had it not been for the valour of the Royalist Cornish foot whose attack succeeded, 'to the wonder and amazement of both friends and enemies'.[132] However Waller's intelligence about the precariousness of Hopton's forces following the attack was not so good, as he was not aware that one more determined push would have sent the Royalists tumbling back to the bottom 'like a heavy stone upon the very brow of the hill.'[133]

Waller clearly appreciated the value of the intelligence given to his scouts by the native population. Using the retreat of Hopton's army after the Battle of Lansdown to his advantage, Waller was able to persuade the local populace of Parliament's supremacy. He thereby obtained much useful intelligence from the locals by reassuring them that 'he had given a notable defeat to the Prince's army, and had broken the whole body of his forces', adding that 'if ... they would now cheerfully come in and shew their zeal ... by joining him ... they might soon make an end of the cavaliers.'[134] Further evidence of the effectiveness of Waller's intelligence operations is provided by his interception and capture of five Royalist ammunition wagons escorted by the Earl of Crawford, a Royalist brigade commander, after a report about the convoy by Parliamentarian scouts.[135]

Yet more primary evidence of how Waller integrated intelligence into his planning was provided when he attacked the Royalist Earl of Crawford's brigade at Alton on 13 December 1643. Waller used the intelligence that had been obtained from his own scouts' reports, and from the interrogation of prisoners, to establish an accurate assessment of the strength of the Royalist garrison, and of when and where the Royalist scouts were placed. He was therefore able to select a route that allowed a carefully selected force to approach 'within half a mile of [Alton], altogether undiscovered by the enemy, our scouts being so diligent, that not a person [had] any opportunity to inform the enemy of our proceedings'.[136] Printed reports added that Waller had 'carried the business so privately that they were upon the enemy [almost at once], he not having notice above a quarter of an hour before'.[137] Although Crawford managed to escape with most of his cavalry, the Royalist foot were left to fight unsupported until they were all killed or captured.

The impact that intelligence-gathering had upon the outcome of these southern campaigns is clear from the evidence of the contemporary accounts. It is evident that Waller in particular made extremely effective use of information and that this enabled him to counter the intelligence being received by Hopton from Royalist sympathisers in the South West. The primary sources indicate that much of the Parliamentarian intelligence came from active scouting, although after Lansdown, Waller's encouragement of the populace to provide his pursuing troops with intelligence demonstrated that he appreciated the importance of local information.

In conclusion, it is clear from the contemporary evidence that both sides made very significant use of intelligence during the 1643 campaigns. Particularly during the Gloucester and Newbury campaign, the primary sources confirm that intelligence-gathering had improved significantly, with accurate information being passed regularly to the commanders in time for them to deploy their forces in order to meet reported threats. Although scouting remained the most widely used form of intelligence, information from spies, intercepted letters and other informants increased steadily during 1643. It also shows that the Royalist army in the North had an effective local intelligence service which, largely due to the interception of messages, was able to provide Newcastle with invaluable intelligence about the movements and intentions of his enemy. Likewise it is clear that the critical significance of the Parliamentarian intelligence information in the northern campaign should not be underestimated. For the Parliamentarian strategy of 'striking when strong and withdrawing when weak' to have worked as well as it did, Lord Fairfax needed to have accurate and constant intelligence of the disposition and strength of the Royalist Army. As the Parliamentarian prospects in the North improved, so too did their supporting intelligence service, probably because more people came forward with information. The evidence suggests that Parliamentarian commanders made better use of their intelligence; both Fairfax in the North and Waller in the South West integrated reports into their plans very effectively. As a result, Fairfax was able to prevent a considerably larger Royalist Army from moving south to reinforce Charles, just as Waller was able to outmanoeuvre Hopton at Lansdown and Alton.

It is equally evident that during the siege of Gloucester, Luke was receiving regular reports from his agents amongst the besieging Royalist forces within a week of the start of the siege.[138] Accurate Parliamentarian intelligence from his scouts not only enabled Essex to get clean away from Gloucester, but also allowed him to capture the Royalists' food supplies. The Parliamentarian scouting reports also enabled him to deploy his forces onto some key topographical strong points on the western edge of the battlefield, occupied briefly the night before by Royalist scouts, during the initial troop deployments immediately prior to the Battle of Newbury. The accounts of the 'race' to London also show that the scouting of both sides was particularly effective, with the commanders constantly aware of the enemy's position.

Both sides appear to have benefited from other sources of intelligence during 1643. For example, deserters to the Royalist cause provided information which allowed Rupert to raid Parliamentarian positions, and Newcastle's army gained an invaluable insight into Parliamentarian plans when Belasis intercepted letters from Sir Thomas Fairfax. Similarly the capture of Hopton's correspondence after the skirmish at Sourton Down gave the Parliamentarian sequestrators some invaluable evidence for their prosecutions of 'closet' Royalist supporters.

As we have seen from the evidence of Luke's extraction of intelligence from the Royalist pamphlet, *Mercurius Aulicus*, it appears perfectly reasonable to believe that news pamphlets increasingly provided useful military information to both sides.[139] Their contemporary accounts show that a significant amount of intelligence was used to inform all the military decisions taken during the main 1643 campaigns. Although both sides had established intelligence-gathering organisations, the Parliamentarian use of the County Committees, supported by information from their garrison commanders, provided them with a more effective intelligence structure.[140] The interception of mail increased steadily during 1643 as commanders realised that captured letters provided both sides with invaluable insights. Luke's appointment as Scoutmaster-General gave the Parliamentarian forces a distinct advantage over their Royalist opponents as his agents provided Essex with critically important intelligence at a number of key moments during 1643.

As the war had expanded across the country, the intelligence services developed in tandem to provide their respective commanders with the information they needed. Waller's action to win the support of the local people after the Battle of Lansdown also indicates how the fighting was beginning to draw everybody into the conflict. What impact would the increasing effectiveness of military intelligence-gathering have upon subsequent campaigns? The next chapter will show how intelligence operations gained credibility as they were increasingly used and developed during 1644.

Notes

1 E. Hyde, *The History of the Rebellion and Civil Wars in England, together with an Historical View of the Affairs in Ireland* (sixteen books, London, 1702–4), Book VI, p.142.

2 S.R. Gardiner, *History of the Great Civil War 1642–49* (four volumes, London, 1893), Volume 2, p.195.

3 Ibid, pp.197–198. See also, J. Day, *Gloucester and Newbury 1643, The Turning Point of the Civil War* (Barnsley, 2007), p.42.

4 Gardiner, *History*, Volume 2, pp.243–244.

5 C.E.H. Chadwyck-Healey (ed.), *Bellum Civile: Hopton's Narrative of His Campaign in the West (1642–44) and Other Papers* (Somerset Record Society, Volume 18, 1902), p.41.

6 T. May, *The History of the Parliament of England* (London, 1647), p.61.

7 J. Rushworth, *Historical Collections* (London, 1659–99), Part III, Volume II, pp.263–265, 268–271, 275 and 279–281.

8 Rushworth, *Historical Collections*, Part III, Volume II, pp.126–127.

9 C.H. Firth, 'Clarendon's History of the Rebellion', *English Historical Review* (Volume 19, 1904), pp.34, 44, and 47–48.

10 Clarendon, *History*, Book VII, pp.177–178.

11 See L. Echard, *History of England* (London, 1707–18); J. Oldmixon, *Critical History of*

England (London, 1724); T. Carte, *General History of England* (London, 1747–55); and C. Macaulay, *History of England from the Accession of James I* (London, 1763–83).

12 S. R. Gardiner, *History of the Great Civil War 1642–1649* (four volumes, London, 1893).

13 See, for example, E.G.B. Warburton, *Memoirs of Prince Rupert and the Cavaliers* (three volumes, London, 1849), Volume II, p.183.

14 C.R. Markham, *A Life of the Great Lord Fairfax* (London, 1870).

15 C.H. Firth (ed.), *The Lives of William Cavendish, Duke of Newcastle and of his wife Margaret, Duchess of Newcastle* (London, 1907).

16 See, for example, A. Woolrych, *Battles of the English Civil War* (London, 1961), pp.43–44; P.Young and R. Holmes, *The English Civil War. A Military History of the Three Civil Wars 1642–1651* (London, 1974), pp.98–114 and 151–158; S. Reid, *All the King's Armies. A Military History of the English Civil War 1642 – 1651* (Kent, 1998), pp.66–80; T. Royle, *Civil War: The Wars of the Three Kingdoms 1638–1660* (London, 2004), pp.250–265; and M. Wanklyn and F. Jones, *A Military History of the English Civil War, 1642–1646* (London, 2005), pp.75–80.

17 D. Cooke, *The Civil War in Yorkshire: Fairfax versus Newcastle* (Barnsley, 2004), pp.29, 48–49 and 55.

18 J. Wilson, *Fairfax. A Life of Thomas, Lord Fairfax, Captain-General of all the Parliament's forces in the English Civil War, Creator and Commander of the New Model Army* (London, 1985), pp.23, 26, 29 and 31–32.

19 S.D.M. Carpenter, *Military Leadership in the English Civil Wars, 1642–1651: 'The Genius of this Age'* (London, 2005), pp.23 and 73.

20 See Carpenter, *Leadership*, p.73; and Wilson, *Fairfax*, p.195.

21 See Chapter 8.

22 Clarendon, *History*, Book VIII, p.56.

23 May, *History*, pp.104–107.

24 Rushworth, *Historical Collections*, Part III, Volume II, pp.292–294.

25 Clarendon, *History*, Book VII, p.75. See also E. 249[5], *A Perfect Diurnall of the Passages in Parliament* (London, 8–15 May 1643); E. 56[11], *Mercurius Aulicus* (Oxford, 10–18 June 1643); and E. 59[12], *The Parliament Scout* (London, 29 June- 6 July 1643)

26 See, for example, Clarendon, *History*, Book VII, pp.176–177, 203–204 and 206.

27 Clarendon, *History*, Book VII, p.158

28 Clarendon, *History*, Book VII, pp.161–164.

29 Gardiner, *History*, Volume II, pp.208–209.

30 Ibid, p.210.

31 See, for example, Warburton, *Memoirs*, Volume II, pp.96, 101, 106, 132, 151 and 184.

32 See Warburton, *Memoirs*, Volume II, pp.203–204 and 287–288.

33 See Warburton, *Memoirs*, Volume II, p.204.

34 Gardiner, *History*, Volume I, pp.150–151

35 Ibid, p.209.

36 See, for example, A. Woolrych, *Battles of the English Civil War* (London, 1961), pp.46–49; P.Young and R. Holmes, *The English Civil War. A Military History of the Three Civil Wars 1642–1651*(London, 1974), pp.142–150; S. Reid, *All the King's Armies. A Military History of the English Civil War 1642–1651* (Staplehurst, 1998), pp.59–65; T. Royle, *Civil War; The Wars of the Three Kingdoms 1638 – 1660* (London, 2004), pp.266–273; and M. Wanklyn and F. Jones, *A Military History of the English Civil War, 1642–1646* (Harlow, 2005), pp.142–150.

37 Young and Holmes, *English Civil War*, p.123. See also F. Kitson, *Prince Rupert. Portrait of a Soldier* (London, 1994), pp.126–127.

38 J. Day, *Gloucester and Newbury 1643. The Turning Point of the Civil War* (Barnsley, 2007).

39 Day, *Gloucester and Newbury*, pp.61, 76 and 97.

40 Day, *Gloucester and Newbury*, pp.120–123 and 125–126.

41 See, for example, Wanklyn, *The Warrior Generals*, pp.48, 50–52, 55, 66 and 73.

42 See May, *History*, pp.40, 56 and 73.

43 See, for example, Rushworth, *Historical Collections,* Part III, Volume II, pp.263, 267–268 and 285.

44 Firth, 'Clarendon's History', pp.50–51. Hopton's manuscripts are Bod. L, Clarendon MSS, 1738, ff. 1, 4, and 6; and Slingsby's manuscripts are Bod. L, Clarendon MSS, 1738, ff. 2, 3 and 7. See also Chadwyck Healey, *Bellum Civile.*

45 See, for example, Clarendon, *History*, Book VII, pp.87, 98, 100, 103, 109, 113 and 116.

46 Clarendon, *History*, Book VIII, p.9.

47 Chadwyck Healey, *Bellum Civile*, p.xvii.

48 M. Coate, *Cornwall in the Great Civil War and Interregnum 1642 – 1660* (Oxford, 1933), p.62.

49 Coate, *Cornwall*, p.65.

50 See, for example, Stucley, *Sir Bevill Grenville,* pp.120, 122–123, 126, and 134–137.

51 See, for example, Adair, *Roundhead General*, pp.56, 58–60, 68, 81, 87, 91 and 93.

52 See, for example, T. MacLachlan, *The Civil War in Wiltshire* (Salisbury, 1997), pp.95–96, 104 and 108–109; and T. MacLachlan, *The Civil War in Hampshire* (Salisbury, 2000), pp.176–177.

53 See, for example, J. Wroughton, *An Unhappy Civil War. The experiences of Ordinary People in Gloucestershire, Somerset and Wiltshire, 1642– 1646* (Bath, 1999), pp.165 and 214–216; and MacLachan, *Civil War in Wiltshire,* pp.158–159.

54 See, for example, M.J. Stoyle, 'Pagans or Paragons? Images of the Cornish during the English Civil War', *English Historical Review* (Volume III, No. 441, 1996), pp.299–323; and M. J. Stoyle, *Loyalty and Locality,* (Exeter, 1994), p.65.

55 M. Cavendish, *The Life of William Cavendish, Duke of Newcastle, to which is added the true relation of my birth, breeding and life* (London, 1667), pp.29, 32, 33, 36 and 43.; and F. Maseres (ed.), *Select Tracts relating to the Civil Wars in England in the reign of King Charles the First* (London, 1815), pp.411–451.

56 E. 245[32], *A Continuation of certaine Special and Remarkable Passages from both Houses of Parliament, 26 January-2 February* (London, 1643).

57 R. Bell (ed.), *Memorials of the Civil War: The Fairfax Correspondence* (two volumes, London, 1849), Volume 1, p.34.

58 Ibid, Volume 1, p.27

59 Ibid, Volume 1, p.45.

60 Maseres, *Short Memorials*, p.418.

61 Ibid, p.419.

62 Ibid, p.416.

63 Ibid, p.416.

64 Ibid, pp.423.

65 Ibid, pp.421– 423.

66 Ibid, p.416.

67 E. 90[12], *Speciall Passages and Certain Information from Severall Places* (London, 14–21 February 1643).

68 Bell, *Fairfax Correspondence*, Volume I, p.64.

69 Bell, *Fairfax Correspondence*, Volume III, pp.67–75.

70 Cavendish, *Life of Newcastle,* p.39.

71 Ibid, p.32.

72 Ibid, p.24.

73 Ibid, p.36.

74 See, for example, E. 245[36], *Mercurius Aulicus* (Oxford, 15–21 January 1643); E. 266[9], *Mercurius Aulicus* (Oxford, 22–28 January 1643); E. 100[18], *Mercurius Aulicus* (Oxford, 16– 23 April 1643); and E. 56[11], *Mercurius Aulicus* (Oxford, 10–17 June 1643). See also, Wilson, *Fairfax,* p.195. Letter from Belasis dated 17 May 1643.

75 Bod. L, Firth MSS, C6 (2), f. 148. Letter dated 17 March 1644.

76 E. 100[18], *Mercurius Aulicus* (Oxford, 16– 22 April 1643).

77 See, for example, E. 245[32], *A Continuation of certaine Speciall and Remarkable Passages from both Houses of Parliament, and other parts of the Kingdome* (London, 26 January- 2 February 1643); and E. 90[12].

78 See, for example, E. 86[39], *Speciall Passages and certain Informations from Severall places* (London, 24– 31 January 1643); E. 245[32]; BL, E. 101[24], *Certaine Informations from Severall Parts of the Kingdome* (London, 8– 15 May 1643); E. 249[7], *A Continuation of certaine Speciall and Remarkable Passages from both Houses of Parliament and other Parts of the Kingdome* (London, 11– 18 May 1643): and *CSPD, 1641– 43*, p.489.

79 See, for example, E. 61[16], *Certaine Informations from Severall Parts of the Kingdome* (London, 17–24 July 1643); and E. 104[18], *The Kingdomes Weekly Intelligencer* (London, 23– 30 May 1643).

80 See, for example, E. 102[1], *Mercurius Aulicus* (Oxford, 1– 8 May 1643); and E. 249[11], *A Perfect Diurnall of the Passages in Parliament* (London, 22–29 May 1643).

81 See, for example, E. 59 [22], *The Kingdomes Weekly Intelligencer* (London, 4–11 July 1643) for a report on the plot to betray Lincoln; and E. 104[24], *Certain Informations from Severall Parts of the Kingdome* (London, 8–15 May 1643).

82 Fairfax, *Short Memorials*, p.416.

83 E. 100[18], *Mercurius Aulicus* (Oxford, 15–22 April 1643).

84 E. 100[5], *The last Intelligence from his Excellency his Quarters at Reading, since the surrendering of the town* (London, 27 April 1643).

85 E. 249[30], *A Perfect Diurnall of some Passages in Parliament* (London, 24–31 July 1643).

86 E. 249[31].

87 E. 65[8], *Certain Informations from Severall parts of the Kingdom* (London, 7–14 August 1643).

88 E. 63[4], *Speciall Passages* (London, 31 July- 7 August 1643).

89 Bod. L, Tanner MSS, 62, f. 197.

90 I.G. Philip (ed.), *The Journal of Sir Samuel Luke* (three volumes, Oxfordshire Record Society, 1947), pp.126 and 128.

91 E. 64[11], *Mercurius Aulicus* (Oxford, 30 July 1643).

92 E. 65[26], *Mercurius Aulicus* (Oxford, 12 August 1643).

93 E. 65[26], *Mercurius Aulicus* (Oxford, 12 August 1643).

94 E. 67[2], *Mercurius Aulicus* (Oxford, 2 September 1643).

95 BL, Addl. MSS, 18980, f.139.

96 Philip, *Journal*, Volume II, p.133.

97 Ibid, pp.136 and 138.

98 E. 65[24], *Certain Informations from Severall parts of the Kingdom* (London, 14–21 August 1643).

99 E. 67[3], *Certain Informations from Severall parts of the Kingdom* (London, 4–11 September 1643).

100 Philip, *Journal*, Volume II, p.152.

101 Ibid, p.149.

102 E. 69[2], *A True Relation of the late Battell neere Newbery* (London, 26 September 1643).

103 E. 69[2], *A True Relation of the late Battell neere Newbery*. See also, Philip, *Journal*, Volume II, pp.150–154.

104 Philip, *Journal*, Volume II, pp.153.

105 Bod. L, Clarendon MSS, 1738, f. 5.

106 BL, Addl. MSS, 62084B.

107 E. 69[10], *A True and impartiall relation of the battaile betwixt, His Majesties Army, and that of the rebels neare Newbery in Berk-shire, Sept. 20, 1643* (Oxford, 1643).

108 Clarendon, *History*, Book VII, p.207.

109 E. 69[15], *A True and Exact Relation of the Marchings of the Two Regiments of Trained Bands of the City of London, being the Red and the Blew Regiments* (London, 2 October 1643).

110 E. 69[10], *A relation of the battaile neare Newbery, Sept. 20, 1643.*

111 C.E.H. Chadwyck-Healey (ed.), *Bellum Civile: Hopton's Narrative of His Campaign in the West (1642–44) and Other Papers* (Somerset Record Society, 18, 1902).

112 See, for example, Chadwyck-Healey, *Bellum Civile*, pp.27, 29, 34, 36, 38–39, 41, 47 and 55.

113 P.Young (ed.), *The Vindication of Richard Atkyns* (London, 1967), pp.11, 13, and 21.

114 Bod. L, Don MSS, f. 57, *Vindication of the Character and conduct of Sir William Waller, Knight, written by himself.* Waller also wrote a manuscript entitled '*Experiences*' which is preserved in the Wadham College Library, Oxford.

115 Chadwyck-Healey, *Bellum Civile*, p.97.

116 See, for example, Chadwyck-Healey, *Bellum Civile*, pp.14, 19, 22, 26, and 29.

117 Ibid, p.41.

118 Ibid, p.41.

119 Ibid, p.27.

120 *Calendar for the Committee for the Advancement of Money*, 6 August 1649, pp.980–981.

121 Chadwyck-Healey, *Bellum Civile*, p.45.

122 Ibid, pp.28–29.

123 E.100 [17].

124 See, for example, E. 245[6], *A Continuation of certaine Speciall and Remarkable Passages from both Houses of Parliament* (London, 5–12 January 1643); E. 245[20], *A Continuation of certaine Speciall and Remarkable Passages from both Houses of Parliament* (London, 19–26 January 1643); E. 245[32], *A Continuation of certaine Speciall and Remarkable Passages from both Houses of Parliament* (London, 26 January- 2 February 1643); and E. 249[4], *A Continuation of certaine Speciall and Remarkable Passages from both Houses of Parliament* (London, 4–11 May 1643).

125 See, for example, E. 101[24], *Certaine Informations from Severall parts of the Kingdome* (London, 8–15 May 1643) for an account of the skirmish at Sourton Down; and E. 60[9], *Mercurius Civicus* (London, 6–13 July 1643) for the account of the battle at Lansdown.

126 E.247 [26].

127 Chadwyck Healy, *Bellum Civile*, p.91.

128 E. 97[2], *The Victorious and Fortunate Proceedings of Sir William Waller and his Forces in Wales* (London, 1643); E. 247[18], *A Perfect Diurnall of the Passages in Parliament* (London, 27 March-3 April 1643); E. 95[2], *The Kingdomes Weekly Intelligencer* (London, 28 March-4 April 1643); and E. 94[29], *Certaine Informations from Severall Parts of the Kingdome* (London, 27 March-3 April 1643).

129 Philip, *Journal*, Volume 1, pp.50–51.

130 Chadwyck Healy, *Bellum Civile*, pp.52 and 55.

131 E. 249[3], *A Perfect Diurnall* (London, 1–8 May 1643).

132 E. 59[24], *Mercurius Aulicus* (Oxford, 1 July 1643).

133 Chadwyck Healy, *Bellum Civile*, p.96.

134 Ibid, p.97.

135 E. 60[17], *Certain Information* (London, 10–17 July 1643).

136 E. 78[22], *A Narration of the great victory obtained by the Parliament's forces under Sir William Waller at Alton* (London, 16 December 1643). See also, E. 78[19], *The Parliament Scout* (London, 8–15 December 1643); E. 252[11], *A Perfect Diurnall of some Passages* (London, 11–18 December 1643); E. 78[29], *The Weekly Account* (London, 20 December 1643); and E. 78[8], *A True Relation of the Whole Proceedings of Sir William Waller and his Army from 20 November to 9 December1643* (London, 1643).

137 E. 78[19], *The Parliament Scout* (London, 8–15 December 1643).

138 Luke, *Journal*, Volume II, pp.137–138.

139 See Chapter 2.

140 See Appendix for a list of the scoutmasters identified during the research for this book.

6

The Tide Turns – Intelligence Operations in 1644

The contemporary accounts of the final campaigns of 1643 provide clear evidence of a growing appreciation of the importance of intelligence information as both Cavalier and Roundhead commanders came to realise that superior intelligence had played a significant part in determining the outcome of the relief of Gloucester and the First Battle of Newbury.[1] The primary sources describing the subsequent campaigns in 1644 show that this appreciation of the value of intelligence continued to have an increasing influence on the military operations of both sides. So how did this increased awareness of the benefits of accurate information influence the principal military campaigns of that year? In order to answer that question, this chapter will summarise the key military actions before exploring what contribution to our understanding of Civil War military intelligence has been made by other historians who have described these campaigns. The evidence of the primary sources will then be evaluated in order to determine the extent to which intelligence-gathering did in fact influence the outcome of the key 1644 battles. In conclusion, a comparison will be made between the current perception of the impact of the 1644 intelligence operations amongst historians and the evidence of the contemporary accounts. The key military campaigns of 1644 will be assessed in two geographic areas – the North and the South.

Although John Pym had died of cancer on 8 December 1643, it was on 25 September 1643 that his final political act, the signing of the Solemn League and Covenant linking Parliament with Scotland, ensured the provision of much needed military reinforcements from the Scottish Army to assist the battered Parliamentarian forces. Thus the recognised historical record of the principal military events of the 1644 campaigns in the North shows that the balance of military power in that area was dramatically altered when the Scots crossed the border on 19 January to assist their new allies. Although the Scottish advance south was delayed by bad weather, the Royalist Northern Army was forced onto the defensive in Yorkshire as the Duke of Newcastle redeployed his forces to contain the Scottish invasion. This redeployment altered the balance of power in Yorkshire and gave the local Roundheads breathing space, which allowed Lord Fairfax the opportunity to consolidate the Parliamentarian position in Yorkshire, Lincolnshire and Cheshire. Accordingly, the Parliamentarian commander ordered his son, Sir Thomas Fairfax, to march into Cheshire and assist Sir William Brereton who was being besieged in Nantwich, the Parliamentarian headquarters, by Lord Byron.

Following the Cessation in Ireland, Byron's local Royalist forces had recently been reinforced by soldiers brought back from Ireland.[2] Although Brereton had no previous military experience, in 1643 he had been appointed commander-in-chief of the Parliamentarian forces in Cheshire, where he had led an aggressive campaign throughout the northern Midlands.[3] Reinforced by Fairfax, Brereton was able to defeat Byron at the Battle of Nantwich on 26 January. After the battle, Fairfax returned to attack the Royalist forces that had been left by Newcastle to protect Royalist interests in Yorkshire. Newcastle had appointed General John Belasis to command the Royalist Yorkshire forces but their decisive defeat at the Battle of Selby on 11 April gave the Parliamentarian commanders the chance to take control in Yorkshire. To counter this threat to his rear, Newcastle was forced to withdraw from the North and he concentrated his infantry in York whilst sending his cavalry farther south to join Rupert's army. Now unopposed, the Scottish Army marched south and combined with the Parliamentarian armies of Lord Fairfax and the Earl of Manchester to besiege York on 21 April, thereby forcing Newcastle to appeal to the King for help. Having successfully relieved the siege of the Royalist forces at Newark on 21 March, Rupert was ordered to march north to relieve York, which he successfully achieved on 1 July. However, Rupert believed his orders also required him to engage the Roundhead forces about the city. He was decisively defeated by the combined Parliamentarian and Scottish armies at the Battle of Marston Moor on 2 July. Although the battle was a major setback to the Royalist cause, it was the Duke of Newcastle's subsequent withdrawal to the Continent after the battle that effectively gave Parliament control of the North.[4]

Turning now to the South, where the historical accounts show that the military events had become increasingly interwoven with the Thames Valley operations following the concentration of forces of both sides. At the beginning of 1644, the Royalist Army, which had been based in Hampshire for the winter, was endeavouring to threaten London from the south but this plan was thwarted when Sir William Waller and Sir William Balfour defeated the advancing Royalist forces, led by Lord Forth and Lord Hopton, at the Battle of Cheriton on 29 March. Meanwhile, the Royalist Western Army, led by Prince Maurice, had become increasingly embroiled in a protracted and ultimately unsuccessful siege of the small Dorset port of Lyme. While the Royalist armies were so engaged, the combined operations of the Roundhead armies of Essex and Waller in the Thames Valley began to press hard against the Royalist forces defending Oxford. Reversing an earlier Council of War decision to remain on the defensive in the Thames Valley and to reinforce the circle of garrisoned towns protecting Oxford, the Royalists withdrew key garrisons from Abingdon and Reading in late May, which allowed the Parliamentarian armies to close in and threaten Oxford directly.[5] This placed the Royalists at a serious disadvantage, although Charles managed to evade the encircling Roundheads by breaking out of Oxford and marching west.

At this point, Essex decided to separate his army from Waller's forces and to relieve Prince Maurice's siege of Lyme.[6] Waller was ordered to continue the pursuit of Charles' Oxford Army, but he was soon to be defeated by the Royalists at the Battle of Cropredy Bridge on 29 June. Meanwhile, after relieving Lyme, Essex marched farther into the West of England in order to relieve the siege of Plymouth and threaten the Royalist control of Cornwall. Charles, concerned for the safety of his pregnant Queen in Exeter, led his Oxford Army in pursuit of Essex, and to his wife's salvation, in July.[7] Having been forced to withdraw from Lyme when Essex had led his army into the South West, Maurice retreated into Devon. Soon afterwards, he joined up with Charles' advancing army and the combined Royalist armies pursued Essex into Cornwall. This concentration of Royalist armies surrounded – and then forced the capitulation of – the Parliamentarian Army at Lostwithiel in early September. When Charles led his victorious army back towards Oxford, he was confronted by a concentration of several different Parliamentarian armies, which resulted in two indecisive engagements fought around Newbury on 27 October and 10 November. These engagements effectively brought the fighting of 1644 to a close.

How were the intelligence aspects of these events described by subsequent historians? The historical accounts of the role of military intelligence in the northern campaigns of 1644 show that its impact was being acknowledged, probably reflecting the growing appreciation of its contribution to the 1643 campaigns. John Rushworth's *Historical Collections*, for example, which had included only a few references to intelligence-gathering in its account of the years 1642 and 1643, contained numerous descriptions of actions where intelligence information had played a significant part in determining the outcome of military confrontations during 1644. In his description of intelligence operations in the North, Rushworth recounted how the Royalist commander, Belasis, had become informed of the Fairfaxes' intentions and movements from '[many] intercepted ... letters' – intelligence which had led to the concentration of the remaining Royalist forces in Yorkshire and their action with the Roundheads at Selby, and his subsequent defeat by Fairfax.[8] Rushworth provided yet more primary evidence of military intelligence-gathering when he described how it had influenced Rupert's approach march and, consequently, the lifting of the siege of

York.[9] For example, he described how 'the Generals had certain notice that Prince Rupert ... was advancing and ... would quarter that night at Knaresborough.'[10] Even Clarendon's subsequent *History* included more contemporary information about the intelligence-gathering operations conducted in support of the 1644 campaigns. Although Clarendon's chronology of the 1644 northern actions was occasionally suspect (for example, he described the Battle of Nantwich as having taken place after the Battle of Selby), he nonetheless acknowledged the benefits of obtaining accurate information. In his description of the relief of Newark, he recounted how 'the enemy, who had always had excellent intelligence, was so confident that he [Rupert] had not the strength to attempt that work, that he [Rupert] was within six miles of them before [they realised].'[11] Clarendon included no acknowledgement of the military significance of these intelligence operations in his *History*.

Reflecting this change of perception, the increased awareness of the impact of intelligence-gathering is also evident in the subsequent historical accounts. Warburton's *Memoirs* referred to a number of contemporary sources which described how intelligence information had played a significant part in Prince Rupert's northern military successes. For example, he noted that the speed of Rupert's march to relieve the siege at Newark had been clearly reported by the scouts to Sir John Meldrum, the besieging Parliamentarian commander. Warburton remarked that the Parliamentarian commanders 'had heard some rumours of Rupert's approach, but being also well assured of his distance and the small number of his forces, they disbelieved even their own scouts'.[12] He also recounted how Rupert had used intelligence from many sources to inform and influence his operation to relieve Newark and bring the siege to a speedy conclusion. Not only had 'a deserter informed him [Rupert] that they [the Parliamentarians] were in direful want within the Spittal', Warburton observed, but also Rupert had 'found, by an intercepted letter, that Fairfax was advancing,' and therefore that a speedy resolution of his action around Newark was necessary.[13] Warburton also alluded to the value of the information which was available to Rupert when he described the relief of York in June. 'Rupert's scouts brought intelligence that the enemy had drawn off from the siege, in order to concentrate their divided forces.' He went on to describe how Rupert not only used his knowledge about the position of the Parliamentarian and Scottish forces to hasten the speed of his advance, but also his familiarity with the local bridges and roads to decisively out-manoeuvre his opponents. The Parliamentary generals had deployed their forces on Marston Moor, three miles to the west of York in anticipation of a Royalist advance on the city from Knaresborough, but as the map shows (see p.133), Rupert outflanked the Roundhead positions and relieved York from the north.[14]

Relatively few of the other subsequent descriptions of the 1644 campaigns in the North referred to the impact of these intelligence operations. Firth's

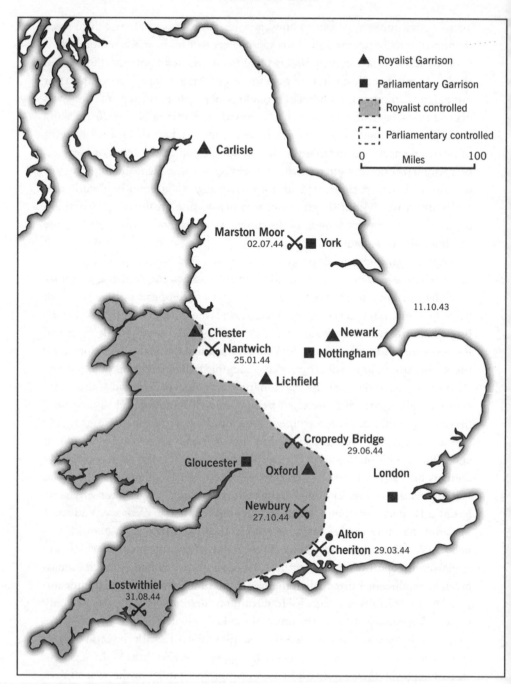

The main battlefields of 1644 and the area controlled by the King at the end of that year.

edition of the life of the Duke of Newcastle did include a brief reference to some important intelligence that the Royalists received, that 'there was some discontent between ... [the Parliamentarian and Scottish armies], and that they were resolved to divide themselves, and to raise the siege without fighting', but this intelligence was not heeded.[15] Later, in 1890, Firth wrote an assessment of two manuscripts relating to the Battle of Marston Moor; one of which had been written by the then Royalist Governor of Scarborough Castle, Sir Hugh Cholmley, whose account included the suggestion that the assault had been initiated following intelligence from a deserting Royalist officer that the Royalist Army was standing down for the night.[16] Perhaps because Prince Rupert himself had subsequently not credited the accuracy of this intelligence, Firth did not accept this suggestion either, even though the Royalist officer suspected of providing the intelligence was under Hurry's command. Hurry himself was to desert again back to the Roundheads a few months later.

The first historian to use the contemporary accounts of intelligence operations to inform his study of the military aspects of the 1644 northern campaigns was Peter Young in his comprehensive account of the Marston Moor campaign.[17] Young acknowledged that Rupert was well aware of the deployment of the besieging armies around York and used this intelligence when planning his approach march to relieve that city.[18] He also described how the besieged Royalists sent messengers to Rupert as often as they could penetrate the tightening ring around the city, and suggested that these messengers would have been able to acquaint Rupert with the position and strength of the besieging armies.[19] Subsequently, Young co-authored a military history of the Civil War with Richard Holmes.[20] Their account recognised the impact that superior Parliamentarian intelligence had upon the outcome of the Battle of Nantwich when it described how Byron's 'relations with the local inhabitants ... [had been] bad, and Byron ... [had been] unable to obtain any useful intelligence'.[21] Holmes and Young went on to describe how Fairfax received better intelligence during that battle and how this enabled him to make more informed decisions, contrasting this with Byron's comparatively poor scouting which led to 'his failure to concentrate against Fairfax when there was still time'.[22] Young and Holmes also described how the intelligence of Meldrum's movements, provided by Rupert's scouts, played a key role in the relief of Newark.[23]

Peter Wenham's detailed account of the siege of York, written in 1970, drew upon contemporary accounts to describe how intelligence played a key role in the Marston Moor campaign.[24] Wenham recounted how an intercepted Parliamentarian letter gave the Royalists' commander, General Belasis, early and accurate intelligence of Fairfax's plans.[25] He also gave examples of intelligence information that reported the progress of the siege; for example, he cited a letter written on 5 May from a Royalist sympathiser, John Frechville, to Lord Loughborough, the Royalist commander in Leicestershire, which described how 'according to the best intelligence we have from York, it is not so distressed.'[26] Wenham also described how 'sundry intelligence that Prince Rupert is already on his march towards Newark, tending northwards' had been reported to the Committee of Both Kingdoms.[27] Wanklyn and Jones' later account of the Marston Moor campaign also acknowledged how the contemporary accounts had provided evidence of the contribution which had been made by intelligence information to the northern campaigns when they recounted how Luke's spies reported Rupert's 'northern designe' to relieve York as early as 6 May.[28] They also noted that the Parliamentarian commanders besieging York were informed of Rupert's position and strength as the Royalist relief army moved north from Shrewsbury.[29] In his later account of the Battle of Marston Moor, Wanklyn included the observation of Sir Hugh Cholmley that the Parliamentarian attack was initiated following a report from a Scottish deserter, which stated that the Royalists were not planning to attack that evening and were standing down.[30]

Further contemporary accounts of the role played by intelligence during the 1644 campaigns in Yorkshire have been included in the recent work of David Cooke.[31] In his review of the Civil War in Yorkshire, and specifically in his more recent exploration of the Marston Moor campaign, Cooke describes how Newcastle received intelligence of the Scots 'massing along the border, in preparation for their long-expected invasion' and how this intelligence allowed Newcastle to march north quickly and in time to confront them.[32] He also notes that Royalist intelligence-gathering provided warning of the Parliamentarian attack on Selby,[33] whilst his description of the Marston Moor campaign also mentions that intelligence reports were received by all of the chief commanders.[34] In particular, Cooke cites contemporary accounts that intelligence of Rupert's advance had been reported to the Parliamentarian commanders around York who reported that they understood that 'Prince Rupert was drawing towards York, with … twenty five thousand horse and foot.'[35] Cooke concludes his summary by citing Cholmley's suggestion that intelligence from a deserting Royalist officer initiated the Parliamentarian assault.[36]

Turning our attention now further south to the subsequent historical accounts of the role played by military intelligence operations in the southern campaigns of 1644, it becomes clear that, as with his account of the northern campaigns, Rushworth's account contained several references to information obtained by intelligence-gathering. In his study of the battle at Cheriton, for example, Rushworth acknowledged how accurate intelligence informed the movements of both armies before the battle.[37] Later, when recounting the operations of Waller and Essex around the Thames Valley that summer, Rushworth also acknowledged that intelligence was used to good effect by both armies in the Cropredy Bridge campaign. He cited primary evidence to describe how a party of horse was sent by Sir Samuel Luke to 'observe [the Royalist Army's] motions', and alluded to the fact that Essex had 'intelligence of the King's departure from Oxford' on 3

June.[38] Similarly, the role played by intelligence-gathering operations during the Lostwithiel and Newbury campaigns was repeatedly acknowledged by Rushworth who described how 'Prince Maurice, being advertised that Essex was advancing as near as Dorchester, [had] thought fit to raise the siege' by 15 June, and that Essex 'had notice of the King's approach further westwards' on 2 August.[39]

Similarly, Clarendon's description of the southern campaigns also contains numerous contemporary references to intelligence-gathering influencing the main battles. He records that during the Cropredy Bridge campaign, 'the intelligence that Waller was still designed for the western expedition, made the King appoint his whole army ... to a rendezvous at Marlborough.'[40] He also notes that, on one occasion, Waller 'had early intelligence of his majesty's motions', and that Charles knew 'upon intelligence that both [Essex's and Waller's] armies followed by strong marches'. Clarendon went on to acknowledge how the intelligence 'that Waller was marched out of Evesham with his whole army towards Worcester' had been particularly useful to Charles when he was returning to Oxford in mid-June, and that Charles 'received good intelligence that Waller, without knowing anything of his [Charles'] motion, remained still in his old quarters'.[41]

Clarendon's use of contemporary accounts of intelligence-gathering during the King's campaign in Cornwall was equally positive and informative, showing how Charles had enjoyed 'the conflux and concurrence of the whole people' whilst in the area.[42] In his *History,* he makes it clear that the Royalists had been receiving – and comparing –information from a number of sources, for when intelligence of the intended breakout by the Parliamentarian horse at Lostwithiel had been given to the Royalists by two deserters from Essex's army, it was found that 'this intelligence agreed with what [the Royalists] had otherwise received.'[43] In this description, Clarendon thereby provided evidence that the Royalists recognised the need to corroborate their intelligence whenever possible. Clarendon also used contemporary accounts of intelligence-gathering to support his assertion that when Charles had decided to return to Oxford after Lostwithiel, the King had received information 'of all the obstructions and difficulties his enraged enemies could lay in his way' and had, in consequence, realised that 'he [Charles] must look to fight another battle before he could reach Oxford.'[44] Clarendon broadened his account to include a description of the defection of Sir Richard Grenville on his return from Ireland and the information he had brought with him describing the Parliamentarian strategic plans, along with the plot to betray Basing House.[45]

The contemporary references cited in the subsequent historical accounts of intelligence-gathering showed clearly the impact that these intelligence operations had had upon the southern campaigns of 1644. For example, in his edition of the *Fairfax Correspondence,* Bell noted that, at the start of the Cropredy Bridge campaign in the first week of June, 'Waller had better intelligence, and sent a body of horse flying after the King to hang upon his rear and harass his progress

until he could come up himself.'[46] Later, in 1933, Mary Coate's account of the
Civil War in Cornwall drew attention to the military and political intelligence
provided by Grenville when he defected.[47] More significantly, Coate evaluated
the intelligence information about Essex's army that the Cavaliers had received
during the Lostwithiel campaign, describing how the strong Royalist sympathies in Cornwall provided 'support [which was] invaluable, [because] it meant
supplies and intelligence'.[48] Her account of the final stages of the Lostwithiel
campaign again emphasised the significance of intelligence. Coate remarked that
Charles was able to out-manoeuvre Essex and deny him key military positions
because Essex's 'intelligence was poor ... [and] he did not appreciate their significance'; Coate also reported how intelligence of the planned breakout of the
Parliamentarian horse was brought in by the two deserters.[49]

The first modern historian to explore the military intelligence aspects of the
1644 southern campaigns in detail was, yet again, Peter Young, who in partnership
with Margaret Toynbee carried out a comprehensive evaluation of the Cropredy
Bridge campaign.[50] Their account included a substantial amount of detail about
the intelligence-gathering operations,[51] and they concluded that intelligence-
gathering during this period was particularly effective.

> Although the intelligence service on both sides in the Civil war is generally
> written off as rudimentary, both Charles and Waller do seem to have been
> apprised pretty quickly of every movement of the enemy during these critical
> weeks of June 1644.[52]

The importance of intelligence information in the Cropredy campaign was also
to be subsequently acknowledged by Wanklyn and Jones who described how
both the King and Waller had been able to monitor each other's movements –
and how the King had been able to evade Waller and return to Oxford when
Waller's scouts were fooled by the Royalist feint towards the north.[53]

Other accounts also provide evidence of intelligence operations, such as the
later biographies of Civil War commanders which include primary evidence
from the contemporary accounts to support their conclusions. Adair's biography
of Waller contains numerous references to contemporary accounts of intelligence
received by both Waller and Charles during the Cropredy Bridge campaign.[54]
Adair described how the King had determined to quit Oxford after 'receiving
intelligence that Essex intended to storm the city next morning', [55] and noted
that the King had later drawn back to Buckingham 'upon intelligence that
[Waller] was ... upon the march'.[56] Similarly Adair described how Waller's scouts
had 'informed him ... that the King's army had marched westwards to Witney and
Burford',[57] and noted that 'the King's army had also halted not 5 miles beyond
the river at the village of Edgecott.'[58] Edgar's biography of Hopton also contained some specific references to the gathering of intelligence during the 1644

campaigns, and described how 'Parliamentary intelligence still bruited the intent of the Royalists to march into Kent upon their old design.'[59] Edgar's account of the Cheriton campaign included descriptions of intelligence being obtained from either prisoner interrogation, or from scouting,[60] before going on to include several references describing how some of the pieces of intelligence received had influenced the outcome of the campaign.

> On 26 March 1644 word came [to Hopton] that Waller, adding to his array 1,800 horse and dragoons under the command of Sir William Balfour, had marched out of Sussex and come … ten miles south-east of Winchester.[61]

Although Adair's later description of the Battle of Cheriton did not specifically acknowledge the impact of intelligence-gathering, he did describe how both sides relied upon their scouts to provide information about the position and strength of their opponents, as well as citing several contemporary sources which described the scouting information received by both sides during the campaign. For example, Adair cited contemporary references which reported that Hopton had 'sent out strong parties of horse severall wayes towards the Enemy, with command not to allarum them, but only to secure the Army from any surprise of theirs,' that these 'scouts brought in some prisoners' and that intelligence had been gained 'as some prisoners confessed'.[62] The account revealed that each side had been well informed of their opponents' position at all stages of the campaign and that no encounter was the result of an 'accidental' meeting.[63] In his biography of Sir William Waller, Adair also detailed the constant use that Waller made of intelligence-gathering during his 1644 southern campaigns and confirmed that Waller's skill in positioning his forces had reflected the accurate intelligence he had received of the Royalist dispositions.[64] Adair's references to Waller's scouting activities are numerous; for example, he describes how Waller had 'despatched six troops of horse to scout towards Winchester, and they returned that night with three prisoners' and added that 'now fully aware … that Hopton had sallied out of Winchester, Waller ordered a rendezvous for his army … next morning.'[65] In his study of Waller's contribution towards the Second Newbury campaign, Adair describes how the Parliamentarian plan was influenced by Waller's intelligence that 'the King expected present [immediate] supply from Prince Rupert and that two brigades of his horse were gone to Banbury [we] thought it fit not to delay.'[66]

A further contribution to our understanding of the impact made on the fighting by intelligence information comes from other, more recent, local historical accounts. Recently, Wanklyn and Jones have explored the strategic significance of intelligence operations on the conduct of the southern campaigns. Of particular interest is their evaluation of the intelligence reported by Grenville when he defected, which informed the Cavaliers of Parliament's 'grand designe' to counter the threat posed by the Royalist Western Army. The Parliamentarian plan was for

Waller to march westwards, receiving his supplies through Lyme, which would become the base for operations against the Royalist forces. Wanklyn and Jones convincingly argue that Maurice's subsequent protracted siege of Lyme, and Forth's reinforcement of Hopton's army to intercept Waller, reflected the confidence that the Royalists had in Grenville's information.[67] Wanklyn's latest work, *The Warrior Generals,* recounts how intelligence was used effectively at Cheriton and during the Lostwithiel campaign.[68] It thus appears that historians are becoming more aware of the fact that intelligence-gathering played a prominent role in the southern theatre in 1644.

So how do historians' subsequent assessments of the conduct of intelligence operations compare with the evidence of the primary sources that describe the conduct of military intelligence operations in the 1644 northern campaigns? A great deal was written by the military commanders, news pamphlets and eye-witnesses about the most significant northern actions of that year, specifically at Nantwich, Newark, Selby and Marston Moor.

Turning our attention first to Nantwich, the part played by intelligence was described in a number of contemporary records, the most important being Sir Thomas Fairfax's account, preserved in his *Short Memorial.* In his description of the Battle of Nantwich, Fairfax recorded that on a number of occasions he received intelligence about the Royalists' movements; for example, he described how he 'had intelligence that the Lord Byron had drawn off his siege, and intended to meet us in the field,' how he was 'informed, that the river which runs through the town, being raised by the melting of the snow, hindered those that lay on the other side of the town from joining with them' and how 'word came that the enemy was in the rear.'[69]

The information contained in these various intelligence reports enabled Fairfax to make decisions that played a critical part in the Parliamentarian victory, such as the intelligence that Byron planned to 'meet them in the field,' which allowed Fairfax to 'put his men into the order in which I intended to fight,' whilst the intelligence he had received about the 'raising of the river due to melted snow' encouraged Fairfax 'to march into the town and relieve them [the Parliamentarian garrison]'. The knowledge that 'the enemy was in the rear' enabled Fairfax to 'face about two regiments ... and relieve those that were engaged'.[70]

Both Parliamentarian and Royalist news pamphlets had been publishing articles reporting the position of Fairfax's relief force for some weeks before the Battle of Nantwich on 26 January. For example, on 16 January, the *Kingdomes Weekly Intelligencer* reported how 'Sir Thomas Fairfax ... on Tuesday 9 January was at Stafford, and joined with Sir William Brereton there and Collonel Kadgeley with 1,000 Morelanders met them also.'[71] This report was confirmed by another pamphlet, the *True Informer,* which went on to say that the relief force was '6,000 horse and foot' although it was not sure if 'Sir William goes with Sir Thomas, or is returned to Nantwich'.[72] Several other pamphlets also reported the progress of Fairfax's force.[73] By monitoring what was being reported in these publications, the Royalist court journal, *Mercurius Aulicus,* was able to declare that 'Sir Thomas Fairfax is gone with 24 troopes of horse to relieve Sir William Brereton.'[74] Later, in its account of the battle, the *Mercurius Aulicus* confirmed that the Royalists had warning of Fairfax's approach for 'Lord Byron, having intelligence of severall bodies of Rebels marching against him, thought fit to fall on part of them before they came together.'[75]

The fact that Byron was receiving intelligence of these Parliamentarian advances was also confirmed by several of the London news pamphlets.[76] The contemporary accounts of this action confirm that the information contained in these reports influenced the military decisions of both sides before and during the action. Like Cromwell, Fairfax believed in the doctrine of providentialism and he usually attributed his victories to 'the mercy of God.'[77] A more significant factor was the more accurate intelligence he collected.

The contemporary accounts also contain primary evidence which reveals that intelligence information played a major part in Rupert's relief of the Parliamentarian siege of Newark. Sir John Meldrum, the Roundhead commander, had been besieging Newark since 29 February. An eyewitness reported that, on 12 March whilst at Chester, Rupert received orders from the King to march to the relief of the garrison.[78] This report described how, when he reached Bingham, Rupert intercepted 'Meldrum's owne letters' from which he learnt that 'the rebels had no more but an uncredited rumour of Prince Rupert's coming.'[79]

The eyewitness also reported how Rupert had derived his intelligence information from a variety of sources describing how Rupert 'had notice from his espials, how the rebels were busy all the morning in sending away their cannon,' and later on, when he had trapped the besiegers in the Spittal, how Rupert had 'notice given him by a prisoner, and by one who came over to us [a deserter], how the rebels were so distressed for want of victuals, that they were not able to live there two days'. This intelligence enabled Rupert to decide that it would be 'cheaper to block up their trenches, than to storm them,' especially as he had received further intelligence – obtained from some other intercepted letters – that 'my Lord Fairfax, and his sonne Sir Thomas, being commanded to march, other places might ere long have need of his presence.'[80] This eyewitness also reported the presence of 'Sir William Neale, Scout Master General' and recounted how Neale helped rescue Rupert when he was surrounded by Parliamentarian troopers during the battle.

Meldrum should have been aware of the intelligence describing Rupert's approach for several of the London news pamphlets had been reporting the position of the relief force ever since Rupert set out from Chester.[81] For example, *The Parliament Scout* had reported that 'Prince Rupert ... draws out from about

Shrewsbury parts, towards Leicester and Newark, but his numbers we hear not, nor whether he will go as far as Newark as is reported.'[82] This report was confirmed by *The Kingdomes Weekly Intelligencer*, which reported that forces were being gathered 'to oppose Prince Rupert's coming to releeve the towne, to whom the Queene hath writ twice to engage his honour to save Newarke'.[83] The various eyewitness accounts describe how Rupert used intelligence information obtained from scouts, spies (espials), deserters, prisoners and intercepted letters. The fact that Sir William Neale, Rupert's scoutmaster, was present at the relief of Newark may well explain why such extensive and effective use had been made of all forms of intelligence. Although the relief of Newark has been described as 'the most impressive feat of arms that [Rupert] had yet performed,'[84] the contribution made by the Prince's intelligencers has yet to be properly acknowledged. All the primary evidence confirms that intelligence played a major part in Rupert's victory, just as Meldrum's defeat can be attributed to his failure to respond to the intelligence reports – 'uncredited' or not – that he received of Rupert's advance. It is, however, quite possible that the Parliamentarian commanders in the north consequently took note of Meldrum's failure for, during the subsequent Selby campaign, they appear to have assessed intelligence received far more carefully.

Both sides received important intelligence during the Selby campaign. In his letter of 12 April to the Committee of Both Kingdoms describing his victory over Sir John Belasis, Lord Fairfax reported how the Royalists had 'intercepted divers of our letters, and thereby became acquainted with our appointments, and so endeavoured to prevent them'.[85] Subsequently, Lord Fairfax was informed by his own intelligence-gatherers that the Royalist commander 'lay in Selby with 2000 men,' and planned to concentrate his troops for an assault on the Royalist forces.[86] The fact that the Royalists had obtained intelligence of Parliamentarian intentions from the intercepted letters is confirmed by a contemporary report in *Hulls Relation*, a Parliamentarian pamphlet describing the exploits of their garrison in Hull. For example, it reported how Belasis had attempted to disrupt the Parliamentarians' 'designe' once he had received intelligence that the Fairfaxes had

> ... united their forces neer Selby, to which place the Governor of York (by letters intercepted, understanding the designe) drew forth all the forces he could make to prevent their meeting, but failing therein he fortified the towne.[87]

Intelligence information thus played a major part in the events which culminated in the Battle of Selby. For, whilst the intelligence supplied to the Royalists prompted Belasis to attack Fairfax's forces, the intelligence supplied to the Parliamentarians enabled the Fairfaxes to concentrate their forces and repel the Royalist assault. This was a key battle that played a crucial part in determining the outcome of the Royalist northern campaign because the destruction of the Royalist forces at Selby led directly to the collapse of Newcastle's resistance to the invading Scots. It seems that the importance of intelligence was recognised at once by the Committee of Both Kingdoms for, in their letter of 5 March, they instructed Lord Fairfax to 'hold continual intelligence with the Scottish army.'[88] The increasingly effective exchange of information between the Parliamentarian and Scottish armies helped to contribute to the next major Parliamentarian victory in the north – the Battle of Marston Moor. On the other side however, there appears to be no comparable evidence that the Royalist commanders ever appreciated the major military advantages to be gained from exchanging accurate and timely intelligence.

Naturally, given the importance of the battle on the outcome of the war, there are numerous primary sources available which describe the military operations conducted during the Marston Moor campaign. However, most of these accounts concentrate on how the battle was fought, and only a few include detailed descriptions of the intelligence-gathering operations that preceded it. Sir Thomas Fairfax's recollection of the battle makes no mention of how Rupert's approach march out-manoeuvred the Scottish and Parliamentarian armies besieging York, nor does he describe any of the intelligence reports which appear to have informed the allied commanders about Rupert's approach.[89] Fortunately, other eyewitness accounts have provided more information about the intelligence reporting Rupert's advance which the commanders around York had, in fact, been receiving. For example, Simeon Ash, chaplain to the Earl of Manchester, described how the Allies 'had certain intelligence that Prince Rupert, with his army, were quartered at Boroughbridge, within twelve miles of York,' whereupon the Allied generals 'resolved … to raise the siege, that they might be able to counter the great forces now ready to assault them.' Ash went on to report how the Allied commanders 'were assured by our scouts that the Prince with his whole body would pass that way [south of the River Ouse]'.[90] Ash's account is corroborated by that of Leonard Watson, Manchester's Scoutmaster-General, who wrote that 'upon notice that Prince Rupert was advancing … we drew off all our forces … and put ourselves into battalia upon Owse-moor, within three miles of York.'[91] As early as the beginning of June, London news pamphlets had been reporting 'constant intelligence [that] Prince Rupert's Army was on their march for the relief of York'[92] with an army of '14,000 horse and foot completely armed'.[93]

Further confirmation of the fact that intelligence of the Royalist approach was being regularly reported by scouts is contained in letters written by soldiers serving with the Allied forces. One Captain Stewart later wrote that:

Understanding that Prince Rupert with about twenty thousand foot and horse did march towards us, the whole army arose from the siege and marched towards Long Marston Moor … but the Prince, having notice of our march, passed with his army by the way of Borough bridge.[94]

These contemporary reports not only confirm that Rupert was aware of the position of the Allied armies around York, but also that the Allied commanders had been receiving regular intelligence from their scouts who were seemingly monitoring the approach of the Royalist relief force very closely. Although well aware of the position of Rupert's army as he approached York, the Allied commanders were misled by the speed and direction of the Royalists' final approach to the city. They seem to have been deceived by a feint made by the advance guard of the Royalist horse towards the Allied armies drawn up on the west side of the river Ouse – this feint served to convince them that their interpretation of the Royalists' route was correct.[95] Finally, according to Sir Thomas Fairfax's account of the battle, Parliamentarian intelligence reports indicated that the Royalist forces totalled 'about 23 or 24,000 men'.[96]

The primary evidence contained within the contemporary accounts confirms that the Royalist commanders were equally well aware of the Allied positions and knew the size of the Scottish and Parliamentarian armies besieging York.[97] Rupert's success in the gathering of reinforcements during his approach, as well as his successful selection of the final route for his final descent upon the city, shows that he had accurate intelligence of the enemy forces and their positions – including knowledge of the bridge of boats connecting the two banks of the Ouse. The Duke of Newcastle possessed yet more information about the tensions between the Allied commanders and advised Rupert to wait upon events for 'he had intelligence that there was some discontent between them, and that they were resolved to divide themselves.'[98] Newcastle therefore advised Rupert to wait on events. Although this was good counsel, Rupert apparently considered that his orders from Charles required him to fight regardless, and neither Newcastle's information nor his advice was heeded.

Sir Hugh Cholmley, the Royalist Governor of Scarborough Castle, provided yet another contemporary report of intelligence which may have had a significant impact on the outcome of the battle. This account, which has hitherto appeared to receive little attention, described how 'a Scottish officer amongst the Prince [Rupert] his horse, whilst the armies faced one another, fled to the Parliament army and gave them intelligence.'[99] According to Cholmley, this intelligence provided 'the reason why they [the Allied armies] fell thus suddenly upon the Prince'.[100] If, as Cholmley believed, the unknown Scottish officer's intelligence advised the Allied commanders that the Royalist commanders, expecting no action that day, were standing down their forces, then the subsequent Allied victory owed much to this information. Leonard Watson, the Parliamentarian scoutmaster and seemingly another believer in predetermination, preferred to attribute the Allied decision to attack simply to 'the help of God'.[101]

The evidence of all of these primary sources makes it perfectly clear that intelligence operations played a decisive part in all the main military actions fought in the northern theatre during 1644. They also reveal that the

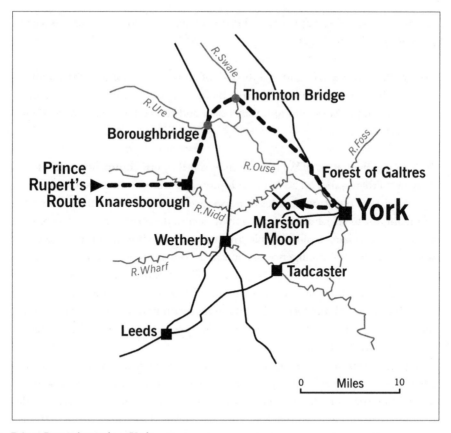

Prince Rupert's march on York.

Parliamentarian commanders appreciated the significance of intelligence-gathering far more than their Royalist opponents – thus Sir Thomas Fairfax would have been well aware of just how important intelligence had been to the final Parliamentarian victory.

So how do the accounts of the southern campaigns compare with those of the north? Once again the primary sources provide a great deal of evidence about the conduct of intelligence and its subsequent impact on the outcome of the key battles, the Battle of Cheriton (29 March), the Battle of Cropredy Bridge (29 June), the Battle of Lostwithiel (20 August to 3 September) and the Second Battle of Newbury (27 October).

Starting with the Battle of Cheriton, we are fortunate that two of the army commanders, Sir Ralph (Lord) Hopton and Sir William Waller, later wrote accounts of the campaign which included descriptions of the intelligence that influenced their decisions. Whilst the objectivity of these reports has to be treated with some caution, they nonetheless provide an interesting insight into the individual commanders' consideration of intelligence-gathering and the use they made of the information they received. It would appear that Hopton's intelligence-gathering network had been effective for, in the last week of March, it was reported to him that:

> Sir William Waller had gotten a recrewt of about 1,800 horse and dragoons, under the command of Sir William Balfour joyn'd to him and therewith advanced out of Sussex towards Winchester and was come as far as Warneford and West Meon.[102]

On learning the details of Waller's advance, the Royalist commanders decided to 'draw up to them', and, on 26 March, Hopton accordingly reinforced his scouting screen and 'sent out strong parties of horse severall ways towards the enemy, with command not to allarum them, but only to secure the Army from any surprise of theirs.'[103] The evidence of this deployment provides a clear insight into Hopton's awareness of Waller's intelligence operations as well as his determination to counter the work of the Parliamentarian scouts. The Royalist knowledge of Waller's advance clearly influenced the deployment of their army, a hypothesis supported by the Royalist Colonel Walter Slingsby, who recounted that, upon 'hearing that some Footte and horse of his [Waller] first Troopes quarter'd within eight miles of Winchester, we drew out ... our whole body.'[104]

Hopton continued to receive intelligence reports from his scouts and was speedily informed that the Parliamentarians 'having discovered one of our parties the night before were drawne out, and embattaild upon a hill'. Another Royalist scouting party 'brought word of their marche,' causing Hopton to begin to suspect that 'the Enemyes designe might be to send Sir William Balfour with his horse and dragoons to possess Alsford [Arlesford].'[105] Having obtained intelligence of the Roundheads' objective from this moment on 27 March, Hopton deployed his troops to counter Waller's movements. Subsequently, the two armies received constant reports of each other's movements until Hopton 'marching himself with Sir Edward Stowell in the head of his brigade, did plainly discover Sir William Balfour's troopes marching in the lane level with them, and they were not a mile asunder.'[106] Royalist intelligence-gathering continued as the scouts 'hunted about ... and at last discovered his whole strength, horse, foote and artillerye, in a low meadow within half a mile of us'.[107] On the morning of 28 March, the day before the battle, Hopton 'sent out a little party, to discover where the enemy were, which was quickly met by light parties of the enemy'.[108]

The Parliamentarian intelligence-gathering was equally effective; contemporary accounts reveal that their scouts promptly detected the Royalist advance. Of particular interest to the Parliamentarian scouts was the fact that the planning of the Royalist advance had been based upon a detailed understanding of the Parliamentarian Army routines. As one of the Roundhead officers, Elias Archer, later reported, 'we discovered the enemy, who took some few of our men that were straggling from their colours, and soon after appeared in a great body... intending (as some prisoners confessed) to take us at Church.'[109] Waller was able to monitor Hopton's progress and, although he lost the race to Arlesford, his intelligence reports enabled him to make one of his celebrated manoeuvres during the night before the battle when he ordered a force of infantry to occupy Cheriton Wood, a commanding height on the flank of the Royalist position. Parliamentarian scouting continued until early the next morning for, as one Captain Harley recounted to his brother, 'in the morning before day, I sent a party of horse to discover which way the enemy did lie.'[110]

Further Parliamentarian intelligence of Hopton's movements was provided by Sir Samuel Luke's spies. As early as 5 January, Luke reported that 'Hopton is dayly expected at Winchester with his forces, which are reported to be 9 or 10,000.'[111] Further reports followed and, by 28 January, Luke was reporting that 'all [men] in the county of Hampshire from 16 to 60 [are] to be at Winchester on Friday last to take up arms against Sir William Waller.'[112] This primary evidence of the intelligence provided by Luke's agents continued as they went on to report that it was Hopton's intention 'to fall upon them [Waller's forces] very shortly'.[113] Further reinforcements of Hopton's forces were reported by Luke's spies on 6, 10 and 15 March.[114] The appointment of Lord Forth to join with Hopton was also reported (albeit somewhat belatedly) on 24 March.[115] Waller's plans to advance, along with the latest estimate of Hopton's army as '10 or 12,000 horse and foote', were made on 26 March.[116] Thus the Cheriton campaign provides yet another example of the way in which the rival commanders' decisions were influenced by the constant stream of intelligence they received from their scouts. Both Hopton and Waller were well aware of their opponents' intentions and at no stage of the campaign was there any uncertainty over the enemy's position. Although Waller followed up his victory by occupying a number of local Royalist towns,[117] further intelligence that a Royalist Army was being formed around Marlborough, coupled with a lack of money to pay his London brigades, prevented Waller from exploiting his victory to the full.[118]

Turning now to the Cropredy Bridge campaign, described by Sir Edward Walker, the Secretary to the Royalist Council of War. His account provides an invaluable insight into the decision-making process of the senior Royalist commanders, for he describes how intelligence was fully integrated into Royalist planning, particularly during the early stages of the campaign when the movements of the Parliamentarian armies, led by Essex and Waller, were being regularly reported to the Royalist Council of War. These reports were used to determine Royalist responses to the threat posed by the two Parliamentarian armies, as is shown by Walker's statement, in mid April 1644, that:

Upon intelligence that a considerable force of Rebels was drawing towards Aylesbury, orders were sent not to stir from Marlborough except they had certain Intelligence that Waller would attempt to go into the West.[119]

Walker's account reveals just how frequently intelligence was received by the Royalist Council of War during the campaign, such as when in June 1644, 'certain intelligence was brought that the Rebels of Waller's army had passed at Newbridge.'[120] This was important information as it made it perfectly clear to Charles that Waller had reacted to his feint or 'grimace' towards Abingdon, knowledge which, in turn, enabled the King to evade both his opponents' armies and march out of Oxford 'having our scouts abroad'.[121] Contemporary sources reveal that reports continued to flow into the Royalist headquarters throughout the campaign. For example, when the King was at Evesham on 6 June, 'upon intelligence that Waller was advancing with his whole army, His Majesty altered his purpose and marched to Worcester.'[122] Later in the campaign, when Charles was planning his return to Oxford from the far side of the river Severn, the Royalist intelligence report that the Parliamentarians had no 'intelligence that Waller knew of our retreat or was moved from his quarters' was a major factor in the King's decision to cross the river at Worcester and head for the Cotswolds by the fastest route. Even so, contemporary accounts reveal that Charles would not move until he 'had perfect intelligence that Waller was not moved and that those passes were secured'.[123]

The Royalist Council of War held on 22 June was thus well aware of the positions of both Essex's army as it marched to the west, and Waller's army as it pursued the King. On 27 June, Sir Edward Walker recalled that 'upon more certain notice that Waller was not far from Banbury, it was thought best to march thither and to lay hold of a fit opportunity to give the Rebels battle.'[124] The close proximity of the two opposing armies during the Cropredy Bridge campaign in the final days of June was clearly an important factor, as it allowed the scouts on either side to keep in close touch with the opposing forces, as well as reducing the time it took to deliver their news to their respective commanders. Walker reports that 'certain intelligence … that a body of 300 Rebel horse were within 2 miles of our van,' caused the Royalist advanced guard to move forward swiftly thereby creating a gap which, subsequently, Waller tried to exploit by advancing his troops across the river by Cropredy Bridge.[125] This Parliamentarian lunge across the river Cherwell led to battle being joined. After the battle, intelligence reached Charles that Waller's army was about to be reinforced by another Parliamentarian force, led by General Brown. On receipt of this information, Charles, 'observing the Probability of Waller's and Brown's sudden conjunction, whereby they might overpower him,' decided to 'bend his course … where they should not speedily follow him' and withdrew his army to Evesham.

Turning now to the Parliamentarian accounts of the campaign, we should note that, in his letters to the Committee of Both Kingdoms, Waller also made a number of observations about the intelligence he received during the campaign. For example, on 4 June, Waller reported that his scouts had brought him news of the King's flight from Oxford and that he was in pursuit, hoping to catch up with the King at Witney.[126] Later, on 13 June, Waller recorded that he had received 'information that the enemy was in Kidderminster ... being two miles from Bewdley, where the King and his army lay and yet remain.'[127] On 20 June, Waller had reached Gloucester when his scouts reported that the King had marched to Witney and Burford.[128] Having been ordered by the Committee to follow the King eastwards, Waller was able to report that:

> Upon intelligence that we were upon the march [the King] drew all back to Buckingham again. By the best intelligence we can get they are 10,000 horse and foot, 8 field pieces, four pieces of battery, and a great mortar piece.[129]

By 27 June, both armies were in close contact and Waller's scouts reported that the King had halted five miles beyond the river Cherwell at Edgecote. A London news pamphlet provided a detailed description of how intelligence was gathered by the Parliamentarian forces.

> Wee discovered their army to be upon the march towards Daventry: and as some (who were since taken prisoners) affirme, their intent was from hence to York; whereupon command was given ... to advance after them and fall upon their reere.[130]

There is also clear primary evidence that Luke's men were reporting the movements of the King. On 4 June, they reported that Charles' army was at Burford, while the following day it was reported that the King's forces 'were gone that night towards Worcester.' On 6 June, Charles was stated to be at Winchcombe, en route to Worcester itself, and on 11 June, he was said to have arrived there.[131] Further contemporary references to the intelligence the Parliamentarians possessed appeared in the London news pamphlets; for example, later in the campaign, *Mercurius Civicus* was reporting how 'we had certain intelligence that His Majesty had gotten over the Severn ... and is fled to Worcester with all his horse and dragoons.'[132]

In summary, therefore, it appears that Walker's account of the Royalist decision-making process provides excellent contemporary evidence of the growing Royalist awareness of the significance of intelligence-gathering. The reports which appeared in *Mercurius Aulicus* at this time – reports which detailed Waller's movements very accurately indeed – also reveal that by this point the Royalists were obtaining much more effective intelligence.[133] Parliamentarian intelligence was similarly informative; Waller's letters confirm that he was using accurate information when making his military decisions. From the moment Charles's flying army left Oxford, its movements were promptly and reliably reported by both Parliamentarian scouts and pamphleteers. Every move of this campaign reflected the constant and accurate flow of intelligence to the army commanders.

Similarly the Cornish campaign of 1644 provided a further demonstration to both sides of the military advantages to be gained from receiving accurate intelligence; the difference was that the Royalists had abundant information whilst the Parliamentarian forces had little or none. The superior Royalist intelligence enabled Charles to win a decisive victory – one which, to a certain extent, offset the defeat of his army at Marston Moor. Yet again, Walker's account is a vital source of primary evidence for the Royalist commanders' conduct and use of intelligence during the Lostwithiel campaign. Walker shows that it was information about the diverging movements of the armies of Essex, Waller and Brown that determined the King's decision to march in pursuit of Essex and 'disturb him before Waller could possibly come to his assistance'.[134] Walker also reported that Essex had been misinformed by Lord Robartes about the level of support the Parliamentarian Army could expect to receive if it marched into Cornwall. He made it clear that once the Royalist Army entered Cornwall, a county which he describes as 'exceedingly affectionate to His Majestie and his cause,'[135] intelligence began to pour into the King's camp. For example, on 1 August Charles 'had intelligence that Essex was gone from Liskeard to Bodmin'.[136]

Of particular importance is the startling revelation of Walker's surprise at the amount of intelligence coming from the civilian population who, in Cornwall, were generally friendly towards the King. As this was now the third year of the war, it is most revealing to discover the low level of appreciation of the significance of intelligence still held by some of the senior Royalists. Walker noted that it was

> ... not until now ... [that] we [were] sensible of the great and extraordinary advantage the Rebels had over His Majesty's armies throughout the Kingdom, by intelligence (the life of all warlike actions) ... which, by the loyalty of this people, the Rebels were deprived of.[137]

To put it mildly, this is a startling insight into Royalist intelligence operations at this stage of the war. The intelligence reported by local people allowed the Royalists to dominate the campaign and to determine how it would be fought. As Walker went on to state, 'the [Rebel] army was no sooner quartered at Liskeard but we had hourly notice of the Rebels actions.'[138] Walker also noted that later in the campaign when Essex's army was isolated at Lostwithiel, two deserters brought intelligence of the proposed breakout by the Parliamentarian horse: '[the] intelligence was very particular, and being confirmed from other parts, was believed.'[139] This evidence reveals that to some degree the Royalists were beginning to appreciate the importance of corroborating intelligence.

By comparison, the Parliamentarian commander was in no doubt about the intelligence disadvantages of being isolated in enemy territory. Writing from Lostwithiel, Essex reported that 'Intelligence we have none, the country people being violently against us, if any of our scouts or soldiers fall into their hands, they are more bloody that the enemy.'[140] It is interesting to note that Luke recorded no reports on affairs in the far South West at this time, presumably because his agents were unable to procure any information in Royalist Cornwall – or, if they had managed to obtain any intelligence, to get that intelligence out of the county.[141]

The Parliamentarian pamphlets published details of the earlier movements of the opposing forces; *The Spie* reported that, after the relief of Lyme, Essex's 'next design is in generall for the west,'[142] and, later in June, *Mercurius Civicus* reported that Essex had 'possessed himself of Dorchester'.[143] Having relieved the siege of Plymouth, Essex was advised by Lord Robartes, the local Parliamentarian magnate, to march into Cornwall. This advice – and the King's decision to march in pursuit – was also duly reported,[144] but the gradual tightening of the Royalist ring around Essex and his army steadily reduced the flow of intelligence so that, in the end, all that appeared in the Parliamentarian press were repeated reports that the Parliamentarian Army was isolated in Cornwall.[145]

From the point of view of this examination of Civil War intelligence, the most remarkable aspect of the Lostwithiel campaign is the fact that, if we are to believe Walker, it took the Royalists so long to appreciate the very considerable benefits bestowed by superior intelligence; the Royalists had been 'walking in the dark'. It reveals that the Royalists fought for over two years before they began to fully appreciate the importance of intelligence; but secondly, and in many ways far more significantly, it shows just how much benefit the Parliamentarian commanders had been deriving from their own intelligence-gathering operations compared to those of their Royalist opposite numbers. With only one more major campaign ahead of them, this realisation may well have come too late for the Royalists. Certainly, the primary sources suggest that the King's destruction of Essex's army at the culmination of the Lostwithiel campaign owed much to the fact that, on this occasion, it had for once been the Royalists who had enjoyed superior intelligence.

Turning now to the manoeuvrings before the Second Battle of Newbury, partly described by Sir Edward Walker,[146] who provides a most revealing description of how intelligence informed the military decisions of the Royalists during the last major campaign of 1644. At a council of war held in Exeter in the last week of September, Charles was informed that Essex's foot had reached Southampton, that Waller, with new recruits of foot, was at Shaftsbury, where he had joined Middleton and his horse, and that 'Manchester with at least 5,000 horse and foot' was at Reading.[147] Walker observed that, notwithstanding these reports of the Roundhead concentration, Charles was determined to assist the besieged Royalist garrisons at Banbury, Donnington and Basing, and that this requirement did much to shape the conduct of the Second Newbury campaign. As Charles marched eastwards, the contemporary accounts reveal that the scouts of the opposing forces made contact, and that this generated the first of the many intelligence reports informing the decisions taken on both sides during the following weeks.

Walker describes how intelligence reports led to skirmishes and raids; for example, on 1 October, His Majesty 'had intelligence that a party of horse ... had beaten up a quarter of Waller's horse at Whitchurch and ... had taken a captain and about 20 prisoners ... which probably caused Waller to dislodge from Blandford'.[148] Reports about the Parliamentarian forces continued to come in; on 15 October, for example, Charles was told that 'Manchester was about Reading with 5,000 horse and foot and 24 pieces of ordnance, and that four regiments of the Trained Bands of London were coming towards him ... Essex was at Portsmouth ... and Waller was at Andover with 3,000 horse and dragoons'.[149] Unfortunately for the Royalists, Colonel Hurry, who had deserted to the King the year before, now deserted again, this time to the Parliamentarian commanders with details of Charles' plans, which led to 'the Rebels knowing His Majesty's strength as their own'.[150]

On the Parliamentarian side, too, much use was made of their intelligence information. Waller regularly reported back to the Committee of Both Kingdoms during the early stages of the Second Newbury campaign; on 17 September he informed the Committee that he had instructed his troops at Salisbury 'to send out continual parties into the west to gain intelligence'.[151] Waller was not the only Parliamentarian commander to seek intelligence. On 3 October, Manchester reported to the Committee how he had established from the reports of his own scouts, and from intelligence from Sir William Waller, that the King was marching fast to the east via Newbury and Abingdon to Oxford.[152] On 4 October, *The True Informer* reported that:

> Parliament received letters from the Earl of Manchester, whereby it was certified that he had received intelligence from Sir William Waller that the King with the main body of his army on Wednesday last was seven miles on this side of Dorchester and that he was resolved to come on with a swift march ... for Oxford ... and that ... he conceives them to be 12,000 horse and foot.[153]

On the same day, the Committee informed Essex that 'we have received advertisement that the King's forces were upon Wednesday advanced 5 miles on this side of Dorchester.'[154]

On 11 October, the contemporary accounts show how the Committee of Both Kingdoms used the intelligence reports they had received about the Royalist Army in an attempt to coordinate the Parliamentarian forces' interception of the King as they 'had certain intelligence he is marching eastwards'.[155] The Parliamentarian scouts had been, by this time, delivering some extremely detailed reports; for example, on 18 October, General Browne reported from Abingdon that:

A scout assures me that the King was yesterday in Salisbury with his foot, and his horse quartered in the villages on this side, and that Sir William Waller was then at Andover. This man, who has spent seven days in the King's quarters, reports that the only designe of the Royal army was for Abingdon, though their horse may go out of the direct course as a blind.[156]

Browne's report also included the information that 'the Royalists ... be not fewer than 16,000, whereof 8,000 are horse.' From these pieces of information, the Committee were able to provide Essex with a comprehensive intelligence update of Royalist intentions on 20 October.[157] Reports like this enabled the Parliamentarian forces to concentrate in the path of the Royalists' eastwards march.[158] However, the Royalist scouting detected the Parliamentarian concentration which caused Charles to alter the direction of his march to the north. This change caught the Parliamentarian commanders by surprise; internal dissent appears to have slowed their reactions and this, in turn, allowed the Royalists to occupy a strong defensive position between the Kennet and Lambourn rivers. The resulting battle was inconclusive when it could have been a resounding Parliamentarian victory – particularly when the subsequent withdrawal of the Royalist Army was detected – but as no scouts were deployed to shadow the Royalists, the Roundheads did not exploit the fact.[159]

This was not the end of this sorry state of Roundhead intelligence operations. After the Second Battle of Newbury had been fought on 27 October, the effectiveness of Parliamentarian intelligence-gathering was further bedevilled by internal dissent between the Earl of Manchester and his second-in-command, General Oliver Cromwell. The Royalists' intentions to recover their artillery from Donnington Castle were known to the Parliamentarian commanders, for Manchester wrote on several occasions to the Committee informing them 'of certain intelligence that the King is to come to Wallingford with his whole army and that he intends to march to fetch away the artillery and ammunition in Donnington Castle'.[160] However, apparently due to some misunderstanding, Cromwell had not ordered the placing of Parliamentarian scouts to watch the Wallingford Bridge and thus the Parliamentarians did not detect the advancing army in time to concentrate their forces in open country to block the Royalists' march to the castle. As was reported in the news pamphlets, 'we cannot plead ignorance of the King's motions, it being traced by us day by day.'[161] This second failure of the Parliamentarian forces around Newbury – in reality a skirmish but which has subsequently been described as the Third Battle of Newbury – resulted in the members of the House of Commons demanding an inquiry into the perceived military failures.[162]

In drawing together a conclusion of the use of intelligence in the campaigns of 1644, it appears reasonable to suggest that the primary evidence confirms that there was a steady increase in the use of intelligence in all theatres of the war during the year, and that this increase reflected the commanders' growing awareness of the value of accurate and timely information. By the end of 1644, a number of significant intelligence-gathering centres had been established by both sides. Sir Edward Nicholas controlled the Royalists' intelligence operations from Oxford, and a similar organisation was also about to be established at Bristol, as part of the new Western Association. Controlling this western Royalist intelligence service would be the responsibility of Sir John Culpepper.

The Parliamentarians had also established a somewhat larger intelligence-gathering structure by the end of the year – but one very similar to that established by the Royalists. In addition to the intelligence sub-committee of the Committee of Both Kingdoms, about to be run by Samuel Bedford, the Roundheads also had intelligence-gathering centres in most counties – perhaps the most effective of which were those in Cheshire, controlled by Sir William Brereton, and at Newport Pagnell, run by Sir Samuel Luke. Leonard Watson, Scoutmaster-General to the Parliamentarian Army of the Eastern Association, also controlled an effective team of intelligence-gatherers, supporting the military actions of the Earl of Manchester and Cromwell.

In view of these substantial intelligence activities, and the significant amounts of information they provided to their respective commanders, it would therefore appear that the assertion that 'most civil war battles were more often the result of armies meeting accidentally' is simply not supported by the significant quantity of surviving primary evidence describing the main battles of 1644. In fact this evidence suggests precisely the reverse for no major engagement occurred 'accidentally' during the 1644 campaigns. Indeed the contemporary accounts indicate that the outcomes of all of these battles were influenced – if not decided – by accurate and timely military intelligence. Furthermore, the failure of the Royalists to intercept Essex's cavalry at Lostwithiel and the failure of the Parliamentarians to intercept Charles's army as it withdrew from the Second Battle of Newbury provide clear evidence of failures to react to intelligence. So, if the intelligence-gathering of both armies was seemingly capable of providing accurate information, what intelligence operations were conducted in 1645 that allowed the Roundheads to beat the Royalists decisively – and thereby win the war?

Notes

1 J. Day, *Gloucester and Newbury 1643. The Turning Point of the Civil War* (Barnsley, 2007), p.217. See also pp.23, 111, 142, 156 and 166.
2 T. Fairfax, *A Short Memorial of Thomas, Lord Fairfax* (London, 1699), p.434.
3 J. Morrill, *Sir William Brereton* (DNB).
4 E. Hyde, *The History of the Rebellion and Civil Wars in England, together with an Historical*

View of the Affairs in Ireland (sixteen books, London, 1702–4), Book VIII, pp.77–79.

5   S.R. Gardiner, *History of the Great Civil War* (four volumes, London, 1893), Volume 2, pp.345–346.

6   J. Rushworth, *Historical Collections* (London, 1659–99), Part III, Volume II, pp.670–671.

7   Gardiner, *History,* Volume 2, p.351.

8   Rushworth, *Collections*, Part III, Volume II, pp.617–618.

9   Ibid, pp.623, 631–632 and 636.

10 Ibid, p.631.

11 Clarendon, *History*, Book VII, p.416.

12 E.G.B. Warburton, *Memoirs of Prince Rupert and the Cavaliers* (three volumes, London, 1849), Volume II, p.393.

13 Ibid, p.396.

14 Ibid, pp.441–444.

15 C.H. Firth (ed.), *The Lives of William Cavendish, Duke of Newcastle and of his wife Margaret, Duchess of Newcastle* (London, 1907), p.60.

16 C.H. Firth, 'Two Accounts of the Battle of Marston Moor', *English Historical Review* (Volume 5, No. 18, 1890), pp.345– 352.

17 P. Young, *Marston Moor 1644. The Campaign and the Battle* (Kineton, 1970, Re-printed Moreton-in-Marsh, 1997).

18 Young, *Marston Moor*, pp.82–83.

19 Ibid, p.80.

20 P. Young and R. Holmes, *The English Civil War. A Military History of the Three Civil Wars 1642 – 1651* (London, 1974).

21 Ibid, p.174.

22 Ibid, p.176.

23 Ibid, pp.177–178, 184–185 and 191–192.

24 P. Wenham, *The Great and Close Siege of York 1644* (Kineton, 1970).

25 Ibid, p.2.

26 Ibid, p.21.

27 Ibid, p.13.

28 M. Wanklyn and F. Jones, *A Military History of the English Civil War, 1642 – 1646* (Harlow, 2005), p.174.

29 Wanklyn and Jones, *Military History*, p.181.

30 M. Wanklyn, *Decisive Battles of the English Civil Wars* (Barnsley, 2006), p.125.

31 D. Cooke, *The Civil War in Yorkshire. Fairfax versus Newcastle* (Barnsley, 2000); and D. Cooke, *The Road To Marston Moor* (Barnsley, 2007).

32 Cooke, *Civil War in Yorkshire*, pp.96–97.

33 Ibid, p.101.

34 See, for example, Cooke, *Marston Moor*, pp.29 and 44.

35 Ibid, p.82.

36 Ibid, pp.91–92.

37 Rushworth, *Collections*, Part III, Volume II, pp.654–655.

38 Ibid, pp.670, 672, and 674–675

39 Ibid, pp.682 and 690.

40 Clarendon, *History*, Book VIII, p.22.

41 Ibid, pp.50, 54 and 56.

42 Ibid, p.93.

43 Ibid, p.115.

44 Ibid, p.144.

45 Ibid, p.140.

46 R. Bell (ed.), *The Fairfax Correspondence* (two volumes, London, 1849), Volume I, p.105.

47 M. Coate, *Cornwall in the Great Civil War and Interregnum 1642 – 1660* (Oxford, 1933), p.132.

48 Coate, *Cornwall*, p.141.

49 Ibid, pp.146–147.

50 P. Young, *Marston Moor1644. The Campaign and the Battle* (Kineton, 1970), pp.78–84; and M. Toynbee and P. Young, *Cropredy Bridge 1644. The Campaign and the Battle* (Kineton, 1970), pp.43–46, 58, 61, 65–66, 68–69 and 72–75.

51 See, for example, Waller's letter to the Committee of Both Kingdoms written on 4 June 1644. BL, Harleian MSS, ff. 83– 83v; and E. Walker, *His Majesty's Happy Progress and Success from the 30ᵗʰ of March to the 23ʳᵈ of November 1644* (London, 1705).

52 Toynbee and Young, *Cropredy Bridge*, p.73.

53 Wanklyn and Jones, *Military History*, pp.165–170.

54 J. Adair, *Roundhead General. The Campaigns of Sir William Waller* (Stroud, 1997).

55 Adair, *Roundhead General*, p.160.

56 Ibid, p.188.

57 Ibid, p.187.

58 Ibid, p.188.

59 F.T.R. Edgar, *Sir Ralph Hopton. The King's man in the West (1642 – 1652)* (Oxford, 1968), p.156

60 Ibid, pp.158 and 160.

61 Ibid, p.158.

62 J. Adair, *Cheriton, 1644. The Campaign and the Battle* (Kineton, 1973), pp.117, 119 and 120–122.

63 For numerous examples, see Adair, *Cheriton*, pp.117–125.

64 J. Adair, *Roundhead General. The Campaigns of Sir William Waller* (Stroud, 1997).

65 Adair, *Roundhead General*, p.157. See also pp.159–162.

66 Ibid, p.212.

67 Wanklyn and Jones, *Military History*, pp.159–161.

68 Wanklyn, *The Warrior Generals*, pp.83, 115–117 and 127.

69 Fairfax, *Short Memorial*, pp.434– 435.

70 Ibid, p.435.

71 E. 29[4], *Kingdom's Weekly Intelligencer* (London, 9–16 January 1644). Fairfax had spent some time in Lancashire gathering forces together before advancing to the relief of Nantwich.

72 E. 29[18], *True Informer* (London, 13–20 January 1644)

73 See, for example, E. 252[17], *A Perfect Diurnall of Some Passages in Parliament* (London, 15–22 January 1644); E. 29[20], *Certaine Informations From Severall parts of the Kingdome* (London, 15–22 January 1644); E. 30[7], *Mercurius Civicus London's Intelligencer* (London, 18–25 January 1644); and E. 30[11], *The Parliament Scout* (London, 19–26 January 1644).

74 E. 30[1], *Mercurius Aulicus* (Oxford, 13 January 1644).

75 E. 32[17], *Mercurius Aulicus* (Oxford, 27 January 1644).

76 See, for example, E. 31[7], *The Parliament Scout* (London, 26 January - 2 February 1644); and E. 31[10], *The True Informer* (London, 27 January-2 February 1644).

77 Fairfax, *Short Memorial*, p.436.

78 E. 38[10], *His Highnesse Prince Ruperts Raising of the Siege at Newark* (Oxford, 1644). This report was repeated in E. 40[6], *Mercurius Aulicus* (Oxford, 16 March 1644).

79 E. 38[10].

80 E. 38[10].

81 See, for example, *Mercurius Civicus, London's Intelligencer* (London, 21–28 March 1644).

82 E. 37[21], *The Parliament Scout* (London, 8–15 March 1644).

83 E. 38[13], *The Kingdomes Weekly Intelligencer* (London, 13–21 March 1644). See also E. 38[14], *Mercurius Civicus London's Intelligencer* (London, 14–21 March 1644); E. 40[6], *Mercurius Aulicus* (Oxford, 16 March 1644); and E. 38[18], *The Parliament Scout* (London, 15–22 March 1644).

84 C.V.Wedgwood, *The King's War 1641–1647* (London, 1974), p.301
85 Rushworth, *Collections*, Part III, Volume II, p.618.
86 Fairfax, *Short Memorial*, p.436.
87 E. 51[11], *Hulls managing of the Kingdoms cause or, a brief Historicall Relation of the Severall Plots and Attempts against Kingston upon Hull* (London, 18 June 1644).
88 *CSPD, 1643–44*, p.35.
89 Fairfax, *Short Memorial*, p.437.
90 E. 2[1], *A Continuation of True Intelligence from the English and Scottish Forces in the North* (London, 16 June – 10 July 1644).
91 E. 2[14], *A more exact Relation of the late Battaile neere York, fought by the English and Scottish forces, against Prince Rupert and the Earle of New-Castle* (London, 1644).
92 E. 51[3], *A Particular Relation of the most remarkable Occurrences from the united forces in the North* (London, 1–10 June 1644). See also, E. 53[12], *Exact and Certain News from the Siege at York*, (London, 1644); E. 252[41], *A Perfect Diurnall of some Passages in Parliament* (London, 3–10 June 1644); E. 50[26], *The Kingdomes Weekly Intelligencer* (London, 4–11 June 1644); and E. 50[32], *The Spie* (London, 6–13 June 1644).
93 E. 51[10], *The Kingdomes Weekly Intelligencer* (London, 11–18 June 1644).
94 E.54 [19], *A Full Relation of the Late Victory*, (London, 1644). See also, E. 54[11], *A Relation of the Good Success of the Parliaments Forces* (London, 1644).
95 Firth, *Life of Newcastle*, p.59.
96 Fairfax, *Short Memorial*, p.437.
97 See, for example, E. 54[11].
98 Firth, *Life of Newcastle*, p.60.
99 Bod. L, Clarendon MSS. 1764. See also, C.H. Firth, 'Two Accounts of the Battle of Marston Moor', *English Historical Review* (Volume 5, No. 18, 1890), pp.345– 352; and J. Binns (ed.), *The Memoirs and Memorials of Sir Hugh Cholmley of Whitby, 1600–1657* (Yorkshire Archaeological Society, 2000), p.136.
100 Bod. L, Clarendon MSS. 1764.
101 E. 2[14].
102 C.E.H. Chadwyck-Healey (ed.), *Bellum Civile: Hopton's Narrative of His Campaign in the West (1642–44) and Other Papers* (Somerset Record Society, 18, 1902), p.78.
103 Ibid, p.78.
104 Ibid, p.100.
105 Ibid, p.79.
106 Ibid, p.79.
107 Ibid, p.101.
108 Ibid, p.81.
109 E. 40[9], *Winchester taken, Together with a Fuller Relation of the Great Victory obtained (through God's Providence) at Alsford, on Friday 28 March 1644* (London, 1644).
110 BL, Portland MSS, Volume 3, pp.106–110.
111 I.G. Philip (ed.), *Journal o f Sir Samuel Luke* (3 volumes, Oxfordshire Record Society, 1953), Volume III, p.231.
112 Ibid, p.241.
113 Ibid, p.256
114 Ibid, pp.261, 264 and 265.
115 Ibid, p.269.
116 Ibid, p.270.
117 Winchester surrendered by the end of the month. Christchurch was captured on 5 April and Bishops Waltham was occupied on 9 April.
118 E. Walker, *His Majesty's Happy Progress and Success from 30ᵗʰ March to the 23ʳᵈ of November 1644* (London, 1705), p.8.
119 Walker, *Happy Progress*, p.8.

120 Ibid, p.18.

121 Ibid, p.20.

122 Ibid, p.20.

123 Ibid, p.25.

124 Walker, *Happy Progress,* p.30.

125 Ibid, p.32.

126 *CSPD ,1644,* p.206. Letter from Waller and Haselrig to the Committee dated 4 June 1644.

127 Ibid, p.246.

128 Ibid, p.252.

129 Ibid, p.279.

130 E. 53[18], *An Exact and full Relation of the last Fight, Between the Kings Forces and Sir William Waller* (London, 5 July 1644).

131 H.G. Tibbutt (ed.), *The Letter Books of Sir Samuel Luke,* Historical Manuscripts Commission, JP4, (London, 1963), pp.661– 667.

132 E. 51[16], *Mercurius Civicus, London's Intelligencer* (London, 13–20 June 1644).

133 See, for example, E. 52[7], *Mercurius Aulicus* (Oxford, 8 June 1644); E. 53[5], *Mercurius Aulicus* (Oxford, 15 June 1644); and E. 54[5], *Mercurius Aulicus* (Oxford, 22 June 1644).

134 Walker, *Happy Progress,* p.37.

135 Ibid, p.49.

136 Ibid, p.49.

137 Ibid, p.50.

138 Ibid, pp.50–51.

139 Ibid, p.70.

140 *CSPD, 1644,* p.434; and M. Stoyle, *Loyalty and Locality* (Exeter, 1994), p.234.

141 Tibbutt, *Letter Books,* p.26.

142 E. 50[32], *The Spie* (London, 6–13 June 1644).

143 E. 51[16], *Mercurius Civicus* (London, 13–20 June 1644).

144 E. 54[20], *The Parliament Scout* (London, 4–11 July 1644).

145 See, for example, E. 6[12], *The Kingdomes Weekly Intelligencer* (London, 6–14 August 1644); E. 6[16], *The Parliament Scout* (London, 8–16 August 1644); E. 254[20], *A Perfect Diurnall of some Passages in Parliament* (London,12–19 August 1644); E. 7[33], *True Informer* (London, 24–31 August 1644); and E. 254[29], *A Perfect Diurnal of some Passages in Parliament* (London, 2–9 September 1644).

146 Walker, *Happy Progress,* pp.110–113.

147 Walker, *Happy Progress,* p.88.

148 Ibid, p.99.

149 Ibid, p.105.

150 Ibid, p.110.

151 *CSPD, 1644,* p.478.

152 *CSPD, 1644–45,* p.8.

153 E. 11[3], *The True Informer* (London, 28 September – 5 October 1644).

154 *CSPD, 1644–45,* p.13.

155 *CSPD, 1644–45,* p.32. See also *CSPD, 1644–1645,* pp.38–39 for a further example of this coordination.

156 *CSPD, 1644–45,* p.52.

157 *CSPD ,1644,* p.521.

158 *CSPD, 1644–45,* p.65.

159 See, for example, Wanklyn, *Warrior Generals,* pp.135–136.

160 *CSPD, 1644–45,* pp.100, 106 and 108.

161 E. 17[4], *The Parliament Scout* (London, 8–15 November 1644).

162 E.256 [34], *A Perfect Diurnall of Some Passages in Parliament* (London, 4–11 November 1644).

7

The Triumph of Intelligence Operations – The Campaigns of 1645

Although Charles did not surrender to the Scots until the following year, the campaigns of 1645 effectively decided the outcome of the English Civil War. Contemporary evidence supports the conclusion that accurate Parliamentarian intelligence-gathering played a decisive part in determining the outcome of the battles of Naseby and Langport. Whilst these two battles effectively destroyed the remaining Royalist field armies, the final 'mopping-up' engagements took place in 1646 at Torrington on 16 February when Hopton was defeated attempting to relieve Exeter, and at Stow on 21 March when Lord Astley – who had commanded a brigade at Edgehill – surrendered the last Royalist field force. Although the impact of intelligence upon the outcome of Naseby and Langport was recognised in the contemporary descriptions of these actions, it has taken some time for it to be acknowledged in subsequent historical accounts. Why did it take so long for the part played by intelligence-gathering to be recognised?

The accepted historical account of the sequence of military events in 1645 shows that the winter of 1644/45 was used by both sides to review and restructure their armed forces. For the Royalists, these changes were mainly focused upon the senior ranks where a number of professional soldiers replaced the local magnates who had formerly been appointed to command the King's armies. Thus Sir Richard Grenville assumed command of the Royalist forces remaining in the West, Prince Maurice took command of the Royalist forces along the Welsh borders, and Prince Rupert replaced the Earl of Forth in overall command of the Royalist armies.[1]

By comparison, the Parliamentarian reorganisation was far more fundamental and extensive for they created a completely new army from the amalgamation – and enhancement – of the existing Roundhead forces. Sir Thomas Fairfax was selected to command this army – known to history as the 'New Model Army' and wearing for the first time the scarlet coats for which the British Army subsequently became world famous. The second major change to the Parliamentarian forces followed the passage through Parliament of the Self Denying Ordinance, a piece of legislation that required all officers who were Members of Parliament to surrender their commissions. The officers of the New Model Army would henceforward be selected for their military, rather than their political, skills and experience.[2] This upheaval generated considerable concern and speculation on both sides and was still in progress when the New Model Army took to the field in May 1645.[3] Indeed, concerns that the Royalists would deploy their forces before the New Model Army had been formed had caused the Committee of Both Kingdoms to order Cromwell to attempt to delay the junction of the Royalist forces at the beginning of the 1645 campaigning season by conducting a series of cavalry raids around Oxford.[4] Notwithstanding the success of Cromwell's subsequent operations, some Royalist leaders were heartened by the inevitable disruption caused by the Parliamentarian reorganisation, believing that the introduction of the 'New Nodel', as some Royalists 'scornfully termed this Army',[5] offered them the opportunity to win a decisive victory.

The Royalist high command's 'grand design' for 1645 identified two priorities – the recovery of their supremacy in the North and the consolidation of their power base in the South West. Although the recovery of the North and the relief of the besieged Royalist garrisons at Chester and Pontefract was possibly a higher priority, the need to recapture Taunton and thereby consolidate the Royalist hold on the South West was viewed as an equally urgent task.[6] Unable to determine their priorities, the Royalist commanders, having concentrated around Stow on 8 May, divided their forces. General Goring was detached from the main Royalist field army, with 3,000 horse, to recapture Taunton, while Charles and Rupert led the rest of the army north – initially to eliminate the Parliamentarian threat to Chester, but principally to restore Royalist supremacy in the area and to cooperate with James Graham, the Marquis of Montrose, and his small, largely Highland, army, which had already won several astonishing victories against larger Covenant forces in Scotland since September 1644.[7]

Although Parliamentarian intelligence about the 'grand design' of the Royalist armies was accurate,[8] the Roundhead commanders were still involved in the restructuring of their armies until early May. This meant that they were unable to take decisive action to pre-empt the intentions of the Royalists. However, the Committee of Both Kingdoms, aware of the immediate risk of the surrender of the Parliamentarian garrison at Taunton, determined that their first priority was to disperse the besieging Royalists, and it was this task that was assigned to the newly formed New Model Army. Thus, on 1 May, Fairfax led some 16,000 men into the west, reaching Blandford a week later. Meanwhile, as Fairfax moved to the west, the Royalist Army marched eastwards and concentrated around Oxford. This concentration caused the Parliamentarian leaders in London to change their plans – an example of 'back-seat-driving' that was to become commonplace during the early days of the New Model Army. Cromwell was ordered to shadow the Royalist forces while Fairfax, at Blandford, was ordered to detach a brigade to relieve Taunton, whilst he retraced his steps with the rest of the New Model Army to attack the Royalist forces concentrating around Oxford.[9] Fairfax so skilfully detached the brigade, under the command of Colonel Weldon, to relieve Taunton that the Royalists prematurely lifted the siege, believing that the whole New Model Army was still marching westwards to engage them. The Western Royalists, once they realised their error, reinvested Taunton, thereby preventing Weldon's brigade from rejoining the New Model Army at Oxford.

While Fairfax marched back east towards Oxford, Charles – shadowed by Cromwell – marched north to relieve Chester. Although the initial Parliamentarian plan was to defeat the King's army by using the combined forces of the Scottish Army in England and the local Parliamentarian forces led by Sir William Brereton,[10] the victories of Montrose understandably distracted the Scottish commanders and delayed their advance south to face the oncoming Royalists. Finding himself outnumbered, Brereton was forced to lift the siege of Chester and to withdraw into Lancashire where he deployed to bar any further Royalist advance to the west of the Pennines.[11] In an attempt to draw Charles away from his northern venture, on 15 May Fairfax was ordered to besiege Oxford.[12] By 19 May, Fairfax was encamped around the city. Cromwell was also ordered to join Fairfax at Oxford, after detaching a brigade under Colonel Vermuyden to reinforce the slowly advancing Scots.

Although Charles had raised the siege of Chester, his route to the North through Lancashire was blocked. Accordingly, the Royalist Army sought an alternative route and marched eastwards towards Newark. As the Committee of Both Kingdoms perceived this movement to be a threat to the Eastern Association, on 26 May Cromwell was ordered to leave the siege of Oxford and to reinforce the Isle of Ely so as to block any Royalist approach to the Eastern Association.[13] However, the news of the siege of Oxford, coupled with a report that the city was unexpectedly low on supplies, had caused consternation in the Royalist Council of War.[14] In an attempt to draw Fairfax away from Oxford, the Royalist commanders decided to attack Leicester, which was duly stormed on 31 May. Charles then paused in the Daventry area whilst he sent a convoy south to re-supply Oxford.[15]

The news of the fall of Leicester came as a shock to the Parliamentarian leaders and they immediately ordered Fairfax to march north to deal with the Royalist Army. Fairfax left Oxford on 5 June and by 12 June had reached Kislingbury, only five miles away from the Royalists, without Charles being alerted to the close proximity of the New Model Army. Although the Oxford convoy escort had rejoined the Royalist Army, the Parliamentarian Army, reinforced by 13 June with the forces of Cromwell and Vermuyden, significantly outnumbered the Royalist Army. The Parliamentarian forces were also too close for Charles to evade so the Royalists turned south to engage Fairfax. The Parliamentarians won a decisive victory at Naseby on 14 June 1645 and, shortly afterwards, retook Leicester. After the battle the King fled west to South Wales while Rupert attempted to gather the scattered Royalist forces into another field army. Informed by his intelligence reports of the immediacy of the Royalist threat to Taunton, Fairfax moved swiftly to restore Parliamentarian supremacy in the Midlands, before marching rapidly into the South West to engage Goring and the remaining Royalist field army. Fairfax's defeat of Goring's army at Langport on 10 July was the last major engagement of the First Civil War, but fighting continued for another year as the New Model Army methodically eliminated the remaining pockets of Royalist resistance.

How was the role of military intelligence in the campaigns of 1645 described by the subsequent historians? The first account of the 1645 campaign was provided by Joshua Sprigge, Fairfax's chaplain, who published a history of the New Model Army in 1647.[16] Sprigge's book, *Anglia Rediviva*, includes a good deal of detail about the use of intelligence during the Naseby campaign; for example, it contains a wide range of contemporary reports, as well as information that appears to come from eyewitnesses.[17] Although some doubt has recently been raised as to whether Sprigge was actually present on the field of battle,[18] rather than witnessing the engagement from the wagon train,[19] his account has nonetheless gained acceptance over the years as being a 'principal authority for the battle'.[20] Sprigge's narrative contains numerous references to intelligence being used to determine Fairfax's decisions. For example, it recounts how, on 13 June:

> Scoutmaster-General [Leonard] Watson (whose continued diligence in getting timely intelligence of the Enemies' motion, then, and always, redounded not a little to the enablement of the army) brought him certain notice, that the enemy was drawing off Burrough-hill towards Harborough.[21]

Sprigge reported the receipt of an even more significant piece of intelligence on 15 June, the day after the battle, when he described how a packet of letters was brought to Watson by one of his spies, who was in the employment of Sir Edward Nicholas (Charles' Secretary of State, who was based in Oxford). These letters included one from Goring to the King, reporting that Taunton was about to fall, and asking the King not to engage Fairfax until 'his forces were joyned with his Majesty'. As Sprigge comments, 'this intelligence did withal much quicken us to make speed to relieve Taunton.'[22] The date that this intercepted letter was actually received by Fairfax, and its relevance to intelligence operations during the Battle of Naseby, will be considered in more detail later in the chapter.

Sprigge also described how intelligence continued to flow into Fairfax's headquarters as he moved southwest to engage Goring around Taunton. The lifting of the siege of Taunton and Goring's subsequent movements were all reported accurately and quickly to Fairfax.[23] The wealth of information pertaining to intelligence that appears in *Anglia Rediviva* may explain why subsequent accounts of the 1645 military campaigns also contained numerous descriptions of the contribution of intelligence. Although John Rushworth was secretary to the New Model Army's council of war and had been present at the Battle of Naseby, his own book, *Historical Collections* which was published in 1659, nevertheless drew very heavily upon Sprigge's book. Indeed, Rushworth's account of the Naseby campaign often repeats Sprigge's account verbatim, with only an occasional additional sentence. For example, at the very beginning of the campaign, Rushworth described how intelligence of the Royalist plan to move their artillery train from Oxford led the Committee of Both Kingdoms to send orders to Fairfax to delay the Royalist concentration of forces by despatching 'some horse beyond Oxford … to intercept that convoy, and hinder the King and his Train from passing out'.[24] He also went on to describe how intelligencers had kept the Parliamentarian commanders informed of the position and size of the Royalist armies at all times during the campaign. Rushworth stated that reports on the Royalist forces were being received from a number of sources. For example, he noted that on 2 May the commander of the Coventry garrison reported to the Committee of Both Kingdoms that 'we have this morning received Intelligence, that the two princes Rupert and Maurice this last night came with all their forces to Evesham.'[25] Rushworth also reproduced a letter from the Parliamentarian Committee of Northampton (dated 4 June) which reported that 'we have at this instant received certain intelligence that the King's army is advanced this way, and that a great party both of horse and foot come as far as Harborough.'[26]

But the most interesting part of Rushworth's account relates to the occasion upon which Fairfax was given the intelligence about Goring's army's movements contained in the letter intercepted by Watson's agents. Rushworth (following Sprigge's account) states that Fairfax had not been given the intercepted letters from Goring to the King until the day after the battle (i.e. 15 June). As Sprigge had done before him, Rushworth describes, in some detail, how Watson had a spy working for Sir Edward Nicholas, and how this spy brought a package of letters to Watson on the day after Naseby. Significantly however, at this point Rushworth amended Sprigge's account, and inserted a sentence claiming that 'Fairfax seemed unwilling to open [these letters] … [until] Cromwell and Ireton [had] prevailed [upon him] to open them.'[27] Amongst the package of letters, there was the one from Goring to Charles declaring that:

> In three weeks time (nine days whereof were then expired) General Goring was confident to master the forces at Taunton and by consequence to settle the west of England [and therefore] … advising the King … to stand on the defensive, and not engage till his forces were joyn'd with his Majesty's.[28]

Clearly the intelligence that Goring was committed to continuing the siege at Taunton was of crucial importance to the commanders on both sides. For the Royalists, the information contained in Goring's letter would surely have made the King reluctant to engage with the New Model Army until after he had been reinforced by Goring. For the Parliamentarians, the letter would have informed them that they had a definite – and probably decisive – advantage in numbers over the Royalist Army, especially in cavalry. The letter would also have made it clear to Fairfax that this numerical advantage would not last forever as it would end as soon as Goring's force rejoined the King. Certainly both Sprigge and Rushworth appreciated the significance of the information for Charles as they both concluded that:

> Had these letters been presented to the King (as they might have been but for this Defeatment) in all probability his Majesty had declined fighting for the present ... but as the want of this Intelligence was so fatal to his Majesty, so the notice thereof quickened Fairfax to make speed to relieve Taunton.[29]

On the other hand, neither Sprigge nor Rushworth appear to have acknowledged the significance of this intelligence for Fairfax. For, as indicated above, had he read the intercepted letter before the battle, he would have known that he significantly outnumbered the Royalist Army – especially in cavalry – and that he needed to engage them before they were reinforced by Goring. The question of when Fairfax actually received this important intelligence will be discussed later.

Clarendon's *History,* which was published some 40 years after Rushworth's book, also seems to have made more use of contemporary sources for he too included a number of references to the use of intelligence-gathering during the Naseby and Langport campaigns. Clarendon, however, was highly critical of Royalist intelligence-gathering during the Naseby campaign, describing how, after Leicester had been taken, 'the army marched to Daventry in Northamptonshire where, for want of knowing where the enemy was, or what he intended to do, the King [was] in a quiet posture for the space of five days.'[30] Clarendon was also very critical of Royalist intelligence-gathering for, on the morning of the Battle of Naseby, he recorded that:

> It began to be doubted whether the intelligence they [the Royalists] had received of the enemy was true. Upon which the scoutmaster [Sir Francis Ruce] was sent out to make farther discovery; who, it seems, went not far enough; but returned and averred, that he had been three or four miles forward, and could neither discover nor hear any thing of them: and presently a report was raised in the army that the enemy was retired. Prince Rupert thereupon drew out a party of horse and musketeers, both to discover and engage them, the army

remaining still in the same place and posture they had been in. And his highness had not marched above a mile, when he received certain intelligence of their advance, and in a short time after he saw the van of their army.[31]

On this occasion, Clarendon was undoubtedly correct to suggest that the Royalist intelligencers had been ineffective and that this helped to pave the way for the disaster that was to follow. Unsurprisingly perhaps, when Clarendon wrote his account, he was not aware of just how great an advantage the Roundheads' superior intelligence had given the New Model Army. Later in his *History* he went on to describe the failures of Royalist intelligence at the subsequent Battle of Langport, citing the surprise of Porter's troops just before that battle.[32] He also mentioned the 'fantastical' action at which Royalist forces engaged each other by mistake when Goring was approaching Taunton to reinforce the Royalist forces besieging the Roundhead garrison.[33]

The more extensive use of contemporary evidence in the accounts by Sprigge, Rushworth and Clarendon describing the conduct of intelligence operations at Naseby and Langport clearly set an example for later historians to follow. Writing in the nineteenth century, Warburton's *Memoirs* contained numerous references to the intelligence reports received by Rupert during the first six months of 1645. In particular, Warburton described how Sir Edward Nicholas had provided the Royalist commanders with the bulk of their intelligence on the movements and intentions of the Parliamentarian forces.[34] Warburton also noted how little information about the advancing New Model Army appears to have been provided by the Royalist scouts, and argued that the laxity of the scouts had limited the options open to the Royalist Council of War as the provision of such late intelligence seriously restricted the time the Council had to plan. In addition, Warburton supplied a coruscating verdict on the Royalist scoutmaster's reconnaissance on the day of the battle, one which concluded that 'the scoutmaster was sent out to reconnoitre, and with the usual worthlessness of the King's servants, he returned with the assertion that there was no enemy in the neighbourhood.'[35] Clearly Warburton agreed with Clarendon that the failure of Royalist intelligence had lost the King both of the battles, and reflected Charles' ignorance of the fact that the excellence of the Parliamentarian intelligence had given Fairfax a significant advantage before either battle began.

Writing 40 years later, S.R. Gardiner also showed a keen awareness of the contemporary accounts which had emphasised the important role that intelligence had played in the Naseby and Langport campaigns.[36] Gardiner's description contained more references to intelligence information than any of his descriptions of the earlier campaign had done; for example, he described how, on 29 April, 'the Committee must have had secret intelligence from Oxford to have known ... [of Goring's march from Taunton to Oxford] so early.'[37] Gardiner also referred to the intelligence which, in May, had been offered to the Committee of Both

Kingdoms by the Royalist Lord Saville, who had suggested that Oxford would be surrendered should the Parliamentarian armies besiege it.[38] Saville's intelligence proved to be inaccurate and Fairfax was most unhappy at being ordered to besiege Oxford whilst the Royalist Army marched about the country unopposed by the New Model Army.[39] The lack of effective Royalist intelligence during the crucial days before the Battle of Naseby was firmly attributed by Gardiner to a failure on Rupert's part when he stated that on 12 June Rupert 'knew no more of Fairfax's movements than if he had been in another island'.[40]

Although he made frequent use of Sprigge and Rushworth in other parts of his *History*, Gardiner was the first historian to suggest that Goring's letter to the King had been intercepted by Watson and shown to Fairfax the day *before* the Battle of Naseby. Gardiner clearly set aside their accounts of when Goring's letter was intercepted, for he stated that:

> On the evening of the 13th ... Fairfax learnt that he was freed from one danger which had been imminent. Scoutmaster Watson brought in an intercepted letter which proved to be a despatch from Goring to the King announcing the impossibility of his leaving the West, and begging Charles to postpone a battle till he was able to join him.[41]

In support of his claim that the intelligence had reached Fairfax the day before the battle, Gardiner cited two items of contemporary evidence; firstly he mentioned a Parliamentarian news pamphlet, published on 20 June 1645, and, secondly, a sermon given by Hugh Peters on 2 April 1646. (We will return to these sources a little later.) Gardiner then went on to describe the failure of the Royalist scoutmaster to discover the approaching New Model Army on the morning of the battle, and Rupert's subsequent and more successful personal reconnaissance.[42] Gardiner's research suggested that the intelligence, which Sprigge and Rushworth declared had only been available to Fairfax *after* the battle, had in fact been made available to him *before* it. Indeed, Gardiner implied that it was the receipt of this intelligence on the night of 13 June which determined Fairfax to launch an immediate attack on the Royalist Army. Gardiner also described how intelligence had enabled Fairfax to attack Goring in his strong defensive positions based on the rivers Yeo and Parrett; he went on to note how poor Royalist intelligence had enabled Massey to trap General Porter's force of Royalist horse while they were stood down and bathing in a river.[43]

The significance of intelligence-gathering during the 1645 campaign continued to be appreciated by early twentieth-century historians. In Sir Charles Firth's books on Oliver Cromwell and the New Model Army, for example, the contemporary evidence of the intelligence aspect of the Battle of Naseby were explored in some depth.[44] Firth described how, in April, a Parliamentarian intelligence report that 'the King was about to take the field' had led to Cromwell being 'despatched to Oxfordshire to prevent the King from joining Prince Rupert'.[45] In his account of Naseby, Firth stated that Rupert had received inaccurate information from his scouts which had 'deluded him into the belief that Fairfax's troops were retiring'.[46] In *Cromwell's Army*, Firth described the intelligence-gathering structure of the New Model Army, and recounted how 'just before the Battle of Naseby, Watson did very valuable service by intercepting Royalist despatches.'[47] As has been noted earlier in this book, Firth also stated that one of the chief 'causes of the success of Fairfax and Cromwell was the efficiency of their intelligence department'.[48]

Writing some 50 years after Firth, C.V. Wedgwood also made use of contemporary evidence to describe the key role played by intelligence in the 1645 campaigns.[49] Wedgwood recounted how faulty Royalist intelligence had enabled a brigade of Fairfax's army to relieve Taunton, and how the intelligence of a 'mischievous and groundless' plot to betray Oxford submitted by Lord Saville – the 'uncertain Royalist'[50] – had led the Committee of Both Kingdoms to order Fairfax to besiege the city.[51] Wedgwood also described how Fairfax had 'feared, from what he had learnt from prisoners, that Goring's forces would soon be added to those of the King', adding that 'his best hope, as he saw it, was to force the King to fight before this junction could be made.' Wedgwood also agreed with Gardiner in claiming that, on 13 June, Fairfax had 'had in his hands ... an intercepted letter from Goring to Rupert ... which announced Goring's objection to the summons he had received' from the King. Fairfax saw his opportunity, Wedgwood observed, 'and took it.'[52]

In 1961, Austin Woolrych used contemporary evidence in his re-evaluation of the Naseby campaign. He too attributed the Parliamentarian success to their superior intelligence.[53] He noted that Parliament had been receiving intelligence information throughout the campaign; how Brereton had 'sent confident intelligence' of the Royalist march towards Chester; and how Lord Saville's intelligence that Oxford 'would open the gates to a besieging army' had caused 'the reducing of Oxford to be the main action of the campaign'.[54] Woolrych argued that Fairfax had had 'excellent intelligence of the royalists' movements from Brereton and Luke whilst Charles and Rupert had 'had no idea that evening [11 June] that the New Model was within a dozen miles of them.'[55] Woolrych, like Wedgwood, followed Gardiner in suggesting that Watson gave Fairfax the crucial letters from Goring on the evening before the battle.[56] After recounting the failure of Ruce, the Royalist Scoutmaster-General, to find Fairfax's advancing army on the day of the battle,[57] Woolrych concluded that 'Brereton's prompt and accurate reports of the royalists' movements from West Drayton to Leicester, and Luke's remarkably efficient intelligence service ... greatly helped the New Model.'[58] Finally, Woolrych drew attention to 'the contrast in efficiency between the Scoutmaster-Generals of the two sides'.[59]

In 1974, Antonia Fraser provided an overview of the intelligence information received by the Parliamentarians in her account of Cromwell's life when she wrote that 'intelligence varied from the brilliant to the negligible.'[60] Fraser also cited the primary evidence when she stated that 'Fairfax was now aware of Goring's recalcitrance from Royalist papers captured in a skirmish, and realised that he must be in a position of enormous numerical superiority over the King', whereas neither Charles nor Rupert 'had any idea how close the New Model actually was'.[61] Fraser was one of the first subsequent historians to acknowledge the impact of intelligence on the outcome of the battle when she concluded that 'Fairfax had already won a tactical victory over the King before the first shot of Naseby was fired.'[62]

The next writer to make a significant contribution to our understanding of the topic was Peter Young, who published a detailed analysis of the Battle of Naseby in 1985.[63] Although this analysis concentrated on where and how the battle was fought, it also described some of the intelligence operations in detail.[64] Young drew attention to a number of operations that had subsequently influenced the outcome of the campaign; for example, he showed how information had been regularly exchanged between the Scottish and New Model commanders and the Committee of Both Kingdoms.[65] In particular, he noted how, at the start of the campaign, information about the concentration of the Royalist Army in April had led to the deployment of Cromwell 'to march beyond Oxford … to intercept … [Rupert's horse], and keep the King and his train from passing out [of Oxford]'.[66] Young recounted how subsequently Fairfax's detachment of Colonel Weldon's brigade to relieve Taunton in May had fooled 'the Western Royalists, whose intelligence left something to be desired'.[67] Young went on to explain how intelligence influenced the selection of Leicester for assault later on in the campaign.[68] However, he did not describe the events between the fall of Leicester and the Battle of Naseby, as his account moved directly to a description of the battle itself; thus he did not assess the impact of intelligence during the days immediately before the battle. This omission meant that he expressed no opinion on the intelligence that had informed Fairfax's march from Oxford to intercept the King.

The contribution made by intelligence to the 1645 campaigns has continued to be recognised in historical and biographical accounts. In his acclaimed study of the New Model Army, for example, Ian Gentles recounted the affair of the letter from Goring intercepted and brought to Fairfax. In particular, Gentles noted that:

> The messenger who carried this and other letters was either a renegade or a double agent, since he delivered them not to Royalist headquarters but to Scoutmaster-General Watson, who brought them to Fairfax. The general at first refused to open the King's mail, but Cromwell and Ireton at length prevailed upon him to conquer his scruples. What they read convinced them of the necessity of fighting the King at once and then moving quickly to smash Goring at Taunton.[69]

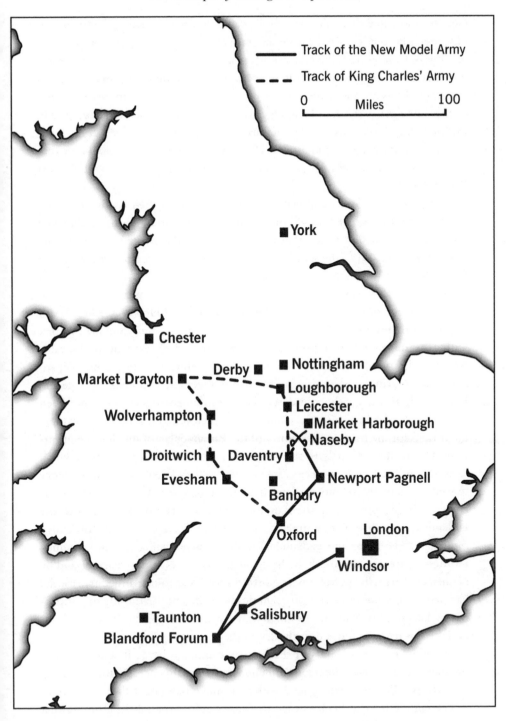

The Naseby Campaign, 1645.

Gentiles also stated that failures in the Royalist scouting had led to the surprising of General Porter's cavalry brigade the day before battle was joined at Langport on 10 July. Gentles described how 'Porter's men were relaxing by a stream, their horses at grass in the meadow, the men bathing, drinking or strolling along the riverbank. Massey caught them unawares.'[70] Gentles went on to describe how further intelligence informed Fairfax of Goring's intentions before Langport. He explained how 'from scouts and local inhabitants, he [Fairfax] learned that Goring was without his baggage and artillery.' From this intelligence, Fairfax knew that his opponent 'had already opted for a retreat' and this information 'emboldened [Fairfax] to strike'.[71]

In 1995, Glenn Foard published a substantial review of the Naseby campaign, which included a great deal of contemporary information about intelligence operations and which noted that the New Model Army 'had twenty scouts under the command of the scoutmaster, Major Watson'.[72] Foard recounted how Rupert's scouts had captured some New Model soldiers on 10 June, and how a suspected Royalist spy had been held in custody for a week to prevent intelligence of the approach of the New Model reaching the King.[73] However, whilst Foard concluded that the New Model Army's intelligence-gathering provided Fairfax with a constant series of reports on the position and strength of the Royalist Army, he did not comment on the intelligence significance of the intercepted letter from Goring on the timing of the Battle of Naseby. Following Sprigge and Rushworth, Foard clearly considered that the intercepted letters had not been brought to Fairfax until after the battle.[74] Nonetheless, Foard was keen to explore the reasons for the marked superiority of the Parliamentarian intelligence operations. He ascribed it partly to the lack of any local Royalist garrisons – which were 'the most effective sources of intelligence as they knew their own territory so well' – and partly to 'information gained from the interception of correspondence' and 'from spies within the Royalist garrisons'.[75] Foard concluded that the Parliamentarians had gained superior intelligence because the Royalist Army's route had taken them into Parliament's most effective intelligence and communications network, run jointly by Sir Samuel Luke in Newport Pagnell, and by Nathaniel Sharpe, the postmaster at Northampton. Foard also claimed that Fairfax had denied the Royalist Army any significant intelligence-gathering opportunities by keeping his army out of range of the patrol areas of the Royalist scouts until he was ready to move directly against them.

The most recent accounts of the Naseby campaign have all acknowledged the decisive impact of superior Parliamentarian intelligence. Writing in 2004, for example, Trevor Royle agreed with Gardiner's assessment that the content of Goring's letter had been known to Fairfax before the battle, claiming that 'the New Model Army had ... evolved a better system of reconnaissance.'[76] Writing a year later, Malcolm Wanklyn and Frank Jones similarly observed that accurate intelligence about the Royalist armies had enabled the Committee of

Both Kingdoms to seize and maintain the military initiative throughout.[77] Their review of the primary evidence supported their assessment that a report from Nicholas in Oxford had caused the King to believe that Fairfax 'seemed to be retreating in a north-easterly direction towards Bedford, apparently to protect the eastern approaches to the [Eastern] Association'. They suggested that this erroneous report had misled the Royalist commanders at a critically important time and, following an examination of Goring's correspondence, they concluded that the letter from Goring did come 'into Sir Thomas Fairfax's hands on 13th, 14th, or 15th June'.[78] In his most recent publication, *The Warrior Generals,* Malcolm Wanklyn recounted how intelligence information enabled Fairfax to 'know exactly where the Oxford Army was'.[79] Thus the accounts of the subsequent historians have shown clearly that the contribution made by intelligence information to the outcome of the 1645 campaigns has been widely recognised. But what else does the evidence of the primary sources actually say about the conduct and outcome of intelligence-gathering during that year?

As the King's army was the first to take the field, it is perhaps logical to start with the account of the Royalist operations written by Sir Edward Walker. This source provides an invaluable insight into the role played by intelligence information in the planning and conduct of Charles' campaign, for Walker's account described how the Royalist strategy was bedevilled by internal disagreements. Walker described how Royalist intelligence concerning the plight of the besieged Parliamentarian garrison at Taunton, coupled with intelligence about the similar predicament of the Royalist garrisons at Chester and Pontefract, caused the division of the main Royalist Oxford Army into smaller forces which 'laid the Foundation of our future Ruin'.[80] Nicholas had provided the Royalist Council of War with accurate intelligence regarding the state of Chester and the strength of Parliamentarian forces in that area when it had met at Stow on 8 May to finalise plans for the 1645 campaign.[81] The Royalist commanders had received regular intelligence reports from Nicholas, who controlled Royalist intelligence-gathering operations from Oxford, and his information influenced Charles' decision to detach Goring into the West to capture Taunton, whilst the rest of the Royalist Army moved north, initially to relieve Chester.

However, execution of the Royalist 'grand design' was hampered by poor local intelligence-gathering by the Royalist Army sent to capture Taunton. For example, when Fairfax detached a brigade under Colonel Weldon to relieve Taunton, the brigade commander, Colonel Weldon, described how the Royalist scouts had not detected the splitting of Fairfax's forces and thus 'could not believe but we [Weldon's brigade] were my Lord Goring's forces, [as] we were within four miles of the town before they would believe we were come, and then … they confusedly ran every way.'[82] The advancing Parliamentarian commander concluded that, as his forces 'never discovered one Scout of theirs,' that the Royalists 'took our army for Goring's'.[83] This significant failure of Royalist intelligence led to a premature withdrawal from the siege, which allowed Weldon to relieve Taunton unopposed. Although Goring's forces re-imposed the siege, the Parliamentarian reinforcement meant that Taunton's capture took more time. This delay not only hampered the eventual concentration of the Royalist armies, but also had a critical impact on their overall campaign strategy.

The Royalists' northern campaign also ran into problems. The army's march to the North was swiftly detected by the local Parliamentarian local commanders – Sir William Brereton commanding the Parliamentarian forces besieging Chester, and Sir Samuel Luke commanding the garrison at Newport Pagnell.[84] Like Luke, Brereton had established a reliable and responsive intelligence network to monitor the movements of the Royalist forces. Brereton reported to the Committee of Both Kingdoms on 2 May, that he had 'received intelligence, which originally came out of the mouth of one of the Prince's secretaries that the Princes are upon their advance this way to relieve Chester'. [85] The Committee replied on 9 May informing him that 'by the intelligence we have received, we conceive the King's march to be towards your parts.'[86] Understandably, the approach of the Royalist Army was being closely monitored by Brereton's own agents and intelligence organisation.[87] However, despite Brereton's requests for the Scottish Army to march south to reinforce him, on 17 May he had to abandon the siege of Chester when the Royalist Army – totalling some 8,000 men – reached Stourbridge.[88] Brereton continued to observe the movements of the Royalist Army and, on 22 May, reported that the Royalists were 'heading for Newark' with '10,000 to 12,000 men'.[89] The accuracy and frequency of Brereton's reports were much appreciated for they undoubtedly assisted the Parliamentarian commanders to plan their own movements, as Lord Fairfax acknowledged in a letter to Brereton on 24 May:

> I thank you for your frequent intelligence and vigilance to know all the motions of the enemy, which I very much depend on. [Your reports] have better enabled me to direct the union of the forces that are appointed to the securing of these parts.[90]

Thus the Royalists' plan to march north to revitalise their support in Yorkshire and then join up with Montrose's victorious forces, was not only disrupted by Weldon's relief of Taunton and Fairfax's subsequent siege of Oxford, but it was also rapidly detected by the Parliamentarian intelligence-gatherers. Once Chester was relieved and the Royalist Army turned eastwards, reporting intelligence of their movements was increasingly the responsibility of Sir Samuel Luke who was based in Newport Pagnell. His letter books provide extensive evidence of his intelligence reports. For example, on 24 May, Luke reported that 'it is thought that he [Charles] will march to Newark.'[91] After the capture of Leicester, on 4 June, Luke reported to Leonard Watson – Fairfax's scoutmaster – that 'his Majesty intends to quarter this night at Market Harborough.'[92] This was one of a series of regular reports that Luke made to Watson over the next ten days, including one which recounted the fact that 'Royalist prisoners say the intention is to join with Goring and then fight Fairfax, afterwards, if successful, going north.'[93] However, Luke did not always receive correspondingly frequent intelligence reports from Watson; indeed he wrote to him on 14 June 'demanding intelligence – having given two letters and received none.'[94] As this was the day that Naseby was fought, Watson may perhaps be excused for having higher priorities at that time than writing to Luke.

Digby conceded that the Parliamentarian actions had 'staggered our Designe', and had then 'retarded' the Royalist march to the North because Charles feared he would lose Oxford.[95] Although, on 6 June, Walker had reported that Fairfax's army had left Oxford and 'that he was marching towards Buckingham,' the news did not alter Charles' determination to delay the Royalists' march north while he re-supplied Oxford. Walker described how the Royalist Army 'marched to Daventry, and there stayed five days, both to mark the motions of Fairfax and to [await the return of his forces] from Oxford'. For a whole week, Nicholas was unable to provide any further intelligence about Fairfax's movements until 13 June, when 'intelligence [was] given of the Advance of Fairfax to Northampton.' Thus the first intelligence the Royalists received of the Parliamentarian Army's advance did not appear until 'Fairfax and his army were quartered within five miles of us.' Indeed, a letter from John Rushworth to Sir Samuel Luke, written on the evening of 13 June, stated that some Royalist prisoners, captured that day, believed 'that the rebels [Roundheads] were gone into Cambs [Cambridgeshire]'.[96] Even on the day of the battle, Royalist intelligence-gathering continued to be unreli-able; Walker recounted how 'one Ruce, the Scoutmaster, was sent to discover; who, in short time returned with a Lye in his mouth, that he had been two or three miles forward, and could neither discover or hear of the Rebels.' It was only some time after receiving this report that Rupert's own scouting patrol obtained 'certain Intelligence of their [the New Model Army] Advance'.[97] This lack of fresh Royalist intelligence at a critical time of the campaign placed Charles and his Royalists at a clear military disadvantage, as their knowledge with regard to the position of the Parliamentarian Army was clearly inaccurate.

The Royalists might have gained a great deal of information about military movements from the London news pamphlets – although there is no contempo-rary record of the Royalist intelligencers using this source. If they *did* read them, they would have seen that their plan to relieve the siege at Chester had been known to Parliament as early as mid April.[98] Two weeks later, the London press reported the plan of 'Sir Thomas Fairfax and Major General Skippon to advance into the west with 8,000 horse and foot for the relief of Taunton'.[99] Later still, on 10 June just before the Battle of Naseby, the pamphlets accurately reported the Royalist Oxford Army as being 'not above 13,000'[100] 'on Danes' Hill [Borough Hill, near Daventry]'[101] and were expecting 'daily a supply of horse from Goring out of the west.'[102] Charles had not been receiving any comparable intelligence on the position of the New Model Army.

Clearly these primary sources confirm that intelligence-gathering played a crucial part in determining the positioning of the opposing forces before the Battle of Naseby, describing how the pursuing Parliamentarians had 'full knowledge' of the Royalists movements before both that battle and the Battle of Langport.[103] In addition, before the Battle of Naseby, Parliamentarian intelligence operations provided Fairfax with a further crucial piece of intelligence – information which had given him a decisive military advantage.

This key piece of intelligence was referred to in the Parliamentarian news pamphlet, *Perfect Occurrences,* published on 20 June. It noted that, on 13 June, the King ordered Goring to 'send him speedily 2,000 horse and 3,000 foot' to reinforce his army so that he might engage Fairfax. The pamphleteer stated that, having received this order, Goring had then given the answer which had been intercepted by Parliamentarian intelligencers:

> May it please your Majesty,
> We are now in a fair way of taking Taunton, and the whole west will be easily reduced to your obedience, this designe we are upon is of exceeding great confidence, and if we should send away any part of our forces, (the Rebels being 4,000 within the towne, our whole strength not above 9,000), our designe would be then quite spoiled and the west in danger to be lost if 5,000 should be drawn away, now I humbly desire that your Majesty would be pleased to send your commands, by this bearer (who will returne within five days) to which I desire to submit, and continue,
> Your most affectionate servant,
> Goring.[104]

The pamphleteer went on to claim that, as Goring had received no response from the King – at least one copy of this letter having been intercepted – the Royalist commander 'thought that his judgement was approved of, and that the King did not desire the forces'.[105] Contemporary corroboration of this report was provided by Hugh Peters, the Chaplain to the ordnance train. In a sermon that he preached to both Houses of Parliament on 2 April 1646, Peters referred to the fact that 'the King's letters from Goring [had been] taken by the great care of our honest and vigilant Scout Watson, the night before the Naseby battell.' Peters also stated that, had the King received this letter from Goring, he would have been 'wholly disswaded from fighting with us then'[106] Peters did not provide any corroboration for his assertion – such as the date of the letters, or when they were intercepted by Watson – nor did he give any indication of how he had obtained this information; presumably he didn't want his sermon to get bogged down in details. However, although there is no definite evidence that the letter quoted in the news pamphlet and the letter described by Peters are the same, both sources make it clear that Fairfax received intelligence from an intercepted letter about Goring's intentions the night before the battle. Peters' account seems never to have been challenged, either at the time of his sermon or subsequently. He was a close associate of the senior Parliamentarian commanders, had frequently visited the general headquarters, and was thus well placed to record the actions of the chief Roundhead officers before the battle.

The question of whether Goring's intercepted letter was shown to Fairfax the night before the engagement, or the night after it, is an important one for the overall assessment of the effectiveness of the 1645 intelligence-gathering operations. As this intercepted letter has been cited by many later historians as evidence that Fairfax knew of Goring's continued action outside Taunton, and that he therefore could not rejoin the King, it is important to explore the other contemporary accounts that mention its interception. The two most contemporary accounts – the report in *Perfect Occurrences* and the sermon of Hugh Peters – have both provided clear evidence that this critical piece of information about the intentions and location of Goring's force – with its strong complement of cavalry – had been known to Fairfax *before* the battle. Contradicting this evidence have been the reports of Sprigge and Rushworth which stated that Fairfax had not received the letter until the day *after* the battle.

The corroborative evidence of Rushworth mentioned earlier is of particular relevance to determining the time the letter was seen by Fairfax, as a sentence in his account stated that both Cromwell and Ireton had had to persuade a reluctant Fairfax to open the King's intercepted correspondence.[107] As Ireton is known to have been seriously wounded during the battle – so seriously that at least one contemporary writer feared that he would die[108] – it seems very unlikely that he would or could have been summoned to help Cromwell persuade Fairfax to open the letters the day after the battle. The fact that Cromwell and Ireton had had to persuade Fairfax to open the letter, coupled with the contemporary evidence of the report in *Perfect Occurrences* and Hugh Peters' sermon, provides compelling evidence that a letter from Goring stating his intention to continue the siege at Taunton – and thus not to join the King – was intercepted by the Roundheads *and read* by Fairfax before the battle. As Fairfax was very concerned about the relative strength of his cavalry compared to that of the Royalists, there can be little doubt that Fairfax would have been particularly keen to receive any intelligence that would have helped resolve this major concern.[109] The intelligence contained in the intercepted letter revealed that he had an immediate opportunity to engage the Royalist Army while he enjoyed a decisive superiority in numbers – especially in cavalry. Armed with this specific intelligence, it is unsurprising that Fairfax subsequently decided to engage the King as soon as possible.

Further support for this conclusion is contained in a letter written to the Speaker on 17 February 1646, in which Fairfax acknowledged the 'diligent and faithful service performed by John Tarrant, a Scout ... who very often hazarded his own life in bringing unto me from the enemy's quarters exact intelligence of their [the Royalists'] affairs and most especially at the Battle of Naseby.'[110] Regrettably, Fairfax's letter does not specify whether Tarrant delivered Goring's intercepted letter before or after the battle. Nevertheless, the fulsomeness of Fairfax's commendation of Tarrant's intelligence work makes it tempting to surmise that he believed Tarrant to have played a key role in helping to bring about the victory – and therefore that he had received his intelligence before the engagement took place.

It is difficult to say why both Sprigge and Rushworth have stated that this significant piece of intelligence was not received until after the battle, if, in fact, it had been received the night before. One possible explanation is that they made a mistake about the timing of a report which they both viewed as peripheral to the main action. As Luke reported, 13 June was a busy day for the Parliamentarian commanders and their Council of War, and there is a letter from Rushworth – secretary to Fairfax's Council of War – apologising for the loss of a letter from a Mr Knightly, a member of the Parliamentary Committee of Prisoners. In his letter, Rushworth explained how 'amongst our great engagement yesterday in securing the papers and letters, this letter of Mr Knightly, which the general received the night before the battle, is so mislaid as for the present it cannot be found.'[111] Another possible explanation is that, as the position of the Royalist Oxford Army was already known to the Parliamentarians, and as there had been no reports of Goring's forces being anywhere near Naseby, Sprigge and Rushworth could well have considered the contents of Goring's letter to be largely irrelevant as it merely confirmed what they already knew. On the other hand, it must be remembered that when Sprigge wrote *Anglia Rediviva* he was keen to emphasise the contribution made by the New Model Army to the overthrow of the King, and this determination may have led him to diminish not just the numerical superiority enjoyed by the New Model Army over the Royalists, but also the extent of the intelligence which they possessed. Most modern historians have concluded that Fairfax *did* receive the intercepted letter before the battle, and the research into the contemporary evidence for this book tends to support this conclusion. Certainly, it confirms the Battle of Naseby was emphatically not 'the result of armies meeting accidentally'.[112]

What is not in dispute is that the intercepted letter gave Fairfax a clear idea of the straitened circumstances of the Parliamentarian garrison at Taunton and, having recaptured Leicester, he moved swiftly to their aid. The London news pamphlets quickly reported the Royalist movements after the Battle of Naseby; for example, in the last week of June, *Mercurius Civicus* published that 'His Majesty was gone to Bristol ... Goring had drawn off his forces from Taunton to join him.'[113] The following week, the pamphlets reported the junction of Fairfax's and Massey's forces 'near Lyme',[114] and a week later still, Goring's force was reported to be '6 or 7,000 horse, 2,500 foot and 8 pieces of ordinance'.[115] These reports were repeated in other news pamphlets.[116] Fairfax himself reported how '1500 Royalists having no intelligence of his [Massey] being in motion, were surprised in a careless posture [when] Major-General Massey fell on them.'[117] As at Naseby, Parliamentarian intelligence during the Langport campaign proved more accurate than that available to the Royalists, and enabled Fairfax to win another decisive victory.

In conclusion, it seems evident that historians have made much more use of the contemporary sources describing the role played by military intelligence in the 1645 campaigns than in any of the campaigns that had preceded them. Far from being a campaign in which 'intelligence activities were on a primitive level', the Parliamentarian campaign of 1645 was one in which intelligence-gathering was accurate, effective and swiftly integrated into the military decision-making process. Even Clarendon agreed that accurate intelligence enabled Fairfax to track the movements of the Royalist Oxford Army from a distance outside the effective range of the Royalist scouts, whilst he determined the best time to attack. At all times during these campaigns, the Parliamentarian commanders knew the precise location of the Royalist forces, and had a reasonably accurate idea of their intentions. The contemporary accounts confirm that, although Fairfax was never in any doubt as to the position of his opponents, he was concerned about the operational potential of the Royalist horse commanded by Goring and did not wish the Royalist forces to combine before his attack. The interception of Goring's letter thus provided him with the key piece of intelligence he needed – and one which allowed him to decide to attack the Royalist Army when he knew he had a decisive advantage. The Royalists, on the other hand, appear to have had comparatively little idea where their opponents were and, from the very beginning of the campaign, news of the movements of the New Model Army came as a surprise to them. Inadequate intelligence of the whereabouts of the Parliamentarians before the battles of Naseby and Langport was one of the major factors that caused the Royalist armies to be defeated so decisively – and thus lose the First English Civil War.

Notes

1 E. Hyde, *The History of the Rebellion and Civil Wars in England, together with an Historical View of the Affairs in Ireland* (sixteen books, London, 1702–4), Book VIII, p.168.
2 C. Firth, *Cromwell's Army. A History of the English Soldier during the Civil Wars, the Commonwealth and the Protectorate* (London, 1902), pp.40– 41.
3 Clarendon, *History,* Book IX, p.6.
4 J. Sprigge, *Anglia Rediviva: England's Recovery* (London, 1647), p.10.
5 Sprigge, *Anglia Rediviva,* p.12. See also, Clarendon, *History,* Book IX, p.36.
6 Clarendon, *History,* Book IX, pp.12, 24 and 27.
7 Ibid, p.35.
8 See, for example, *CSPD, 1644–45,* pp.331, 334 and 341.

9   Sprigge, *Anglia Rediviva,* pp.16–17.
10 *CSPD, 1644–45,* pp.409, 452 and 455.
11 See R.N. Dore (ed.), *The Letter Books of Sir William Brereton,* (two volumes, The Record Society of Lancashire and Cheshire, 1990), Volume I, p.446; and CSPD, *1644–45,* p.505.
12 *CSPD, 1644–45,* p.497. Letter dated 17 May from Committee of Both Kingdoms to Sir Thomas Fairfax.
13 *CSPD, 1644–45,* p.530.
14 E. Walker, *Brief Memorials of the Unfortunate Success of His Majesty's Army and Affairs in the year 1645* (London, 1705), p.127.
15 Ibid, p.128.
16 J. Sprigge, *Anglia Rediviva; Englands Recovery* (London, 1647).
17 See, for example, Sprigge, *Anglia Rediviva,* pp.27, 29, 31 and 33.
18 See, for example, G. Foard, *Naseby: The Decisive Campaign* (Barnsley, 1995), p.403.
19 See P. Young, *Naseby 1645: The Campaign and the Battle* (London, 1985), p.xx.
20 See, for example, E.G.B. Warburton, *Memoirs of Prince Rupert and the Cavaliers* (three volumes, London, 1849), volume I, p.101; Young, *Naseby,* p.xix; and M. Wanklyn, *Decisive Battles of the English Civil War* (Barnsley, 2006), p.168.
21 Sprigge, *Anglia Rediviva,* p.31.
22 Ibid, pp.47–48.
23 Ibid, pp.60–64.
24 J. Rushworth, *Historical Collections* (London, 1659–99), Volume I, p.23.
25 Ibid, p.28.
26 Ibid, p.37.
27 Ibid, p.49.
28 Ibid, p.49.
29 Ibid, p.49.
30 Clarendon, *History,* Book IX, p.36.
31 Ibid, pp.38–39. See also Warburton, *Memoirs,* Volume III, p.103.
32 Clarendon, *History,* Book IX, p.57.
33 Ibid, p.45.
34 Warburton, *Memoirs,* Volume III, pp.91 and 97.
35 Ibid, p.103.
36 S.R. Gardiner, *History of the Great Civil War 1642–1649* (four volumes, London, 1893).
37 Gardiner, *History,* Volume II, p.207.
38 Ibid, p.212.
39 Sprigge, *Anglia Rediviva,* pp.24–25.
40 Gardiner, *History,* Volume II, p.240.
41 Ibid, pp.242–243.
42 Ibid, p.244.
43 Ibid, pp.269–270.
44 C.H. Firth, *Oliver Cromwell and the Rule of the Puritans in England* (Oxford, 1900), pp.119–123; and C.H. Firth, *Cromwell's Army. A History of the English Soldier during the Civil Wars, the Commonwealth and the Protectorate* (London, 1902), pp.63–67.
45 Firth, *Oliver Cromwell,* pp.119–120. On 24 April, Cromwell had routed three regiments of Royalist horse at Islip.
46 Ibid, p.123.
47 Ibid, p.65.
48 Ibid, p.67.
49 C.V. Wedgwood, *The Great Rebellion: The King's War 1641–1647* (London, 1958).
50 Wedgwood, *The King's War,* p.174
51 Ibid, p.446.
52 Ibid, pp.450–451.

53 A. Woolrych, *Battles of the English Civil War* (London, 1961), pp.138–139.

54 Ibid, pp.107–108.

55 Ibid, pp.113, 115 and 139.

56 Ibid, p.117.

57 Ibid, p.121.

58 Ibid, pp.138–139.

59 Ibid, p.139.

60 A. Fraser, *Cromwell: Our Chief of Men* (London, 1974), p.153.

61 Ibid, p.154.

62 Ibid, p.155.

63 P. Young, *Naseby 1645: The Campaign and the Battle* (London, 1985).

64 Ibid, pp.xvii, and 216–220.

65 Ibid, pp.220–221.

66 Ibid, pp.205–206.

67 Ibid, p.213.

68 Ibid, pp.228–229.

69 I. Gentles, *The New Model Army in England, Ireland and Scotland, 1645 – 1653* (London, 1992), p.55. During a conference on the Battle of Naseby held at Kelmarsh Hall on 29 June 2008, Gentles was later to state that one of the reasons why Parliament won the battle was 'because their intelligence was so good'.

70 Gentles, *New Model Army*, p.67. See also, Clarendon, *History*, Book IX, p.57.

71 Ibid, p.68.

72 G. Foard, *Naseby: The Decisive Campaign* (Barnsley, 1995), p.202.

73 Ibid, pp.91, 121, 164 and 167.

74 Ibid, p.322.

75 Ibid, pp.159–160.

76 T. Royle, *Civil War: The Wars of the Three Kingdoms 1638 – 1660* (London, 2004), p.326.

77 M. Wanklyn and F. Jones, *A Military History of the English Civil War, 1642–1646* (Harlow, 2005), pp.231–244.

78 Ibid, pp.242–243.

79 M. Wanklyn, *The Warrior Generals. Winning the British Civil Wars 1642–1652* (New Haven and London, 2010), pp.160–162.

80 Walker, *Brief Memorials*, p.125.

81 Clarendon, *History*, Book IX, p.29.

82 E. 284[9], *An Exact Relation of the raising of the siege, and relieving of the town of Taunton* (London, 1645).

83 E. 284[11], *A Great Victory obtained against the Enemy, at the raising of the Siege from before Taunton* (London, 1645).

84 R.N. Dore (ed.), *The Letter Books of Sir William Brereton* (two volumes, Lancashire and Cheshire Record Society, 1984–90); I.G. Philip (ed.), *Journal of Sir Samuel Luke* (3 volumes, Oxfordshire Record Society, 1953); and H.G. Tibbutt (ed.), *The Letter Books of Sir Samuel Luke,* Historical Manuscripts Commission, JP4, (London, 1963).

85 Dore, *Letter Books*, Volume I, p.343.

86 Ibid, p.384.

87 Ibid, p.420.

88 Ibid, p.446.

89 Ibid, p.480.

90 Ibid, p.488.

91 Tibbutt, *Letter Books*, p.286.

92 Ibid, p.299.

93 Ibid, p.563.

94 Ibid, p.320.

95 Walker, *Brief Memorials*, p.127.

96 Tibbutt, *Letter Books*, p.575.

97 Ibid, p.129–130.

98 E. 278[13], *Mercurius Civicus* (London, 10–17 April 1645).

99 E. 284[1], *Mercurius Civicus* (London, 24 April-1 May 1645). This deployment was also reported in the *Weekly_Account* and the *Kingdomes Weekly Intelligencer*. See also, E. 282[3], *Weekly Account* (London, 30 April–7 May 1645), and E. 282[2], *Kingdomes Weekly Intelligencer* (London, 29 April- 6 May 1645).

100 E. 288[8].

101 E. 288[2].

102 E. 262[8].

103 For example, see E. 288[22], *A True Relation of a Victory obtained over the King's forces, by the army of Sir Thomas Fairfax* (London, 1645).

104 E. 262[10], *Perfect Occurrences of Parliament* (London, 13–20 June 1645).

105 E. 262[10].

106 H. Peters, *Gods Doings and Mans Duty* (London, 1646), p.19

107 Rushworth, *Historical Collections*, Volume I, p.49

108 E. 288[21].

109 Sprigge, *Anglia Rediviva*, p.33.

110 Bod. L, Tanner MSS 59, f. 750.

111 Tibbutt, *Letter Books*, p.577.

112 Marshall, *Intelligence and Espionage*, p.18.

113 E. 289[10], *Mercurius Civicus* (London, 18–25 June 1645).

114 E.292 [1], *Mercurius Civicus* (London, 26 June – 3 July 1645).

115 E.292 [18], *Mercurius Civicus* (London, 3–10 July 1645).

116 See also, E.262 [11], *A Perfect Diurnall*, (London, 16–23 June 1645); , E.262 [21], *A Perfect Diurnall*, (London, 7–14 July 1645); E.293 [1], *A Perfect Diurnall*, (London, 8–15 July 1645); E.292 [15], *Kingdom's Weekly Intelligence* (London, 1–8 July 1645) and E.293 [1], *Kingdom's Weekly Intelligence* (London, 8–15 July 1645).

117 E.261 [4], *Copies of Three letters from Sir Thomas Fairfax* (London, 1645). See also, E.292 [28] and E.292 [30].

8

The Impact of Historical Perceptions On Our Understanding of Civil War Operations

As has been seen, there are a large number of varied contemporary sources that provide abundant primary evidence that intelligence-gathering did, in fact, play a significant part in determining the outcome of virtually all the major battles that were fought between 1642 and 1646. Indeed, even before the fighting began, the Parliamentarian leaders were receiving accurate and useful intelligence from sympathisers holding senior positions in the Royalist court, and from members of the public. Once the fighting began it is clear that not only did military intelligence play a significant part in all the major engagements, but also that it was used to good effect in many of the minor skirmishes. It is therefore relatively straightforward to document how intelligence information influenced the outcome of the First English Civil War.

What is far more difficult to explain is why the majority of the subsequent historical accounts of the English Civil War have not included any reference to the impact that this substantial amount of information had upon the outcome of the fighting. Whilst more has been written about Civil War intelligence operations since the end of the Second World War, it is really only within the last five to ten years that the true significance of these intelligence operations has begun to be recognised and their impact explained. Even against the background of this emerging emphasis, the most recent general overviews of the fighting have continued to overlook the impact that intelligence information had upon the conflict. Indeed, one of the latest accounts of the Civil War continues to describe military intelligence operations as 'rudimentary'.[1]

Historical researchers appear to have been wary of assessing the cumulative impact of the increasingly accurate intelligence reports that were flowing into the camps of the opposing commanders: even Julian Whitehead's most recent account of intelligence operations during the Civil War and

Commonwealth does not specifically assess their impact upon the outcome
of the war between 1642 and 1646.[2] Why is there this seeming reluctance
to challenge historical perceptions – or misconceptions – and acknowledge
the relevance of the primary evidence in the contemporary accounts which
describe how effectively intelligence-gathering operations were conducted
throughout the war?

Any answer to that question will have to address several different – albeit
interlinked – issues. A researcher needs to be convinced of the accuracy and reliability of the information contained in the contemporary accounts before using
them. To establish the accuracy of eyewitness accounts, what the writers saw – or
thought they saw – needs to be verified by another independent contemporary
account, just as the credibility of the source needs to be considered. As maps and
time-keeping were imprecise in the seventeenth century, it is often difficult – if
not impossible – to verify precisely contemporary descriptions of multi-faceted
and lengthy events, especially if some time has passed between the event itself
and the subsequent compilation of the account of that event. However, whilst
these particular problems may well have made it more difficult to reconstruct
precise and complex events exactly, such as how a battle developed, uncertainty
about exact timings or locations would not necessarily have a significant impact
upon the relevance of contemporary reports describing some other events, such
as more general intelligence information received before a battle.

In the case of contemporary or subsequent reports of events written by people
who were not witnesses, it is necessary to establish the potential bias of the report.
Knowledge of the individual political preferences can be useful as can independent corroboration of the report by comparison with other independent accounts
of the same event. For example, many news pamphlets reports were produced by
each side to provide their version of events; these were often written by people
who had not witnessed the events they described and thus these accounts were
equally vulnerable to the errors identified above. Depending on when they were
written or published, any account could easily contain hearsay information and
the 'wisdom of hindsight'. Nevertheless, although the accuracy and objectivity of contemporary accounts written after the events they describe must pose
concerns, this does not necessarily mean that all the views expressed therein are
valueless. This is especially true if elements of an account are independently sub-
stantiated, for if certain facts can be verified it is reasonable for them to be used
even if they come from an account which is otherwise unreliable.

Thus, having taken these concerns into consideration, it is therefore perfectly
possible to identify information contained within contemporary accounts that is
free from these potential weaknesses – and therefore valid to cite and co-relate
with other reliable sources. Not all the primary evidence about intelligence-
gathering is dependent upon precise timings or exact geographic positions; the
accuracy and relevance of some reports can be accepted if they are corroborated

by other items of primary evidence, and if the accuracy of their evidence is otherwise unchallenged. Clearly any evaluation of contemporary accounts has to be careful and systematic, but at least some of their information can be relied upon when cautiously assessed and any potential bias is identified and taken into account. For example, it is generally accepted as a fact that the Battle of Naseby was fought on 14 June 1645. Similarly, there is little doubt that Charles I's army was defeated by the New Model Army commanded by Sir Thomas Fairfax. But exactly where it was fought, by how many soldiers, and how the battle developed – all these aspects remain imprecise and uncertain. The reason why we accept the accuracy of the date of the battle – and the identity of the commanders – is because those facts are corroborated by several contemporary sources.

It is also important to be aware of exactly which sources were available to – or have been used by – previous historians to inform their conclusions. Understandably, the earliest accounts of the Civil War published in England were written in the seventeenth century by the supporters of Parliament during the Interregnum, and this is reflected in the opinions they contain. Although these accounts of the conflict began to be compiled almost as soon as the fighting ceased in 1646, their authors made little mention of intelligence-gathering; nor did they make any attempt to assess the impact that intelligence operations had had on the outcome of the war. Their silence may be readily explained by the fact that intelligence-gathering has traditionally been shrouded in secrecy and the operations conducted in the seventeenth century were no exception. Thus, in 1647 when Thomas May, one of the official secretaries to the House of Commons, published his *History of the Parliament in England*, his account of the military actions was not only brief (and concluded with the First Battle of Newbury in September 1643),[3] but his descriptions of intelligence-gathering were also extremely limited. Although his *History* contained a few references to the intelligence aspects of the conflict, they were generalised observations, and did not include any assessment of the impact of intelligence operations.[4]

More interestingly, in the same year that May published his *History*, Joshua Sprigge, Sir Thomas Fairfax's former chaplain, published an influential book entitled *Anglia Rediviva*. Although it did contain a brief summary of the earlier years of fighting (when Fairfax was not in command), as Sprigge had been appointed by Fairfax to be secretary to the New Model Army, *Anglia Rediviva* was essentially an account of the actions of that army whilst under the command of Fairfax himself.[5] What is of particular relevance to this book, however, is that, probably due to his personal insight into the factors which influenced the operations of the New Model Army, Sprigge's work described the significant contribution that intelligence-gathering had made to Parliamentarian campaigns. Consequently, military intelligence reports were mentioned in substantially more detail than in May's narrative. For example, Sprigge gave a detailed account of the extensive and precise intelligence received by Fairfax during the weeks preceding the battles of

Naseby and Langport.[6] Sprigge's account is also corroborated by contemporary news pamphlet reports as well as other contemporary accounts. It thus not only appears to be valid, but it is also the first published work to acknowledge the important contribution made by intelligence information. Therefore, it is of particular significance that contemporary publications recognising the part played by intelligence were thus available to subsequent historians as early as 1647. Although *Anglia Rediviva* was reprinted in 1854, few subsequent historians appear to have taken the opportunity to evaluate the validity of Sprigge's recognition of the role played by intelligence-gathering.

It is of equal importance that corroboration of Sprigge's account was not long in coming. John Rushworth's *Historical Collections* – first published in 1659 – also acknowledged the impact that intelligence information had had upon the eventual outcome of the conflict. Although Rushworth's position both as Cromwell's secretary and as a long-term Parliamentarian civil servant made him vulnerable to immediate Royalist challenges of bias, distortion and suppression, there is no reason to discredit his description of intelligence operations as long as his accounts are verified wherever possible. As with many of the news pamphlet reports, Rushworth's account can be verified by comparison with reports in the *Calendar of State Papers Domestic* (*CSPD*) and in the journals of both Houses of Parliament, as these documents also contained numerous contemporary references to information provided by intelligence operations.

Rushworth's account is equally reliable when it details the variety of sources used to provide intelligence. For example, he describes how a letter from Colonel Goring in Holland to the King's secretary, Sir Edward Nicholas, was intercepted and read out to Parliament.[7] Rushworth also provided an early insight into the intelligence operations relating to the interception of mail, and he described the countermeasures introduced to stop intelligence reports from scouts and informants reaching the enemy, citing in this case the restrictions placed by Parliament on travel between Oxford and London.[8] His statement is verified by other contemporary accounts subsequently published in the *CSPD*.

It is interesting to contrast the limited presentation of intelligence in May's original work with the fuller accounts in Sprigge's *Anglia Rediviva* and Rushworth's *Collections* published just before the Restoration. Given their close connection with the army commanders, it is surely reasonable to conclude that Sprigge's and Rushworth's more detailed accounts reflect the fact that they witnessed the intelligence operations they described, and that by the end of the fighting in 1646 the Parliamentarian commanders were substantially more aware of the significance of military intelligence on the conduct of their campaigns earlier in the war than they had been when May was gathering information for his book. Sprigge's description of the intelligence received by Fairfax before the Battle of Naseby is a particularly good example of this increased awareness.[9] Whilst the primary evidence shows that the value of intelligence information was clearly understood by the Parliamentarian commanders, there is later contemporary evidence that the attitude of the Cavalier commanders towards intelligence-gathering was very different.

Understandably, it was not until the Restoration that Royalist accounts of the fighting began to be published in England. As these were by now describing events that had taken place up to 20 years before, their accuracy was even more vulnerable to challenge – especially as much of the relevant Royalist intelligence documentation may have been burnt before Oxford was surrendered in June 1646.[10] In these Royalist accounts, the conduct of, and impact made by, military intelligence received minimal attention. The Royalist authors tended to concentrate on the more strategic issues – such as the causes of the war – and they tended not to provide a detailed analysis of military events. The absence of any apparent Royalist recognition of the significance of intelligence-gathering operations conducted during the conflict is especially striking when compared with the clear descriptions – and associated awareness – of the role played by intelligence that had been displayed in several Parliamentarian accounts.

It is, therefore, particularly significant that Clarendon's *History* contains a most interesting description of the character of Lucius Carey, Viscount Falkland, which was written after his death at Newbury in 1643. This description provides a most revealing insight into some of the more senior Royalists' perceptions of intelligence-gathering. As Charles' Secretary of State, Falkland was not only one of the King's most senior and closest advisers, but he was also the man with overall responsibility for intelligence-gathering for the crown, just as Thomas Cromwell, Cecil and Walsingham had carried out this duty for the Tudor monarchs. According to Clarendon, Falkland considered that, whilst the use of military scouts was honourable and their reports were therefore trustworthy, the use of spies to obtain information through deception and other clandestine methods was inherently deceitful and the information obtained thereby was therefore unreliable. Clarendon recorded that Falkland would not trust people who 'by dissimulation of manners, wound themselves into such trusts and secrets as enabled them to make discoveries for the benefit of the state', because 'such instruments must be void of all ingenuity and common honesty.'[11] Clarendon went on to add that Falkland considered that the 'opening of letters upon a suspicion that they might contain matter of dangerous consequence' was a 'violation of the law of nature, that no qualification by office could justify a single person in the trespass.'[12] Falkland's evident reluctance to employ spies may help to explain why, at least during his time in office, the Royalist high command took such an ambivalent approach to the gathering of intelligence. However, whilst intelligence-gathering by military personnel developed as the war progressed, Falkland's reservations regarding duplicitous behaviour can only have served to limit Royalist spying. If this opinion was widely held by Royalist commanders, it is hardly surprising that the Cavaliers' use of intelligence was comparatively hesitant.

Initially, however, it is possible that the more senior – and possibly more traditional – commanders on both sides had reservations about the methods used to obtain intelligence information. Even as late as 1644, Essex wrote to the Committee of Both Kingdoms that 'scouts are useful to prepare officers and men for the worst but well grounded intelligence is to be obtained only from a party of the army commander by one whom we may confide in.'[13] This statement suggests that Essex was not entirely persuaded by the intelligence that was being received, and that he would only believe information that came from individuals whom he himself personally knew and trusted. It was many years before the premise that honest people could use deceitful means to obtain reliable information became more widely accepted.

This Royalist ambivalence was reflected in Sir Edward Hyde's (Clarendon's) *History of the Rebellion* when it finally appeared between 1702 and 1704.[14] The completed work was a substantial publication of sixteen books bound together in six volumes. It was viewed as historical writing on a grand scale and, as Clarendon had been an active participant in many of the political events he described, the book achieved a degree of credibility which many of the earlier contemporary publications had lacked. Due to Clarendon's descriptive analysis and personal comment, his *History* provided a level of insight that was unmatched by the other contemporary histories of the Civil War. However, as Clarendon had no military background and had not witnessed all the battles that had been fought during the conflict, he had to rely on the accounts of others for much of his commentary on military matters. Thus, although his *History* endeavoured to assess the outcome of military operations in a more comprehensive manner than had been attempted by earlier contemporary historians, Clarendon was often merely repeating what he had been told.[15] Nevertheless he did make some general assessments, including, on several occasions, evaluations of the contribution which had been made by intelligence information.[16] Crucially, Clarendon appears to have been most unimpressed by the value of intelligence and his *History* includes some very dismissive comments about the effectiveness of intelligence-gathering.[17] So, although Clarendon's is the most celebrated Royalist account, and has found great favour with many subsequent historians, his description of military intelligence-gathering is hardly as balanced or impartial as present-day historians might wish. So how valid are Clarendon's assessments of the Civil War – including his perception of intelligence-gathering – and do they merit the credibility that subsequent historians have given them?

The background to Clarendon's *History* is complicated but relevant to an understanding of the shape and scope of the final publication. From the very beginning of the enterprise in March 1646, when Charles I had agreed that Clarendon should write the Royalist historical account of the Civil War, the latter had formed a clear view of the purpose of the work. The expectations of the two men appear to have differed from the start for, while Charles was seeking to produce a justification of his political and military actions, Clarendon believed that he was required to write a private paper of advice which would be presented to the King for his personal attention.[18] Clarendon made a good start on this paper (which would later be incorporated into the book), writing at some length about the political build-up to the outbreak of war, a series of events in which he had been personally involved. However, as his own experience of the subsequent fighting was very limited, he had to seek contributions from the relevant Royalist commanders. Here Clarendon encountered significant problems as neither Prince Rupert nor the Duke of Newcastle would contribute to his *History*. Clarendon had to stop work while he sought alternative descriptions from other senior Royalists. He eventually received contributions from Sir Edward Walker, who had been the King's military secretary; Sir Hugh Cholmley who had been governor of Scarborough at the time of the Battle of Marston Moor; and Sir Ralph Hopton, who had been commander of the Royalist Western Army.[19] The accuracy of parts of Hopton's account may be verified by comparison with those of other Royalist commanders such as Colonel Slingsby. When the King was executed in 1649, Clarendon temporarily stopped his work as Charles' death led him to review his reasons for writing the book. He had already completed the first seven books; these described the political and military events that had taken place before Prince Rupert's relief of Newark in 1644.

In 1660 Clarendon returned to England with Charles II and was appointed Chancellor. He did not take up his pen again until some time after 1667 when he was banished to France for a second time as a result of his involvement in the failure of the Second Dutch War. As Clarendon had not taken any of his papers with him when he left England at the start of this second banishment, when he returned to his writing in France, he concentrated upon his autobiography, a piece of work which inevitably became a justification of his own personal and political activities. It was only when his son visited him in 1671 – bringing with him the unfinished manuscript of his *History* and the associated papers – that Clarendon decided to complete it. As he remained determined to 'earn literary fame as a historian',[20] Clarendon decided to combine the manuscript of his autobiography with the manuscript of his earlier work in order to produce an updated and more comprehensive version of events.

Although Clarendon's decision to proceed in this way is perfectly understandable, the consequence of his decision was that the finished *History* became especially vulnerable to accusations of bias, inaccuracy and distortion. Of particular relevance to any assessment of military intelligence is the animosity that Clarendon bore towards Prince Rupert and other Royalist military commanders.[21] This animosity seems very likely to have distorted Clarendon's account of the effectiveness of Royalist military intelligence because Prince Rupert's appointment as Lieutenant-General of Horse gave him key responsibilities in this particular area of military operations. Therefore those aspects of Clarendon's conclusions that reflect upon Prince Rupert, and any associated intelligence-gathering operations, need to be checked especially carefully to confirm that they are accurate.[22] It is particularly important to note that Clarendon's *History* included comments on the quality, as well as the content, of the military intelligence which was received and acted upon by Civil War commanders. His comments therefore provide the only Royalist equivalent to the similar qualitative assessments which were made by the Parliamentarian historians. Although Clarendon based the factual content of his *History* on the contributions of others, he could not resist the temptation to add comments and summaries of his own. It was thus inevitable that the self-justification that was evident in Clarendon's autobiography would also influence and distort the objectivity of his *History*.[23] It is necessary to make this point because, of all the contemporary published accounts of the English Civil War, Clarendon's *History* appears to have been the account most heavily relied upon by subsequent historians.

Not all of Clarendon's *History* is totally suspect, as parts of it were based on the first seven books completed by 1648; these books covered earlier political events in which Clarendon had been closely involved. However, because of Clarendon's personal animosities and aversions, it is prudent to be sceptical about some of the statements which appear. Perhaps the historians of the eighteenth and nineteenth centuries – who often relied upon Clarendon's work as an accurate primary source – were unaware of the potential weaknesses of his text. This was perhaps unsurprising, as many of the contemporary Civil War texts which questioned the accuracy of Clarendon's account had not yet been placed in the public domain. A source of possibly even greater illumination was the increased availability of primary source material which was made possible by more ready access to the resources of the British Museum. For example, the foundation of the Camden Society in 1838 and the Chetham Society in 1843, followed by the publication of the Calendars of State Papers and the creation of a new Public Records Office (1862), the Historical Manuscripts Commission (1869) and the *English Historical Review* (1886) all encouraged the growth of more critical analysis of the events of the 1640s. The significance of this analysis was that it shone more light on some of the more specific and local aspects of intelligence-gathering operations during the Civil War – light that may not have been available to earlier historians. Although reservations about the political objectivity of Clarendon's *History* were voiced almost as soon as the book appeared, questions about its historical accuracy only began to be considered when, in 1904, Sir Charles Firth published a series of articles in the *English Historical Review* when he questioned the accuracy of Clarendon's work and suggested that historians should check with other contemporary sources before relying on the *History*.[24] However, for whatever reason, Clarendon's account continued to be widely used, and seemingly without being corroborated against many – or sometimes any – of these other more recently available primary sources.

And so the situation remained largely unaltered for almost 200 years, for the next major contribution to our understanding of Civil War intelligence operations did not take place until Sir Charles Firth, the eminent Victorian historian, wrote a number of books and articles which reflected his particular interest in intelligence operations. As Firth conducted more research into the contemporary accounts, he was able to describe the intelligence operations in more detail, and he was thus the first historian to not only to acknowledge the crucial role that intelligence-gathering had played in the English Civil War, but also to identify military intelligence-gathering as being one of the key factors in the Parliamentarian victory. Indeed in his assessment of the New Model Army, Firth claimed that 'one of the [main] causes of the success of Fairfax and Cromwell was the efficiency of their intelligence department.'[25] There is no evidence to indicate what triggered Firth's sudden interest in Civil War intelligence operations. It may have been due to the fact that Firth was writing at a time when Rudyard Kipling's novels on the Great Game – the intelligence-gathering operations on the North West Frontier of India – were stimulating considerable professional interest as well as attracting a widespread popular readership.[26] This growth in public interest this may well have been a factor in arousing his enthusiasm for the subject of intelligence-gathering.

In January 1897, Firth made an important contribution to the understanding of Civil War military intelligence when he wrote an article for the *English Historical Review* which considered the activities of Thomas Scot – one of Oliver Cromwell's intelligence officers – during the Interregnum.[27] This account concentrated mainly on Scot's work as an 'intelligencer' during the Commonwealth and demonstrated how the intelligence-gathering operations conducted during the English Civil War had been developed and continued during the Interregnum – especially by John Thurloe during the Protectorate of Oliver Cromwell. Firth also edited the Duchess of Newcastle's biography of her husband, which contained a number of references to Royalist intelligence-gathering operations.[28]

However, Firth's main contribution to our understanding of English Civil War military intelligence is contained in his book *Cromwell's Army*, first published in 1902. Although this book concentrated on the equipment and administration of the New Model Army, Firth also included the first overarching assessment of the contribution that military intelligence operations had made to the final outcome of the conflict. Firth was also the first historian to identify some of the Parliamentarian soldiers and civilians who had held and developed the post of Scoutmaster-General during the 1640s.[29] More scoutmasters continued to be appointed during the subsequent fighting during the so-called Second and Third Civil Wars (which ended with the Battle of Worcester in 1651). Indeed, as Cromwell had continued to initiate intelligence-gathering operations during the Protectorate – and had established the basis for future national intelligence operations – Firth's work should have become a logical starting point for historians studying military intelligence after the Civil War period.[30]

Possibly coincidentally, another challenge to Clarendon's perceptions of the value of intelligence-gathering began to emerge towards the end of the nineteenth century when a more focused interest in the impact of the Civil War within particular districts of the country began to emerge in local and regional histories. Reflecting perhaps the greater public access to this seventeenth-century documentation, explorations of local Civil War history began to delve more deeply into the detail of local contemporary records. The authors of these local history studies soon began to discover substantial evidence of local intelligence-gathering activities described in the contemporary accounts. It is probably reasonable to suppose that this contemporary evidence had remained undiscovered by the earlier, and more strategic, national historical assessments as these accounts had had neither the space, nor the need, to delve deeply into the local records.[31] However, although research for several of these local histories unearthed hitherto unconsidered evidence of effective and wide-ranging intelligence-gathering, their authors were understandably aiming to show how these intelligence operations affected local events rather than providing a broader national evaluation of the possible strategic impact of regional operations. It seems, therefore, that no wider conclusions were drawn from the discovery of 'local' evidence of intelligence-gathering – and no more comprehensive or national exploration of these regional accounts was embarked upon at that time. Nevertheless, this regional research suggested two valid conclusions: firstly, it suggested that intelligence-gathering on a local scale had been far more extensive that had been acknowledged hitherto, and secondly that the extent of this local intelligence-gathering, if collated and considered from a national level, would have challenged the widely-held perception that intelligence-gathering had not played a significant role in the outcome of the fighting.[32]

It appears that, increasingly, scholars writing on the local dimensions of the Civil War were being confronted with the dilemma that the primary evidence they had uncovered tended to contradict the perceptions (or misconceptions?) of intelligence-gathering presented by Clarendon in his *History*. One way of dealing with this factual mismatch was to concentrate upon the local situation without drawing any wider implications. For example, J. W. Willis-Bund's account of the action at Powick Bridge incorporated the account of the skirmish provided by Clarendon, even though this account contained a number of statements contradicted by other contemporary accounts of the engagement, but Willis-Bund made no comment on the discrepancy.[33] Another example of how military intelligence operations were reported in these regional studies is provided by Mary Coate's account of the skirmish at Sourton Down (25 April 1643). In a particular passage, Coate recorded how a Parliamentarian Army quartermaster 'saw three of Hopton's scouts and hurriedly rode back to warn Chudleigh (the Parliamentarian commander) that the enemy (Hopton) was within two miles'. Coate concluded that this 'should have taught both armies the necessity of accurate intelligence', a remark that shows that some regional historians, at least, were beginning to appreciate the potential national implications of the military advantages provided by accurate intelligence information.[34] Whilst books like these provided ample evidence of active and widespread intelligence operations being conducted in every community, they seldom if ever included any specific analysis of the part that intelligence might have played on the outcome of the Civil War – either in that particular region, or nationally. The need for a broader, national assessment of Civil War military intelligence was thus often implied, but never satisfied as historians continued to defer to the received wisdom epitomised by Clarendon's work.

Later on, twentieth-century research into the impact that the Civil War had upon local communities and regional operations was increasingly enlightened by the publication of the edited versions of Civil War manuscripts. These local studies continued to reveal the extent to which communities were involved in the conflict and revealed increased emphasis on the intelligence-gathering support provided by local people. Of the more recent local histories, John Wroughton's *An Unhappy Civil War,* describes in detail the impact and nature of local intelligence-gathering operations in Gloucestershire, Somerset and Wiltshire, whilst Tony MacLachlan's accounts of the Civil War in Hampshire and Wiltshire also contain interesting insights into the conduct of intelligence operations.[35] Roy Sherwood's study describes the Civil War in the Midlands, while David Cooke's book about the fighting in Yorkshire draws heavily on an evaluation of the intelligence operations conducted by Fairfax's Scoutmaster-General, Leonard Watson.[36] Although Clarendon continues to be cited regularly in these local histories, it is interesting to note that the regional histories also draw upon a much wider range of contemporary accounts, including Sir Samuel Luke's *Journal* and *Letterbook*, for much of their primary evidence on intelligence-gathering.

Despite all the work carried out by Firth, and the subsequent findings of the local historians, it is nonetheless disappointing to have to record that their initiatives into the impact of nationwide intelligence-gathering upon the outcome of the Civil War, and the questionable reliability of perceptions contained in Clarendon's *History,* were not taken forward for many years. It was not until after the Second World War that historians began to re-evaluate the earlier assessments which had been made of the contribution of intelligence operations to the outcome of the Civil War. The increased awareness of the significance of intelligence was probably due to the military experiences of the 1940s, coupled with the steady increase in editions of contemporary manuscripts which appeared shortly after the war. The publication in 1950 of the *Journal of Sir Samuel Luke*, edited by I.G. Phillip, was followed in 1963 by the publication of the *Letter Books of Sir Samuel Luke,* edited by H.G. Tibbutt.[37] As Luke was the original Parliamentarian Scoutmaster-General, these publications provided historians with an invaluable insight into the depth and breadth of seventeenth-century intelligence work.

It is also possible that public interest in intelligence-gathering and espionage was boosted by Ian Fleming's James Bond and subsequently by John le Carre's

George Smiley novels; perhaps that these novels reflected (and even helped create) a general perception that carrying out intelligence-gathering operations was a commendable occupation. Moreover, those historians who had served in the military between 1939 and 1945 would have fully appreciated the value of intelligence information. With their personal experience to guide them, they were arguably better attuned to the references about intelligence-gathering in the historical sources relating to the Civil War.

Thus a new understanding of military intelligence during the mid-twentieth century led to a fresh appreciation of the significance of English Civil War intelligence-gathering and its impact upon military operations. As mentioned earlier, this coincided with the publication of a number of edited collections of original primary material. These edited collections would prove invaluable to historians as they revealed the true extent of Civil War military intelligence-gathering operations by providing, for the first time, a detailed assessment and description of what intelligence-gathering work had been put in place during the conflict. During the last few decades, scholars have thus enjoyed a much wider variety of contemporary sources. Especially significant in this respect has been R.N. Dore's edition of the *Letter Books of Sir William Brereton*, another senior Parliamentarian commander who, like Sir Samuel Luke, appreciated the need for accurate intelligence.[38] As the Parliamentarian commander in Cheshire, Brereton established an efficient intelligence operation that provided invaluable information, particularly at critical stages of the Naseby campaign. Although lacking a military background, Brereton showed an immediate awareness of the importance of intelligence-gathering and his correspondence contains numerous examples of how the Roundhead intelligence-gathering organisation provided comprehensive, coordinated assessments to the senior Parliamentarian commanders.[39] Equally important was the fact that Brereton's fellow commanders appreciated the value of the intelligence he provided.[40] Regrettably, the relevance of this rich source of information to the broader subject of military intelligence-gathering during the Civil War was not appreciated by the editor of Brereton's *Letter Books* and, as a result, the work has not had the wider effect on the historiography of the topic that it might otherwise have done.

The historian who eventually took up Firth's long discarded initiative to carry out a detailed investigation of the military intelligence aspects of the Civil War was Peter Young, a graduate of Trinity College, Oxford who led a commando brigade during the Second World War. His military experience helped him recognise the full impact of military intelligence on the outcome of individual battles and campaigns.[41] Although the main priority of Young's work was to use contemporary accounts to establish the size and composition of the Royalist and Parliamentarian armies, his detailed analysis of the way Civil War battles were fought explained which factors had influenced the outcome of those battles – and ultimately the outcome of the war. The problem that faced Young was that there was so much contemporary Civil War military material to consider that he had to prioritise the subjects he chose for further assessment. Analysis of the impact that military intelligence had had on the outcome of the Civil War initially took a much lower priority, although he provided useful assessments of the role played by intelligence in each campaign.[42] Although Young never discussed in any detail how each side developed their intelligence capability, nonetheless such operations were never far from his mind, as is evident from the following comment on the Battle of Cropredy Bridge:

> Incidentally, it may be remarked that although the intelligence services on both sides in the Civil War is generally written of as rudimentary, both Charles and Waller do seem to have been apprised pretty quickly of every movement of the enemy during these critical weeks of June 1644.[43]

This was the first time since Firth's day that a historian had acknowledged that some Civil War intelligence operations were being conducted effectively. Young's evaluation of the contemporary evidence had established that the intelligence provided by both sides during the Cropredy Bridge campaign had been accurate and that each side had received regular reports of the enemy position and strength.[44]

Another source of information about intelligence operations may be found in the biographies of Civil War commanders, as the research for these accounts delved more deeply into the evidence of the contemporary accounts, and provided useful insights into the way the men used the intelligence information they received. Perhaps because historians had been inspired by the spate of autobiographies of senior Second World War military commanders published during the 1950s – many of which included discussions of how intelligence-gathering operations had influenced the outcome of campaigns and battles – the 1960s saw a resurgence of interest in the contemporary accounts describing the overall conduct of intelligence operations during the English Civil War.[45] This resurgence took the form of specific research into the contemporary accounts of the Civil War commanders themselves, which revealed the interest the commanders had taken in intelligence operations. The publication of further biographies of the leading Civil War commanders such as Oliver Cromwell and Sir Ralph Hopton shed yet more light on the matter.[46] F.T.R. Edgar's biography of Sir Ralph Hopton was one of the first studies specifically to assess a Royalist commander's use of military intelligence.[47]

During the 1970s, biographers devoted a good deal of attention to the contemporary accounts of the intelligence-gathering activities of Civil War commanders, Prince Rupert being a favourite subject. In 1976, for example, Maurice Ashley published a biography of the Prince which devoted special attention to Rupert's methods of intelligence-gathering and the importance he attached to intelligence information in general.[48] Later biographies, including one by Kitson, confirmed Rupert's enthusiasm for intelligence.[49] Kitson's subsequent assessment of Cromwell's generalship clearly identified the advantages he had gained from the effective use of military intelligence, a fact which had hitherto been obscured by Cromwell's own tendency to attribute his successes to God, 'destiny' and 'pre-determinism' rather than to his intelligence-gatherers.[50]

However, although almost all the biographies produced during this period made some reference to the contemporary accounts of intelligence-gathering, most of them drew no wider conclusions about the overall effectiveness and conduct of nationwide intelligence operations – nor their impact upon the outcome of the war.[51] Recently, a more strategic assessment has been provided by Stanley Carpenter's account of six Royalist and Parliamentarian commanders which has shown that the Roundhead plans in northern England were heavily dependent on precise intelligence.[52] The most recent assessment of the generalship of the Civil War commanders, published by Malcolm Wanklyn in 2010, includes, unlike earlier assessments, a much fuller evaluation of the use of intelligence by the individual commanders.[53] However, as will be described in the next chapter, these biographies did not always attribute the military successes of these commanders to the information they received, but rather to their military intuition.

Further areas of study which have shed light on the nature of Civil War intelligence operations have been investigations into the social dimensions of the conflict, informed by the contemporary primary sources. Over the last 40 years, many publications about the Civil War have enhanced our understanding of how military intelligence-gathering operations were supported at all levels of seventeenth-century society. This research has shown that loyalties were divided right across the country and that even the most humble individuals were often prepared to take sides.[54] The studies have shown that it was possible for each side to receive active support in every part of the country – even if, at times, that support might have had to be covert rather than overt depending on which party had achieved local superiority. Thus it would have been perfectly feasible for 'intelligencers' to have operated throughout the entire kingdom, as reflected by these recent studies.[55]

Foremost amongst these accounts is Charles Carlton's *Going to the Wars* in which the author describes the extent to which intelligence operations had an impact on the lives of civilians as well as on the campaigns. This evaluation of the role played by ordinary people in intelligence-gathering has recently been continued by Diane Purkiss.[56] Further research into contemporary records has also revealed the role that women played in seventeenth-century intelligence-gathering. Antonia Fraser focused attention on this aspect of intelligence operations in her book, *The Weaker Vessel* (1984), which described the involvement of Anne, Lady Halkett in Royalist intelligence work.[57] This theme was continued by Roger Hudson in his book, *The Grand Quarrel,* published in 1993, and Alison Plowden made further pertinent observations in her study of the roles played by women during the English Civil Wars which was published in 1998.[58] But the most detailed account of the part played by women in to appear so far has been produced by Marcus Nevitt.[59] In his study of women and pamphlet culture during the English Civil War, Nevitt describes the life and activities of Elizabeth Alkin whose husband had been executed as a spy by the Royalists. Also known as 'Parliament Joan', Elizabeth played an active and successful role in a wide range of intelligence operations for several years – although perhaps more as a 'Mrs Moneypenny' than as a 'Bond girl'! Nevitt's description of how Alkin provided Parliament's pamphlet editors with some of their information provides much useful background information on the conduct of intelligence operations in the mid-seventeenth century.

In recent years, electronic access to contemporary news pamphlets has become much more widely available. Using the evidence of these pamphlets, the intelligence-gathering associated with the work of Royalist propagandists was described in P.W. Thomas' account of the propaganda work of Sir John Berkenhead, the editor of the Royalist pamphlet, *Mercurius Aulicus*.[60] More recently, Angela Macadam's DPhil thesis has provided an equally interesting comparative insight into *Mercurius Britanicus*, the Parliamentarian rival to *Mercurius Aulicus*, which first appeared at the beginning of 1643. Her account of the Marston Moor campaign describes how the news pamphlets published 'accurate' and 'excellent' intelligence during that campaign.[61]

These studies into contemporary accounts have all helped to establish that the ordinary people of seventeenth-century England had the desire as well as the capability to support and actively contribute to intelligence-gathering operations. They have shown that both civilian and military personnel supported a wide range of spying and scouting tasks, displaying great bravery and innovation. It is now clear that intelligence-gathering operations were conducted across the entire country, and that there were people determined to support their own favoured side, notwithstanding the considerable personal risks they ran.

In recent years, historians of British military intelligence, such as B.A.H. Parritt and Peter Gudgin, have also offered some interesting insights into the intelligence skills that were developed during the war.[62] Other accounts of the international intelligence operations conducted during the Stuart period have, however, relied heavily upon Clarendon's work.[63] A new area of intelligence-gathering has been revealed by a recent exploration of the contemporary accounts of the development of codes and ciphers; these have shown that Parliament could decipher Royalist coded messages from 1643. The work of these scholars has suggested that, whilst the use of codes and ciphers had an increasing impact upon the conduct of military operations during the conflict, their main impact was upon the more strategic and political aspects of the Civil War.[64]

Perhaps as a result of the greater awareness of the significance of intelligence since the end of the Cold War, coupled with greater access to the evidence of the contemporary seventeenth-century accounts, the most recent reappraisals of the Civil War campaigns and major battles have now begun to explore the subject of intelligence in far more detail than hitherto. This long overdue extension of our use of contemporary sources has confirmed the extent of the intelligence-gathering operations.

The research conducted for Barbara Donagan's recent monograph on the Civil War in England has enhanced our understanding of how intelligence operations influenced the outcome of the fighting.[65] It not only supplies the most comprehensive summary to date of the full scope of such operations, but also considers in much more detail than any previous work the contributions of the scouts, deserters, messengers and spies who provided intelligence information during the conflict.[66] The monograph includes discussion of the communication and interception of intelligence and thus provides an invaluable starting point for a further exploration of how intelligence operations materially influenced the campaigns. Most recently of all, Julian Whitehead's more general account has set the conduct of intelligence operations within a broader description of the Civil War and Commonwealth. Only about a third of Whitehead's work discusses the events of the period 1642–1646, and this discussion 'relied heavily' on Clarendon's *History*.[67] Although Whitehead does include references to Luke's writings,[68] as he himself acknowledges, his account draws predominantly upon secondary sources.[69] As a result, his summary of the First English Civil War intelligence operations does not provide the detailed evidence of intelligence-gathering contained in the contemporary accounts – which makes it more difficult for his account to reflect the full contribution made by military intelligence to the events he describes.

It would appear from the research conducted for this book that, although some of the contemporary accounts contained in either seventeenth-century manuscripts, news pamphlets or other publications contain inaccuracies, there remains a substantial body of consistent and corroborated contemporary evidence which confirms that military intelligence-gathering played an increasingly important part in the military operations of the Civil War. As the war continued, the importance of the cross-checking of information became more widely recognised and the variety and sophistication of intelligence sources increased. The evidence of the earliest contemporary accounts, first published by Parliamentarian sympathisers during the Interregnum, has shown clearly that military intelligence-gathering was conducted with increasing effectiveness during the war and that it was recognised to have made a significant contribution to the final decisive battles. Although the Royalist accounts do not reflect a similar appreciation of the importance of intelligence-gathering as has been expressed in Parliamentarian records, given the substantial evidence that is contained in the contemporary accounts of the final battles, it is surprising that subsequent historians do not appear to have recognised the significance of intelligence operations and thus not alluded to it in their later historical accounts.

There are two main reasons for this absence of references to military intelligence in the majority of the historical accounts of the English Civil War. Firstly, military intelligence-gathering operations are traditionally shrouded in secrecy and, as those of the English Civil War were no exception, it is possible that many early historians were just unaware of the available evidence. Secondly, there can be little doubt that the absence of detailed analysis of all the contemporary sources of primary evidence owes much to the perception of ineffective intelligence operations delivered with such a heavy hand in Clarendon's *History*. It is highly likely that Clarendon's dismissive perception that Civil War intelligence-gathering was largely ineffective and irrelevant to the outcome of the conflict influenced many who followed. Not even general histories of military intelligence have assessed Civil War operations;[70] for example, John Keegan's recent analysis starts with the Napoleonic Wars.[71] This lack of attention has served to reinforce Clarendon's misconception about intelligence-gathering for, as recently as 2009, Blair Worden described military intelligence during the English Civil Wars as 'rudimentary',[72]

It was not until specific and tightly focused areas of research led to more penetrating studies of the primary evidence that the full extent of, and contribution made by, Civil War intelligence-gathering was properly revealed. The publication of edited versions of key contemporary accounts has now begun to be reflected in many of the most recent accounts of the Civil War and it is reassuring to note that the significance of the intelligence-gathering operations of Luke, Watson and Brereton have become included more frequently. It is, therefore, particularly encouraging to note that these recent studies have allowed us to better understand the overall contribution made by intelligence information to the outcome of the First English Civil War.

Notes

1 B. Worden, *The English Civil Wars 1640–1660* (London, 2009), p.69.
2 J. Whitehead, *Cavalier and Roundhead Spies. Intelligence in the Civil War and Commonwealth* (Barnsley, 2009).
3 T. May, *The History of the Parliament of England* (London, 1647).
4 Ibid, p.56. Eight years later, May published a further account of the conflict entitled *A Breviary of the History of the Parliament of England* (London, 1655). This follow-up work made even fewer references to intelligence operations; nor did it make any assessment of their impact on military operations. See May, *Breviary*, pp.250–252, 319, and 343–346.
5 J. Sprigge, *Anglia Rediviva. England's Recovery* (London, 1647, reprinted Oxford 1854).
6 Ibid, pp.26–37 and 59–71.
7 J. Rushworth, *Historical Collections* (London, 1659–1699), Part III, Volume II, pp.69–70. Later volumes of Rushworth's work were published in 1699.
8 Ibid, pp.314 and 367.
9 Sprigge, *Anglia Rediviva*, pp.27–33.
10 M. Toynbee (ed.), *Official Papers of Captain Henry Stevens, Wagon-master general to King Charles I, November 1643 – December 1644* (Oxfordshire Record Society, 1961), p.12.
11 Clarendon, *History*, Book VII, p.226.
12 Ibid, p.226.

13 Ibid, p.15.

14 Clarendon, *History,* passim.

15 See C.H. Firth, 'Clarendon's History of the Rebellion', *English Historical Review* (Volume 19, 1904), pp.44–46.

16 See, for example, Clarendon, *History,* Book VI, pp.78–80; Book VII, pp.149–154 and 225–226; and Book IX, pp.36–38.

17 See, for example, Clarendon, *History,* Book VI, p.79; and Book IX, p.38.

18 Firth, 'Clarendon's History', p.32.

19 Ibid, pp.44–46.

20 Ibid, p.465.

21 This animosity is made very clear at various different places in his text. See, for example, Clarendon, *History*, Book VI, p.78.

22 R. Hutton, 'Clarendon's History of the Rebellion', *English Historical Review* (Volume 97, 1982), p.88.

23 Firth, 'Clarendon's History ', pp.24–54, 246–262, and 464–483.

24 See, for example, Firth, 'Clarendon's History ', p.473.

25 C.H. Firth, *Cromwell's Army* (London, 1902, 1962 edition), p.67.

26 Kipling worked as a journalist in India between 1882 and 1889. He wrote *Plain Tales from the Hills* in 1888, *Soldiers Three* in 1892 and *Kim* in 1901.

27 C.H. Firth, 'Thomas Scot's Account of his Actions as Intelligencer during the Commonwealth', *English Historical Review* (Volume 12, No. 45, 1897), p.116.

28 C.H. Firth (ed.), *The Life of William Cavendish, Duke of Newcastle* (London, 1906), pp.29, 32–34, 36, 39, 47–48, 52–53, 56, and 60–62.

29 Firth, *Cromwell's Army*, p.65. Firth obviously concentrated on Parliamentarian scoutmasters and made only passing reference to a few of the Royalist scoutmasters. A number of Civil War scoutmasters are listed in Annex 1 to this book.

30 B.A.H. Parritt, *The Intelligencers: The story of British Military Intelligence up to 1914* (Ashford, 1971), p.4.

31 See, for example, Phillips, *Memoirs of the Civil War in Wales*; Godwin, *Civil War in Hampshire*; and J. W. Willis Bund, *The Civil War in Worcestershire* (Birmingham, 1905).

32 Godwin's *Civil War in Hampshire* provides numerous examples of intelligence operations. See, for example, pp.14, 57, 71, 112, 120, 140–145, and 173–177.

33 See D. Sarkar, *The Battle of Powicke Bridge* (Worcester, 2007). Mr Sarkar highlights the dangers of relying upon Clarendon's accounts of local military actions (p. 8).

34 M. Coate, *Cornwall in the Great Civil War and Interregnum 1642–1660* (Oxford, 1933), p.65.

35 J. Wroughton, *An Unhappy Civil War. The experiences of Ordinary People in Gloucestershire, Somerset and Wiltshire 1642–1646* (Bath, 1999), pp.165 and 214–218; T. MacLachlan, *The Civil War in Wiltshire* (Salisbury, 1997), pp.104, 158 and 198; and T. MacLachlan, *The Civil War in Hampshire* (Salisbury, 2000), pp.176–177 and 319.

36 R. Sherwood, *The Civil War in the Midlands 1642 – 1651* (Stroud, 1992), pp.44–45 and 140–141; and D. Cooke, *The Civil War in Yorkshire: Fairfax versus Newcastle* (Barnsley, 2004), pp.129, 132 and 136.

37 I. G. Philip (ed.), *The Journal of Sir Samuel Luke* (3 volumes, Oxfordshire Record Society, 1950); and H.G. Tibbutt (ed.), *The Letter Books of Sir Samuel Luke: 1644–45* (Historical Manuscripts Commission JP4, HMSO, 1963).

38 R.N. Dore (ed.), *The Letter Books of Sir William Brereton* (two volumes, Lancashire and Cheshire Record Society, 1984–90), Volume I, pp.80 and 172. (The original letters are held in the British Library, Add MSS, 11331–11333).

39 Ibid, pp.118 and 177.

40 Ibid, p.233.

41 See, for example, P. Young, *Edgehill 1642* (Moreton-in-Marsh, 1967); P. Young, *Marston Moor 1644* (Moreton-in-Marsh, 1970); and P. Young, *Naseby 1645* (London, 1985).

42 See, for example, Young, *Edgehill*, pp.74–75; Young, *Marston Moor*, pp.80–84; and Young, *Naseby*, pp.216–221.

43 M. Toynbee and P. Young, *Cropredy Bridge 1644* (Kineton, 1970), p.73.

44 Ibid, p.68.

45 See, for example, A. B. Cunningham, *A Sailor's Odyssey* (London, 1951), p.325; and W. Slim, *Defeat into Victory* (London, 1956), p.186.

46 F.T.R. Edgar, *Sir Ralph Hopton. The King's Man in the West (1642–1652)* (Oxford, 1968); and A. Fraser, *Cromwell: Our Chief of Men* (London, 1974).

47 Edgar, *Hopton*, pp.125–126.

48 M. Ashley, *Rupert of the Rhine* (London, 1976), p.29.

49 P. Morrah, *Prince Rupert of the Rhine* (London, 1976), p.127; and F. Kitson, *Prince Rupert. Portrait of a Soldier* (London, 1994), pp.63–65.

50 F. Kitson, *Old Ironsides. The Military Biography of Oliver Cromwell* (London, 2004), pp.219 – 222.

51 See, for example, Stucley, *Grenville*, p.134; and Adair, *Waller*, p.80.

52 S.D.M. Carpenter, *Military Leadership in the English Civil Wars, 1642 – 1651: 'The Genius of this Age'* (London, 2005), p.73.

53 M. Wanklyn, *The Warrior Generals. Winning the British Civil Wars 1642–1652* (New Haven and London, 2010), pp.6, 18– 20, 22– 24, 39, 48– 52, 59– 60, 69, 73, 94, 110– 111, 115– 117, 137, 149, 160– 162, 255 and 273.

54 D. Underdown, *Revel, Riot and Rebellion* (Oxford, 1985), p.1; and M. Stoyle, *Loyalty and Locality* (Exeter, 1995), p.231.

55 Carlton, *Going to the Wars*, pp.263–264.

56 Purkiss, *Civil War*, pp.410–11. See also B. Donagan, *War in England: 1642 – 1649* (Oxford, 2008), pp.100–106, 110 and 113.

57 A. Fraser, *The Weaker Vessel* (London, 1984), p.211.

58 R. Hudson (ed.), *The Grand Quarrel* (Stroud, 1993); A. Plowden, *Women all on Fire The Women of the English Civil War* (Stroud, 1998).

59 M. Nevitt, *Women and the Pamphlet Culture of Revolutionary England 1640 – 1660* (Aldershot, 2006), pp.97–120.

60 P.W. Thomas, *Sir John Berkenhead, 1617 – 1679 A Royalist Career in Politics and Polemics* (Oxford, 1969), pp.45–47.

61 A. Macadam, 'Mercurius Britanicus: Journalism and Politics in the English Civil War' (unpublished DPhil Thesis, University of Sussex, 2005), pp.73 and 77.

62 Parritt, *Intelligencers*, p.4; P. Gudgin, *Military Intelligence - A History* (Stroud, 1999), pp.2–6.

63 See, for example, P. Aubrey, *Mr Secretary Thurloe, Cromwell's Secretary of State 1652–1660* (London, 1990); A. Marshall, *Intelligence and Espionage in the Reign of Charles II, 1660–1685* (Cambridge, 1994), pp.18–21; and R. Hutchinson, *Elizabeth's Spy Master: Francis Walsingham and the Secret War that saved England* (London, 2006).

64 D. Kahn, *The Code-Breakers: The Comprehensive History of Secret Communication from Ancient Times to the Internet* (New York 1967, revised 1996), pp.166–169, and J. Whitehead, *Cavalier and Roundhead Spies Intelligence in the Civil War and Commonwealth* (Barnsley, 2009), pp.223–229.

65 Donagan, *War in England*, pp.100–106, 110 and 113.

66 Ibid, pp.95–114.

67 Whitehead, *Cavalier and Roundhead Spies*, p.235.

68 Philip, *Journal of Sir Samuel Luke*; and Tibbutt, *Letter Books of Sir Samuel Luke*.

69 Whitehead, *Cavalier and Roundhead Spies*, pp.235–237.

70 See, for example, T. Fergusson, *British Military Intelligence, 1870 – 1914* (London, 1984); and P. Gudgin, *Military Intelligence a History* (Stroud, 1999).

71 J. Keegan, *Intelligence in war: Knowledge of the enemy from Napoleon to Al Qaeda* (New York, 2003).

72 B. Worden, *The English Civil Wars 1640–1660* (London, 2009), p.69.

9

Military Intelligence – A Walk in the Dark or the Deciding Factor?

This book has two aims: to explore the background of the current historical perception that, because military intelligence played no significant part in the English Civil War, it therefore had little impact upon deciding the outcome of the key battles, and secondly to test the validity of the assertion that English Civil War military commanders were quite accustomed 'to walk in the dark' because their military intelligence was so inadequate that they had no accurate knowledge of where their foes were or what they were doing. The detailed exploration of the surviving contemporary accounts, summarised in the preceding chapters, has shown that there exists a substantial body of evidence which demonstrates beyond reasonable doubt that military intelligence played a significant – and at times decisive – part in the military resolution of the conflict. As this assessment represents a new departure from much of the current historiographical orthodoxy, *To Walk in the Dark* will conclude with a review of that orthodoxy before summarising the extent to which military intelligence was a significant factor in determining the outcome of the fighting.

So what has this detailed assessment of the contemporary and subsequent historical accounts told us about the perceptions – or misconceptions – of previous historians? The analysis of the subsequent historical reporting of the impact of intelligence operations on the outcome of the First English Civil War has shown that, although there was a great deal of contemporary evidence to show that intelligence had played a significant part in determining the outcome of the fighting, this evidence had largely been overlooked. As many subsequent accounts appear to have relied upon Clarendon alone for their primary evidence, it is hardly surprising that Clarendon's perception of intelligence-gathering has thereby been perpetuated. Only where historical research has penetrated beyond Clarendon's *History* has the full extent of contemporary intelligence-gathering operations been revealed.

The research associated with this book has shown that previous assessments of the contribution made by military intelligence have tended to reach one of two widely divergent conclusions. The most widely accepted conclusion, normally reached by those historians writing general surveys of the conflict, continues the long-standing tendency to dismiss the role of intelligence as 'rudimentary,'[1] 'primitive,'[2] or 'erratic'.[3] On the other hand, scholars presenting more focused accounts of individual campaigns – or analyses of specific regional or technical aspects of the fighting – have normally reached the very different conclusion that military intelligence played a significant part. This recognition began relatively recently with Firth's 1902 study of *Cromwell's Army,* followed by Godwin's 1904 account of the fighting in Hampshire, and, 30 years later, by Mary Coate's treatment of the Civil War in Cornwall, in which she described the impact of intelligence information in some detail.[4] More recently, this recognition has been emphasised in Jon Day's review of the 1643 Gloucester and Newbury campaign in which he recounted how Essex had received 'a mass of accurate information from Oxford, the camps at Gloucester and Sudeley, and garrisons across central England.'[5] Day's account went on to describe how Luke's men 'had provided real time reporting of Rupert's movements' and that it was one of them who had 'delivered the snippet that saved Essex's army from envelopment north of Tewkesbury'.[6]

The most plausible reason for these widely divergent conclusions is suggested by a consideration of the extent to which primary evidence was explored by the individual historians. The books and articles focusing on particular campaigns and specific issues have invariably drawn on the full range of the relevant available contemporary sources. It is this analysis of the primary evidence that has revealed the existence of an increasingly sophisticated intelligence organisation which delivered a large amount of intelligence information to each side. On the other hand, those historians who have sought to provide a more strategic overview of the Civil War have not needed to explore the military aspects of the conflict in any depth and have therefore, perhaps understandably, been quite content to rely more extensively on the general perceptions of intelligence-gathering presented by Clarendon in his *History.* As the earlier chapters of this book have shown, relying on Clarendon has its risks as there is a substantial body of contemporary evidence to support the conclusion that intelligence operations played a much more decisive part in the Civil War than Clarendon either realised or was prepared to acknowledge. Clarendon's assertion that, during the Edgehill Campaign, 'neither army knew where the other one was'[7] influenced legions of subsequent historians, who tended to simply repeat this statement as if it were an established fact. For example, both Gardiner and Warburton repeatedly echoed Clarendon's assessment, apparently oblivious of the growing number of contradictory contemporary accounts that were by then available.[8] Indeed, Warburton's comment that, at Edghill, 'the two great armies were in total ignorance of each other's movements' would appear to reflect Clarendon's perception exactly.[9]

However, such was Clarendon's academic and political status, the validity of his assessment of Civil War military intelligence operations remained unchallenged until Sir Charles Firth evaluated Clarendon's *History* more thoroughly. As Firth had also explored the role of intelligence-gathering in his account of the New Model Army, he was thus not only the first historian to explore the accuracy of Clarendon's account of the Civil War by testing it extensively against other contemporary accounts,[10] but he was also the first to draw the conclusion that 'one of the causes of the success of Fairfax and Cromwell was the efficiency of their intelligence department.'[11] His exploration identified a number of areas where the primary evidence of the contemporary accounts contradicted Clarendon's conclusions.[12] But, although Firth's warning that Clarendon's account should be used with caution was reiterated by Ronald Hutton in 1982,[13] the orthodox view that military intelligence had been ineffective throughout the war remained unchallenged at the national level. Hardly surprisingly perhaps, the wider implications of the findings of the local historians that intelligence information had played an important part in determining the strategic outcome of the Civil War were not immediately followed up.

Peter Young's later work into the military aspects of the Civil War provided yet another instance of the more detailed 'local' studies contradicting the 'national' perceptions that military intelligence-gathering operations were ineffective. But, because Young focused his research upon the military aspects of the fighting, his assessments of the contribution made by the military intelligencers were inconclusive. Thus his assessments of the key Civil War battles did not include detailed explorations of the impact that intelligence had had upon their outcome. One exception may be found in his joint assessment with Margaret Toynbee of the Cropredy Bridge campaign in which, as we have seen, they acknowledged that 'although the intelligence of both sides in the Civil War is generally written off as rudimentary, both Charles and Waller do seem to have been apprised pretty quickly of every movement of the enemy.'[14]

Since Young's day, the role played by intelligence has continued to be obscured by conflicting scholarly opinion. Some of the more recent assessments of Stuart intelligence operations have continued to reflect Clarendon's perception. For example, Alan Marshall has asserted that 'intelligence activities were on a primitive level and that most civil war battles were more often the result of armies meeting accidentally rather than as any intelligence coup.'[15] Yet, during the same period, many other historians, including Glenn Foard, Jon Day, David Cooke and Peter Reese, have noted that intelligence-gathering operations had a significant impact on the outcome of key Civil War campaigns. Perhaps Peter Reese's account of the life of General George Monck – the Royalist officer captured by Fairfax at Nantwich in 1644, who became Cromwell's commander in Scotland before the restoration of Charles II in 1660 – contains the most revealing comment about the extent to which Civil War commanders had, at last, appreciated the value of intelligence information. Reese reminds us that Monck had written that 'intelligence is the most powerful means to undertake brave Designs and to avoid great ruines.'[16]

A characteristic of many of the 'strategic' historical studies of the Civil War is that the true contributions made by intelligence-gathering often tend to be over-looked. In these accounts, information is cited about an event without necessarily exploring how that information was obtained. For example, several times in his assessment of Civil War military leadership, Stanley Carpenter refers to generals' military 'intuition' which he suggests is 'the firm knowledge of events, terrain, the nature of the enemy and one's own troops.'[17] Whilst this is undoubtedly true, Carpenter does not appear to acknowledge that 'the firm knowledge' is invari-ably based upon analysis of intelligence. Nor does he concede that it is usually intelligence information which, in turn, has provided the basis for the subsequent 'intuition' that successful generals then displayed. If historians do not make any specific correlation between the implicit contributions made by intelligence-gathering and the outcome of consequent military actions, it is hardly surprising that, consequently, the contribution will not be recognised.

This lack of recognition has often hampered any effective assessment of the impact of intelligence upon Civil War military actions. Again, Carpenter's account of the Civil War operations in the North includes several references to Parliamentarian 'superior generalship', but seemingly fails to acknowledge that it was often better-quality intelligence information that had provided the Parliamentarian commanders with the opportunity to demonstrate this superior-ity. For example, Carpenter cites one occasion when the Royalists had been able to seek reinforcements because they 'had heard of [Lambert's] approach',[18] and, in another example in March 1644 during the action around Bradford, Carpenter describes how Lambert had been able to defeat the Royalists because he had 'realised the enemy's vulnerability'. In neither case does Carpenter acknowledge the contribution most probably made by intelligence-gathering. Although the contemporary accounts of Sir Thomas Fairfax provide clear evidence that he himself recognised the need for accurate and timely intelligence to inform his decisions, the significance of this is not specifically acknowledged by Carpenter. This failing can be found in many other historical accounts where generals are said to have 'heard' or 'learnt' of some significant event, without considering the source of the information.[19]

As having accurate intelligence is valueless unless the commanders make use of that information, it is therefore equally important to assess the use the com-manders made of the intelligence they received. The primary evidence shows very clearly that, after an erratic beginning, both sides invested more effort in intelligence-gathering operations as the conflict progressed. As has been shown in the preceding chapters of this book, the memoirs and letters of the main Civil War military commanders, such as Fairfax, Waller, Newcastle and Hopton, contain numerous specific references to the insights offered by their intelligence information.[20] Indeed, these commanders' own accounts provides first-hand evidence that intelligence was frequently critical to their successes.[21] Furthermore, it is equally apparent from the contemporary accounts that, after Edgehill, the Parliamentarian commanders were quicker to appreciate the military benefits of accurate intelligence than their opponents. Consequently they implemented a more comprehensive and effective intelligence-gathering organisation more rapidly than the Royalists – and gained the advantage accordingly.

The contemporary accounts also reveal that the coordination and dissemination of intelligence information was invariably carried out far more effectively by the Parliamentarian Committees than by the Royalist Council of War. The primary evidence indicates that it was not until the victory at Lostwithiel in 1644 that the Royalist Secretaries of State responsible for intelligence-gathering, who were based in the court at Christ Church College in Oxford, began to realise just how much valuable information could be provided by an effective intelligence organisation. However, by mid-1644 there was little opportunity for the Royalist to improve their intelligence organisation substantially enough to influence the outcome of the fighting. By comparison, the contemporary accounts show that the Parliamentarian commanders appear to have realised the value of intelligence information significantly earlier than their Royalist opposite numbers. Indeed, as we have seen, there is good contemporary evidence to suggest that – unlike the majority of their Roundhead opposite numbers – some Royalists regarded the reliability of their intelligencers and their information with an unwarranted degree of suspicion.

On exploring the development of intelligence organisations by Civil War commanders, it appears that Essex was the first Captain General to appoint a Scoutmaster-General. The contemporary accounts also indicate that the Parliamentarians were the first to appoint scoutmasters as part of their County Associations – although these appointments were later to be emulated by the Royalists.[22] Whilst both sides widened the establishment of intelligence organisations as the fighting spread, and improved their postal communications in order to be able to pass the information generated more quickly and securely, contemporary sources provide substantially more evidence of superior Parliamentarian intelligence-gathering. In particular, the writings of Brereton and Luke describe an increasingly responsive and innovative intelligence-gathering operation and this conclusion is supported by the evidence contained in other contemporary accounts; for example, in William Lilley's observations about the Parliamentarian intelligence-gathering organisation in Oxford.[23] We do know that similar Royalist operations were in place; for example, Prince Rupert appointed Sir William Neale as his Scoutmaster later in 1643, and a spy network was set up as late as 1644–45 by John Barwick in London but, as far as we can tell from the primary sources, the impact of Royalist intelligence operations was less decisive.[24]

Certainly there is no evidence that the Royalist commanders ever established a postal interception and deciphering organisation as effective as that run by the Parliamentarians from 1643 onwards. As 1645 progressed, the capture and decoding, first of the King's correspondence at Naseby, and subsequently of Digby's correspondence when it was captured at Sherborn in October 1645, provides clear proof that the Parliamentarians were able to decipher – and subsequently publish – the greater part of their enemies' intercepted messages. This exposure caused enormous damage to the Royalists' integrity and their political plans, and weakened the commitment of their supporters. Moreover, as the Parliamentarians steadily gained control of more territory, so their sources of intelligence increased – and the Royalist intelligence sources diminished accordingly. As the battles of Edgehill, Highnam, Newbury and Naseby had demonstrated to the Parliamentarians (just as Lostwithiel had to the Royalists), there were definite intelligence advantages to be gained from fighting battles in areas where the majority of the local populace favoured one's own cause.

However accurate and timely the intelligence reports, they were of no – or at best only limited – value unless they were used by commanders in time to influence the outcome of military actions.[25] As this book has shown, in the majority of cases, Civil War commanders acted upon their intelligence information in a timely manner, thereby allowing that information to make a potentially important contribution to the outcome of local military actions and skirmishes. Nonetheless, there were occasions when intelligence information was not used to the best possible effect. For example, in 1644, the Parliamentarian armies of Essex and Waller, operating together, had an excellent opportunity to assault Oxford, capture the King, and bring the war to a decisive end. Essex's subsequent decision not to continue to cooperate with Waller, to divide the Parliamentarian forces and then to command Waller to cover and contain the Royalist Oxford Army while Essex led his own army to the west, wasted a rare opportunity for Essex to use the Parliamentarian numerical superiority to defeat Charles decisively at the beginning of 1644. As has been described, further military opportunities were lost by Parliamentarian commanders later in that year during the Second Battle of Newbury. Up until this point, the successes and failures of intelligence operations had been fairly evenly shared between the Royalist and Parliamentarian commanders. Of particular significance perhaps, the Roundhead commanders in the North appear to have had more faith in their intelligencers and they promptly heeded the reports they received. This appears to be particularly true of Sir Thomas Fairfax who, whether he was serving under his father's command when storming Wakefield or serving further south in command of the New Model Army at the decisive battles of Naseby and Langport, always took careful note of his intelligence information. The only Roundhead commander to set aside his intelligencers' reports was Meldrum whilst besieging Newark – a significant error of judgement as Rupert defeated him conclusively a few hours later.

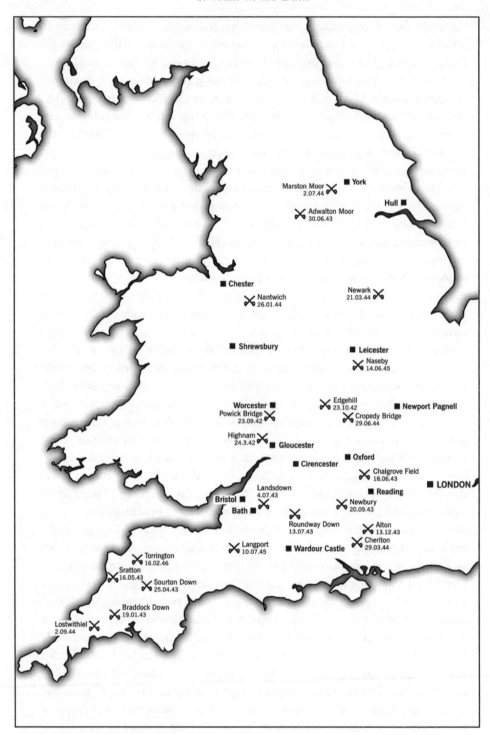

The battlefield sites, 1642–1646.

Despite the concern which some individual Royalists clearly had about the integrity – and hence the reliability – of intelligencers, the senior Cavalier commanders generally responded well to their intelligencers' reports. Research for this book has revealed only two significant examples of accurate and dependable intelligence not being effectively used by Royalist commanders. One was during the Gloucester campaign when the Royalist commanders did not respond quickly enough to their intelligence of Essex's move towards Cirencester after he had relieved the siege of Gloucester.[26] The other is Rupert's rejection of Newcastle's intelligence that the Allied armies before York were likely to split up and go their separate ways once York had been relieved. In both cases, the Royalists lost the subsequent military actions (at Newbury and Marston Moor). Had the Royalists acted promptly upon those pieces of intelligence the subsequent events of the Civil War would almost certainly have been very different. However, in 1645, the contemporary evidence shows that the Royalist intelligence operations were markedly inferior to those of the Parliamentarians. This enabled the more accurate and timely Parliamentarian intelligence to contribute significantly to the decisive victories won by Fairfax at both Naseby and Langport – victories which won the war for Parliament.

The second aim of this book was to establish the impact that intelligence-gathering operations had upon the outcome of the English Civil War. The evidence revealed by the research which has been carried out makes it very clear that intelligence-gathering operations were conducted widely and that intelligence information made a decisive contribution to the Parliamentarian victories at Naseby and Langport (as cited above), just as it had contributed to the earlier Royalist victories at Newark and Lostwithiel. Contrary to Clarendon's perception, much useful military information was derived from a variety of intelligence sources. Not only do the surviving writings of Civil War generals confirm their dependence upon timely intelligence reports, but the wider recognition of the importance of intelligence is also confirmed in the accounts of the fighting by other participants. For example, primary evidence of the passing of intelligence information is provided not only by both Parliamentarian and Royalist soldiers – such as Nehemiah Wharton and Richard Symonds[27] – but also by senior Cavalier and Roundhead officers, such as Colonels Slingsby and Birch.[28] There is primary evidence that the interception of mail and deciphering of messages was used increasingly from 1643 onwards.[29] The news pamphlets of the period also provide numerous examples of the publication of military intelligence. Of course, not all of this information was correct – and some of it was contradictory – but the primary evidence shows clearly that the importance of gathering military intelligence was recognised by both sides from very early on in the war. An analysis of Firth's manuscript copies of Prince Rupert's correspondence with his commanders, held in the Bodleian Library, reveals that almost two thirds of all these letters contained intelligence information about the Parliamentarian forces.[30]

The reporting of counter-intelligence operations also confirms that Civil War commanders recognised the significance of the impact that intelligence was having upon the outcome of the fighting and shows that they were determined to take the strongest actions to block the flow of information to their opponents. The Bullman affair, described in Chapter Two, provides clear evidence of the early determination to eliminate the threat posed by successful enemy intelligencers, and shows how arbitrary and ruthless actions were taken to eliminate such men and the intelligence provided by them. In addition to the traditional sources of information provided by scouts, the very nature of the civil conflict facilitated the active participation of local people. As in any civil war, the participation of the population created considerable problems for both sides as it made identification of the true enemy more difficult, particularly when the conflict offered local people many opportunities to provide information, food and money, or to carry messages. The steady increase in civilian participation in the conflict resulted in correspondingly violent behaviour from the soldiers of both sides as they sought to extract money, information or confessions from local people, and there is considerable evidence of increasing coercion as the war progressed.[31] Indeed, in the printed 'Catechisms' which were produced for the guidance of combatants on both sides, soldiers were increasingly authorised to use 'torments … in some cases … to finde out the truth'.[32] Contemporary accounts have provided many examples of brutal treatment being afforded to civilians on the pretext of legitimate military interrogations. For example the Cavalier journal, *Mercurius Rusticus*, described how the steward of the Royalist Sir John Lucas, was 'pricked with drawn sword [and] a dozen candles [were] lighted … and held to and under his hands, and lighted match [was] applied between his fingers' in an attempt to extract information.[33] The primary sources makes it clear that the soldiers themselves believed that the local population frequently participated in intelligence-gathering operations, and that they drew little distinction between spies, messengers and 'intelligencers'.

For many years, historians have striven to identify the crucial factors which enabled Parliament to defeat the King decisively. It seems unassailably logical to suggest that Parliament won the Civil War because its armies won the final major battles.[34] But which military-related factors enabled the Parliamentarian armies to win those battles? Was intelligence the factor which decided the outcome of the English Civil War? Could intelligence operations have made possible an earlier conclusion to the fighting? Earlier chapters of this book have shown that, although intelligence operations had enabled the Parliamentarian forces to win local superiority by defeating a number of the Royalist commanders, it would not be until Charles himself had been decisively defeated in the field that the Royalists would be forced to negotiate an agreement with Parliament. Several factors have been frequently cited by scholars as reasons for the Parliamentarians' eventual success, for example, the fact that Parliament controlled most of the more densely populated and wealth-producing centres of the country – particularly London.[35] Likewise the Parliamentarian control of the navy has been identified as another major factor in their final victory. Frequently, the superiority of Parliamentarian munitions and materiel has also been cited as a decisive factor – along with their numerical superiority (especially after the intervention of the Scottish Army in 1644).[36] However, the significance of many of these factors has been challenged subsequently. For example, further research has revealed that, due to the continual problem of not having enough ships, the navy was not always able to intercede decisively on all occasions around every part of the coastline.[37] Similarly, it has been suggested that initial shortages of Royalist arms and munitions had been largely overcome by the arrival of the Queen's resupply ships at Bridlington in 1643.[38] But, in addition to these debates, another important factor which goes a long way towards explaining the Parliamentarians' military successes has hitherto been almost entirely overlooked. This factor was intelligence information.

The contribution made by intelligence-gathering grew as each side sought to gain the local superiority needed to facilitate the recruitment of more soldiers and the gathering of more money and supplies. For example, contemporary accounts reveal that the intelligence information received by the heavily-outnumbered Parliamentarian Army in the North was of critical importance in enabling Fairfax to keep the much larger Royalist forces embroiled, and thereby prevent the Earl of Newcastle from sending reinforcements to join the main Royalist field army at Oxford in 1643. Further south, intelligence information was vital to the military success of both Hopton and Waller as they struggled to prevent either side sending reinforcements to their main army. As historians are now beginning to realise, intelligence played a decisive role in a number of the key battles regardless of whether they were won by the Royalists or the Parliamentarians. Whilst the previous chapters have identified strong evidence of active and comprehensive intelligence-gathering operations being conducted throughout the conflict, the most important evidence revealed by this book is that which suggests that military intelligence made a critical contribution to the outcome of the decisive battles fought in the 1645 campaign.

Contrary to Marshall's perception that Civil War battles 'were more often the result of armies meeting accidentally,'[39] the contemporary sources confirm that intelligence informed and influenced every major military action from Edgehill to Langport. Although Clarendon denigrated the contribution made by intelligence operations to the Edgehill campaign, there is clear evidence that the proceedings of the Royalist Council of War during this campaign were being reported regularly to Essex by Blake, the Parliamentarian spy. The contemporary evidence suggests that Essex delayed his pursuit of the Royalist Army as he was planning to trap it between two Parliamentarian armies – his own and the London Trained Bands. It also indicates that the Parliamentarian commanders had intelligence of the Royalist Council of War's intention to assault Banbury

Castle, although they were not aware that Charles subsequently changed this plan after Rupert's scouts reported the latest position of the Parliamentarian Army. Contemporary accounts show clearly that, when the Royalist scouts discovered the Parliamentarian Army on the evening before the battle, this intelligence was received in time for the Royalist Army to concentrate and take up its battle formation without hindrance from the Parliamentarian forces. If the Royalist scouts had not detected Essex's army on the evening of 22 October, it is perfectly possible that Essex's intelligence reports would have enabled him to monitor Charles' progress whilst he concentrated all his regiments and then he would have been well placed to spring his plan and trap the Royalist Army between his entire army and London's reinforced defences. As the confrontation at Turnham Green was to suggest, the result of any such engagement might well have resulted in a decisive Parliamentarian victory – a victory which would have had its roots in superior Parliamentarian intelligence.

There is a great deal of contemporary evidence of intelligence-gathering having an impact on the outcome of the subsequent campaigns in 1643. In a little reported yet decisive engagement, Waller used the intelligence of the Royalist dispositions around Highnam gathered by the Gloucester garrison to destroy Lord Herbert's 'Welsh' army before it could join the King. Later that year, Hopton realised that he had an advantageous opportunity to attack the Parliamentarian Army at Stratton, near Bude, when he received the information that Stamford had unwisely divided his army and detached his horse whilst within striking range of his enemy – a decision that suggests the Parliamentarians were not fully aware of the position and strength of the Cavalier forces. When countering Hopton's advance towards Oxford, accurate intelligence informed Waller's movements before the battles at Lansdown and Roundway Down. But despite the advantages his intelligence had given him, Waller lost those battles because the fighting skills of the Roundheads were outmatched by the remarkable courage of the outnumbered Royalist forces.

Contemporary 1643 accounts of Fairfax's engagements with Newcastle's forces in the North also provide evidence of how intelligence informed the deployment of both armies. It was the failure of his men to carry out his orders that caused Fairfax's Roundheads problems at both Seacroft Moor and Adwalton Moor – not a failure of intelligence because both Fairfax and Newcastle possessed accurate information about their opponents. Intelligence also played a particularly important role in the Roundheads' victories in the Gloucester and Newbury campaigns at the end of the year. Initially faulty Royalist intelligence persuaded Charles that Gloucester would surrender to him personally and caused him to become embroiled in the siege of Gloucester; subsequently accurate and timely Parliamentarian intelligence enabled Essex to manoeuvre his army in such a way as to defeat all Royalist attempts to isolate and overcome him in the Cotswolds. Of crucial importance to the success of the Parliamentarian breakout from Gloucester was the intelligence reported by Luke's spies, for these reports enabled Essex not only to break clear from the steadily encircling Royalist forces, but also to capture a substantial supply convoy that had just arrived at Cirencester; the supplies from this convoy helped Essex to break away (just as their loss hampered the plans of the pursuing Royalists). Although the Royalist Army was subsequently able to win the race and get to Newbury first, the superior Parliamentarian scouting of the battlefield provided important topographical intelligence which enabled Essex's army to gain a decisive advantage by occupying key geographic features on the morning of the battle. At the very end of 1643, Parliamentarian intelligence-gathering gave Waller key information about the Royalist dispositions and scouting activities – information which allowed him to decisively defeat Hopton's forces at Alton.[40]

Clear evidence of the impact of accurate and timely intelligence information also emerged throughout the campaigns of 1644. Accurate intelligence of the problems facing Byron at Nantwich enabled Fairfax and Brereton to combine and win a decisive victory over the Royalist forces on 26 January. A little later and further south, the contemporary evidence shows that both Waller and Hopton were receiving accurate intelligence which informed their manoeuvres before the Battle of Cheriton on 29 March. The contemporary accounts of the battle reveal that it was an impromptu Royalist attack, apparently made without the knowledge or consent of the Royalist commanders, which was the root cause of the Royalist defeat – not faulty intelligence. The contemporary accounts of the subsequent campaigns of 1644 provide a mass of evidence to show that intelligence played a significant part in each action. Rupert's marches to relieve the sieges of Newark and, later in the year, of York, were both informed by accurate information about the Parliamentarian positions. At York, Newcastle possessed relevant intelligence about the inherent instability of the relationships of the Allied army commanders, intelligence which Rupert set aside in his desire to carry out what he considered to be the King's higher priority order to engage the Parliamentarian/Scottish Army at Marston Moor. There is some contemporary evidence to suggest that the late attack of the Allied Army was ordered following the receipt of the information that the Royalist Army was standing down for the evening.

The actions further south at Cropredy Bridge and Lostwithiel also reflect the impact of intelligence-gathering as there is a substantial body of primary evidence which shows that, whilst both Waller and Charles were equally well informed by their scouts and intelligencers during the Cropredy Bridge campaign, the Cavaliers' intelligence was so superior at Lostwithiel that it played a decisive role in the Royalist victory – especially as the Parliamentarian Army received virtually no intelligence throughout the time it had been isolated by the Royalist armies. The fact that Charles' senior advisors were surprised by the amount of intelligence they were receiving from the local people is an important indication of the relative paucity of such information that they must have been

receiving during their earlier operations around Oxford and the Thames Valley.[41]
As the 1644 campaigning season drew to an end, the failure of the Parliamentarian
commanders to win decisive victories around Newbury in the autumn may be
attributed partly to the failure of their intelligence organisation.

The war-winning campaigns of 1645 demonstrated just how decisive intelligence information could be. Both at Naseby and at Langport, it enabled the
New Model Army to engage the Royalist forces from a position of considerable
numerical and tactical superiority – and to win the decisive victories that had
so far eluded them since the indecisive Battle of Edgehill three years before. It
was accurate and timely intelligence that informed Fairfax of Goring's continued
embroilment around Taunton, and consistent intelligence that informed him of
the position of the Royalist Army, which allowed him to attack decisively at a
place and time of his own choosing. After Naseby, it was more accurate intelligence which notified him of the urgent need to move swiftly to the west, and
consequently to defeat Goring's forces decisively at Langport.

The appointment of Fairfax as Lord General was fortunate as it meant that the
New Model Army was commanded by a man whose experience in the northern
campaigns had made him well aware of the importance of using military intelligence to inform his plans. Not only was this awareness crucial to the outcome of
the 1645 campaign, but the movements of the Royalists, initially towards Chester
and then towards Newport Pagnell, also took their army into the areas controlled
by two other Parliamentarian commanders who were equally aware of the importance of intelligence-gathering – Sir William Brereton and Sir Samuel Luke. Yet
again, the evidence of the contemporary sources proves that the accurate intelligence provided by these two Parliamentarian commanders had a decisive impact
on the outcome of both the Battle of Naseby – where it both enabled Fairfax to
deploy the Parliamentarian Army at a distance outside the range of the Royalist
scouts – and also because it informed Fairfax that, as the Royalist Army remained
divided, he consequently had a marked numerical superiority. During the Battle
of Langport, Fairfax's timely intelligence not only allowed him to surprise the
Royalist cavalry the day before the battle, but it also informed him of Goring's
intention to retreat on the day on the day itself – information which allowed him
to attack the Royalist Army as it was off-balance.

The contribution of intelligence information to determining the outcome
of the final battles of the Civil War should not be underestimated. It allowed
Parliament to achieve the decisive victories over the King's armies which it
had sought to achieve since 1642 – victories which led to Charles' surrender
in 1646.[42] Of course, intelligence information did not win the battles by itself,
any more than the intelligence contained in the communications intercepts provided by Bletchley Park alone helped the Allies to win the Second World War.
But the intelligence gathered during the Civil War did a very great deal to help
the Parliamentarian armies to emerge victorious – just as failures in the Royalist

intelligence-gathering at critical times denied their commanders the intelligence they needed to tip the war in their favour. Thus the primary sources contain an overwhelming amount of evidence to show that intelligence operations merit recognition and inclusion as a significant factor in determining the outcome of the First English Civil War.

After the war, it is clear that the Parliamentarian commanders recognised the contribution which had been made by intelligence to their success. Consequently they consolidated and enhanced their recently acquired intelligence-gathering skills during the years of the Protectorate and Interregnum. It is particularly significant that, during his campaigns in Scotland, George Monck strengthened and extended the scoutmaster's role, insisting that it be maintained at a time when Cromwell was seeking to make reductions in Monck's force levels. As Monck wrote to Cromwell opposing his plans:

> There has been as much good service done for the public by the intelligence
> I have gotten by the help of a Deputy-Scoutmaster-General, than hath been
> done by the forces in preventing the rising of parties.[43]

The advantages of efficient scouting had been recognised by the Parliamentarian forces, for their scouting patrols played an important part in determining Cromwell's dispositions for the battles of Preston, Dunbar and Worcester.[44] There was no longer any delay in appointing a Scoutmaster-General to assist in the campaigns of the 1650s. Cromwell appointed a Dr Henry Jones, sometime Bishop of Clogher, to be his Scoutmaster-General during his operations in Ireland, whilst Mr George Downing was appointed as Scoutmaster-General during Cromwell's actions in Scotland.

During the Protectorate, the lessons of the Civil Wars were absorbed and the work of the intelligence services was widened. These improvements were not restricted to the military arena. On 1 July 1649 Thomas Scot was appointed by Parliament to a national position 'to manage the intelligence both at home and abroad'.[45] With the introduction of national postal services came the increased use of the interception and deciphering of mails to obtain intelligence information. Scot described how intercepted letters were 'deciphered by a learned gentleman incomparably able that way, Dr Wallis of Oxford', clearly a continuation and extension of his earlier work during the First English Civil War.[46] While Scot was in charge of intelligence-gathering, the number of informants was also steadily increased and intelligence reports were more widely accepted from loyal members of the local populace.[47] More people became involved in operations; some army officers, such as Colonel Joseph Bampfield, emerged as professional intelligence agents, but women also became more fully involved.[48] Of potentially most significance, however, was the formal acknowledgement of the importance of intelligence to national security when, in July 1653, the responsibility for all aspects of intelligence-gathering was formally placed under the control of John Thurloe, Cromwell's Secretary of State. Thurloe undertook the crucial role of coordinating the intelligence-gathering services and connecting them to the central offices of government.[49] Clearly the effectiveness of the intelligence services operated during the Interregnum was recognised for, at the Restoration, the Protectorate intelligence organisation was taken on by Charles II who thereby acknowledged that much of the national experience of intelligence-gathering had been drawn 'from the experience of its former enemies'.[50] Certainly Thurloe had created a structure which would provide a basis for intelligence-gathering 'for generations to come'.[51]

Research for this book has identified a number of avenues which would profit from further exploration by students of military intelligence in the English Civil War. For example, a detailed exploration of how the role of the scoutmaster was developed in the English regions between 1642 and 1646 would be most illuminating. Equally helpful would be further research into how spying was improved and its results incorporated into the national intelligence organisation that began to emerge during the Protectorate. An evaluation of the conduct of intelligence-gathering by the local county committees and associations would also be invaluable, as would further research into the funding of Civil War intelligence-gathering operations. The very considerable contemporary documentation which is still held in the National Archives relating to the funding and management of local organisations would provide invaluable assistance in this respect. In view of what this book has revealed, it would be interesting to review some more of the orthodox accounts of the other important Civil War campaigns – such as Adwalton Moor, Winceby and Torrington – in order to ensure that the impact of military intelligence upon the outcome of those campaigns has been comprehensively evaluated. Research into these subjects would not only supplement assessments of Thurloe's contribution to intelligence operations during the Interregnum, but would also provide an important link between previous research into Elizabethan intelligence operations and research into the subsequent developments of English intelligence operations after the Restoration.

The research which has been carried out for this book has shown clearly that the contribution made by intelligence operations to the result of the English Civil War was substantially more significant than has been acknowledged for the past 365 years. Even if it might be unjustified to claim that intelligence operations alone determined the outcome of the war, the evidence of the primary sources shows clearly that intelligence information played a much more significant and important role in determining the outcome of all the major Civil War battles than has been acknowledged by many subsequent historians. The intelligence factor in the battles of Naseby and Langport in particular was especially crucial as these engagements, more than any others, won the war for Parliament. The contribution made by military intelligence therefore deserves greater recognition as a key factor which influenced the outcome of the Civil War itself. The massive amount of evidence contained in the contemporary sources shows that, far from being 'primitive', the military intelligence techniques and organisation implemented during 1642 and 1646 not only assisted Parliament to defeat the Royalists, but that they also provided a solid foundation for the future development of military intelligence operations during the Protectorate and Restoration.

Notes

1 M. Toynbee and P. Young, *Cropredy Bridge 1644. The Campaign and the Battle* (Kineton, 1970), p.73.

2 A. Marshall, *Intelligence and Espionage in the Reign of Charles II, 1660–1685* (Cambridge, 1994), p.18.

3 B. Worden, *The English Civil War 1640–1660* (London, 2009), p.69.

4 C.H. Firth, *Cromwell's Army: A History of the English Soldier during the Civil Wars, the Commonwealth and the Protectorate* (London, 1902), pp.63–67; G.N. Godwin, *The Civil War in Hampshire (1642–45)* (London, 1904), pp.14, 18, 71–72, 112 and 173–177; and M. Coate, *Cornwall in the Great Civil War and Interregnum 1642–1660* (Oxford, 1933), pp.62, 65, 71, 75–79, 89, and 91.

5 J. Day, *Gloucester and Newbury 1643. The Turning Point of the Civil War* (Barnsley, 2007), p.217.

6 Ibid, p.217

7 E. Hyde, *The History of the Rebellion and Civil Wars in England, together with an Historical View of the Affairs in Ireland* (sixteen books, London, 1702–4), Book VI, p.79.

8 See, for example, E.G.B. Warburton, *Memoirs of Prince Rupert and the Cavaliers*, (three volumes, London, 1849), Volume II, pp.5–6, 10–11, 62, 101, 132, 209, 273–274, 287, 331, 349, 395 and 442; Volume III, pp.92–93 and 102–104; and S. R. Gardiner, *History of the Great Civil War 1642–1649* (four volumes, London, 1893), Volume I, pp.43, 87, 130, 150, 161–162, 169, 173, 198, 321, 362 and 372; Volume II, pp.16, 31–32, 209–211 and 242.

9 Warburton, *Memoirs*, Volume II, p.10.

10 See C.H. Firth, 'Clarendon's History of the Rebellion', *English Historical Review*, Volume 19 (1904).

11 Firth, *Cromwell's Army*, p.67.

12 See, for example, Firth, 'Clarendon's History', pp.44–46.

13 R. Hutton, 'Clarendon's History of the Rebellion', *English Historical Review* (Volume 97, 1982), p.88.

14 Toynbee and Young, *Cropredy Bridge*, p.73.

15 A. Marshall, *Intelligence and Espionage in the Reign of Charles II, 1660–1685* (Cambridge, 1994), p.18.

16 G. Moncke, Duke of Albermarle, *Observations upon Military and Political Affairs* (London, 1674), pp.35– 40.

17 S.D.M. Carpenter, *Military Leadership in the English Civil Wars, 1642–1651: 'The Genius of this Age'* (Abingdon, 2005), p.26.

18 Carpenter, *Military Leadership*, pp.85–86.

19 See, for example, C. Hibbert, *Cavaliers and Roundheads. The English at War 1642–1649* (London, 1994), p.206; J. Kenyon, *The Civil Wars of England* (London, 1988), pp.142–143; H.C.B. Rogers, *Battles and Generals of the Civil Wars 1642–1651* (London, 1968), p.228; and T. Royle, *Civil War. The Wars of the Three Kingdoms 1638–1660* (London, 2004), p.241.

20 See, for example, T. Fairfax, *Short Memorials of Thomas, Lord Fairfax* (London, 1699), p.416; *CSPD, 1644*, p.301; and Clarendon MSS, 1738, ff. 1, 4, and 6.

21 See, for example, Fairfax, *Short Memorials,* p.435; E. 97[2], *The Victorious and Fortunate Proceedings of Sir William Waller* (London, 12 April 1643); and Clarendon MSS, 1738, ff. 1, 4, and 6.

22 Anon, *A List of Officers claiming the sixty thousand pounds &c. granted by His Sacred Majesty for the relief of his truly loyal and indigent party* (London, 1663), pp.45 and 128.

23 See, for example, BL, Add MSS, 11331, f. 18; and BL, Add MSS, 11332, ff. 80–5; I.G. Philip (ed.), *The Journal of Sir Samuel Luke* (3 volumes, The Oxfordshire Record Society, 1947); and W. Lilley, *The Last of the Astrologers. A History of his Life and Times* (First published 1715, second edition Scolar Press, Yorkshire, 1974), p.77.

24 P. Barwick, *The Life of John Barwick* (London, 1728), p.46.

25 See Chapter 3, above.

26 See Warburton, *Memoirs,* Volume II, pp.203–204 and 287–288.

27 See, for example, *CSPD, 1642,* pp.391–392; and C. E. Long (ed.), *Richard Symonds: Diary of the Marches kept by the Royal army during the Great Civil War* (Camden Society, 1859), p.8.

28 See, for example, Bod. L, Clarendon MSS, 1738, ff. 2, 3 and 7; and J. Roe (ed.), *Military Memoir of Colonel John Birch* (Camden Society, 1873), pp.4, 50 and 70.

29 See, for example, C.H. Firth, 'Thomas Scot's Account of his actions as Intelligencer during the Commonwealth', *English Historical Review* (Volume 13, No. 51, 1897), p.527.

30 Bod. L, Firth MSS, C6 and C7, *Prince Rupert's Correspondence.* 334 out of the 569 letters which are contained in these two volumes reported intelligence about Parliamentarian forces.

31 See, for example, E. 103[3], *Mercurius Rusticus* (Oxford, 20 May 1643); and E. 106[12], *Mercurius Rusticus* (Oxford, 10 June 1643).

32 See R. Ram, *The Souldiers Catechisme* (London, 1646), p.10; and T. Swadlin, *The Souldiers Catechisme* (Oxford, 1645), p.11.

33 E. 103[3], *Mercurius Rusticus* (Oxford, 20 May 1643).

34 See, for example, M. Wanklyn, *Decisive Battles of the English Civil Wars: Myth and Reality* (Barnsley, 2006), pp.200–206.

35 C. Hill, *The Century of Revolution 1603–1714* (London, 1974), pp.99–100.

36 Wanklyn, *Decisive Battles,* p.203.

37 B. Capp, *Cromwell's Navy. The Fleet and the English Revolution 1648–1660* (Oxford, 1989), p.2.

38 M. Wanklyn and F. Jones, *A Military History of the English Civil War, 1642–1646. Strategy and Tactics* (London, 2005), pp.152–153.

39 Marshall, *Intelligence and Espionage,* p.18.

40 See Chapter 6, above.

41 See Chapter 7, above.

42 See Chapter 8, above.

43 BL, Clarke MSS, XL, f. 21.

44 See, for example, H.C.B. Rogers, *Battles and Generals of the Civil Wars 1642–1651* (London, 1968), pp.280–282; P. Reese, *Cromwell's Masterstroke. Dunbar 1650* (Barnsley, 2006), pp.77–78; and M. Atkin, *Cromwell's Crowning Mercy. The Battle of Worcester 1651* (Stroud, 1998), pp.60, 62 and 65.

45 *CSPD, 1649–50,* p.221. See also Marshall, *Intelligence and Espionage,* p.21.

46 C.H. Firth, 'Thomas Scot's Account of his Actions as Intelligencer during the Commonwealth', *English Historical Review* (Volume 12, No. 45, 1897), p.121.

47 Marshall, *Intelligence and Espionage,* p.22.

48 J. Loftus and P.H. Hardacre (ed.), *Colonel Joseph Bampfield's Apology: written by himself 1685* (London, 1993). See also J. Loftus (ed.), *The Memoirs of Anne, Lady Halkett and Ann, Lady Fanshawe* (Oxford, 1979).

49 P. Aubrey, *Mr Secretary Thurloe, Cromwell's Secretary of State, 1652–1660* (London, 1990), p.33.

50 Marshall, *Intelligence and Espionage,* pp.20 and 29.

51 Aubrey, *Mr Secretary Thurloe,* p.128.

Appendix

Royalist and Parliamentarian Scoutmasters

Royalist Scoutmasters

John Bennet
Bennet claimed to have been the King's scoutmaster in Berkshire.[1]

Sir Charles Blunt
Blunt was the son of Sir Richard Blount of Sissinghurst, Kent. He had been knighted in Ireland in 1618 and was appointed to the Oxford Army. Blunt was reported to be Scoutmaster-General to Prince Rupert at Brentford in 1642 and was still in post at Newbury in 1643.[2] In May 1644, Blunt was reported as being deputy governor of Donnington Castle, prior to being appointed Governor of Greenland House in 1644.[3] These appointments would have reflected the increasingly common practice of appointing scoutmasters as governors of front-line garrisons.[4] Shortly after being praised by the Earl of Forth,[5] Blunt was reportedly killed by one of his own officers during a scuffle with a sentry in Oxford in June 1644.[6]

George Bradbury
Bradbury claimed to have been the King's scoutmaster in Stafford.[7]

Ludowick Bray
Ray claimed to have been the King's scoutmaster in Nottingham.[8]

Thomas Cartwright
Cartwright claimed to have been the King's scoutmaster in Stafford.[9]

William Cockayne

Cockayne claimed to have been the Scoutmaster-General and Quartermaster General in Devon.[10]

John Edwards

Edwards claimed to have been the King's scoutmaster in Carmarthen.[11]

Thomas Hancks

Hancks claimed to have been the King's scoutmaster in Stafford.[12]

John Holland

Holland claimed to have been the King's scoutmaster in Leicester.[13]

Colonel Michael Hudson

Born in 1605, Hudson took holy orders and was appointed Rector of Cliffe, Northamptonshire in 1641. He served as a colonel under Newcastle and, in 1644, he was Scoutmaster-General to the Northern Army. He attended Charles I during his flight to join the Scots and was murdered in 1648.[14]

Captain Moore

On 8 April 1645, Moore was reported to have been scoutmaster to the Earl of Northampton.[15]

Sir William Neale

Described as six foot tall, very beautiful in youth, with great courage but a great plunderer and cruel,[16] Neale joined the staff of Prince Rupert in 1643 and was appointed as his Scoutmaster-General. He was present at the capture of Cirencester in 1643 and fought at relief of Newark when he helped save Rupert's life. Neale was appointed Governor of Hawarden Castle, Flintshire in 1644 and was ordered to surrender the castle in 1646. Neale then passed into obscurity; he died on 24 March 1691 and was buried in Convent Garden Church in London.[17]

Ralph Pierpoint

Pierpoint claimed to have been the King's scoutmaster in Hereford.[18]

James Roberts

Roberts claimed to have been the King's scoutmaster in Radnor.[19]

Sir Francis Ruce

Clarendon identified Ruce as the Royalist scoutmaster at the Battle of Naseby.[20]

William Smart
Smart claimed to have been the King's scoutmaster in Stafford.[21]

Mr Smith
Smith was identified as Scoutmaster-General of the Northern Army by the Duchess of Newcastle.[22]

Parliamentarian Scoutmasters

Samuel Bedford
Bedford was initially appointed as deputy to Sir Samuel Luke and was subsequently appointed Scoutmaster-General to the Committee of Both Kingdoms.[23]

George Bulmer
Captain Bulmer was identified as scoutmaster in the Thames Valley in 1643.[24]

John Gardiner
Gardiner was paid as scoutmaster to Colonel Sir John Noxworth's Kent regiment.[25]

John Harding
Harding was paid as scoutmaster to Colonel Sir John Noxworth's Kent regiment.[26]

Theodore Jennings
Jennings was identified as Scoutmaster-General to the Earl of Denbigh when he was captured and taken to Wallingford Castle.[27]

Kirby
When captured by the Royalists, Kirby was identified as the 'scoutmaster of Warwicke'.[28]

Sir Samuel Luke
Luke was appointed by Essex to be his Scoutmaster-General in January 1643. Subsequently he was appointed governor of Newport Pagnell in November 1643 and relinquished his post as part of Self Denying Ordinance (although he was extended in the post during the Naseby campaign).[29]

Name unknown
James Chudleigh, the Parliamentarian commander was clearly unimpressed by the 'intolerable neglect of our Deputy Scoutmaster' at Sourton Down on 25 April 1643.[30]

Major Patson

Patson was reported as being Scoutmaster-General to General Hammond at the surrender of Exeter.[31]

James Pitsom

Pitsom was reported as Sir William Waller's scoutmaster in 1644.[32]

Lieutenant-Colonel Roe

Roe was reported as being Scoutmaster-General to the City of London.[33]

Richard Terry

Terry was reported as being scoutmaster to Coventry.[34]

Leonard Watson

Watson had originally been appointed as Manchester's Scoutmaster-General in the Eastern Association. He was a keen supporter of Cromwell and he was appointed as Scoutmaster-General to the New Model Army in 1645.[35]

Notes

1 Anon, *A List of Officers claiming the sixty thousand pounds &c. granted by His Sacred Majesty for the relief of his truly loyal and indigent party* (London, 1663).

2 B. A. H. Parritt, *The Intelligencers: The story of British Military Intelligence up to 1914* (Ashford, 1971), p.4.

3 I. G. Philip (ed.), *The Journal of Sir Samuel Luke* (3 volumes, Oxfordshire Record Society, 1950), Volume III, p.258.

4 *CSPD, 1644,* p.163.

5 *CSPD, 1644,* p.163.

6 P.R. Newman, *Royalist Officers in England and Wales, 1642–1660* (New York, 1981), p.33. See also E. 50[26], *The Kingdomes Weekly Intelligencer* (London, 4–11 June 1644); and E. 50[32], *The Spie* (London, 6–13 June 1644).

7 Anon, *A List of Officers claiming the sixty thousand pounds &c. granted by His Sacred Majesty for the relief of his truly loyal and indigent party* (London, 1663).

8 Ibid.

9 Ibid.

10 Ibid.

11 Ibid.

12 Ibid.

13 Ibid.

14 N. Cranfield, *Michael Hudson* (DNB). See also, P.R. Newman, *Royalist Officers in England and Wales, 1642–1660* (New York, 1981), p.203.

15 E. 279[8].

16 A. Clark (ed.), *Brief Lives, chiefly of contemporaries, set down by John Aubrey, between the years 1669 and 1696* (two volumes, London, 1898), Volume 2, p.93.

17 See also I. Roy, *Sir William Neale* (DNB).

18 Anon, *List of Indigent Officers.*

19 Ibid.
20 E. Hyde, *The History of the Rebellion and Civil Wars in England, together with an Historical View of the Affairs in Ireland* (sixteen books, London, 1702–4), Book IX, pp.38–39.
21 Anon, *List of Indigent Officers.*
22 M. Cavendish, Duchess of Newcastle, *The Lives of William Cavendish, Duke of Newcastle and of his wife, Margaret, Duchess of Newcastle* (London, 1872), p.32.
23 E.303 [2].
24 E. 249[2]. See also, I.G. Philip (ed.), *Journal of Sir Samuel Luke* (three volumes, The Oxfordshire Record Society, 1947), Volume I, p.68.
25 See TNA, *Commonwealth Exchequer Papers,* SP28/130, ff. 26/27.
26 Ibid.
27 E. 9[5], *Mercurius Aulicus* (Oxford, 24 August 1644).
28 E.40 [32].
29 S. Kelsey, *Sir Samuel Luke* (DNB). See also Philip, *Journal*; and H.G. Tibbutt (ed.), *The Letter Books of Sir Samuel Luke: 1644–45* (Historical Manuscripts Commission JP4, HMSO, 1963).
30 E. 100[6], *A Most Miraculous and Happy Victory* (London, 1643).
31 E. 319[22], *Powtheram Castle at Exeter, Taken by Sir Thomas Fairfax* (London, 31 January 1646).
32 M. Wanklyn, 'A General Much Maligned. The Earl of Manchester as Army Commander in the Second Newbury Campaign', *War in History* (Volume 14, Number 2, 2007), pp.149 and 153.
33 E. 288[38].
34 *CSPD, 1644,* p.149.
35 J. Sprigge, *Anglia Rediviva: England's Recovery* (London, 1647), p 31.

Bibliography

Abbreviations

BL   British Library, London
Bod L   Bodleian Library, University of Oxford
CSPD   Calendar of State Papers (Domestic)
E   The British Library, Thomason Tracts
SP   State Papers
TNA   The National Archives, Kew

MANUSCRIPT PRIMARY SOURCES

The National Archives
SP 21 (Committee of Both Kingdoms)
SP 28 (Commonwealth Exchequer Papers)

The British Library
Additional MSS
11331–3 (Sir William Brereton's papers)
18778–80 (House of Commons Journals)
18979 (Fairfax Papers)
18980–2 (Prince Rupert's Papers)
18983 (Charles/Rupert Letters)
21506 (Civil War Letters)
25708 (Fairfax Memorials)
30305–6 (Fairfax Family Papers)
36913 (Prince Rupert's Papers)
62084–5 (Pyt House Papers)

Egerton MSS 785–7 (The Letter Books of Sir Samuel Luke)

Harleian MSS
986 (Symonds' Notebook)
991 (Marches of the Royalist Army)
6802 (Royalist Council of War papers)
6804 (Royalist Council of War papers)
6851 (Royalist Council of War papers)
6852 (Royalist Council of War papers)
Sloane MSS 1519 (Civil War Papers)
Stowe MSS 190 (The Letter Books of Sir Samuel Luke)

The Bodleian Library, University of Oxford
Carte MSS X, XI (Irish Papers)

Clarendon MSS
21–28 (History of the Rebellion (March 1642 – December 1646)
94 (Royalist Ciphers)

English History MSS c53 (Sir Samuel Luke's Diary, 1642–44)

Fairfax MSS 32, 36, 37 (Fairfax Family Papers)

Firth MSS C6 (Prince Rupert's Letters), C7 (Prince Rupert's Letters)

Rawlinson MSS
A1 (Thurloe)
A306 (Secret Service Money)

Tanner MSS
20 (English Historical Papers)
59–62 (Bluecoat Musters)

Waller MSS Don. d57 (The Vindication of Sir William Waller)

PRINTED PRIMARY SOURCES

Anon, *Instructions for Musters and Armes: and the use thereof* (London, 1631)
Anon, *A List of Officers claiming the sixty thousand pounds &c. granted by His Sacred Majesty for the relief of his truly loyal and indigent party* (London, 1663)
Barriffe, W. *Military Discipline: or the Yong Artillery Man* (London, 1635)

Bulstrode, R. *Memoirs and Reflections* (London, 1721)

Boyle, R. Earl of Orrery, *A treatise on the art of war* (London, 1677)

Cavendish, M. Duchess of Newcastle, *The Life of William Cavendish, Duke of Newcastle, to which is added the true relation of my birth, breeding and life* (London, 1667)

Cruso, J. *Militarie Instructions for the Cavallrie* (Cambridge, 1632)

Davies, E. *The Art of War, and Englands Traynings* (London, 1619)

Dugdale, W. Short View of the Late Troubles in England (London, 1681)

Echard, L. *History of England* (London, 1707–18)

Fairfax, Sir Thomas *Short Memorials of Thomas, Lord Fairfax* (London, 1699)

Heath, J. *Chronicle of the late Intestine War in the Three Kingdoms* (London, 1661)

Hexham, H. *The Principles of the Art Militarie: Practised in the Warres of the United Netherlands* (London, 1637)

Hodgson, J. *Memoirs of Captain John Hodgson* (reprinted Pontefract, 1994)

Hyde, Sir Edward, Earl of Clarendon, *The History of the Rebellion and Civil Wars in England, together with an Historical View of the Affairs in Ireland* (sixteen books, London, 1702–4)

Lilley, W. *Special Observations on the Life and Death of King Charles I* (London, 1651)

Lilley, W. *The Last of the Astrologers: A History of his Life and Times* (London, 1715)

May, T. *The History of the Parliament of England* (London, 1647)

May, T. *A Breviary of the History of the Parliament of England* (London, 1655)

Moncke, George, Duke of Albermarle, *Observations upon Military and Political Affairs* (London, 1671)

Nalson, J. *Impartial Collection of the Great Affairs of State from the Beginning of the Scotch Rebellion in the Year 1639 to the Murder of King Charles I* (two volumes, London 1682–3)

Peters, H. *Gods Doings and Mans Duty,* (London, 1646)

Ram, R. *The Soldiers Catechisme* (London, 1646)

Rich, B. *A Pathway to Military Practice* (London, 1587)

Ricraft, J. *The Civil Warres of England* (London, 1649)

Rushworth, J. *Historical Collections* (London, 1659–99)

Sprigge, J. *Anglia Rediviva: England's Recovery* (London, 1647)

Swadlin, T. *The Soldiers Catechisme* (Oxford, 1645)

Sir James Turner, *Pallas Armata* (London, 1683)

Sir Edward Walker, *Historical Discourses upon Several Occasions* (London, 1705)

Sir Edward Walker, *His Majesty's Happy Progress and Success from the 30th of March to the 23rd of November 1644* (London, 1705)

Walker, Sir Edward, *Brief Memorials of the Unfortunate Success of His Majesty's Army and Affairs in the Year 1645* (London, 1705)

Walsingham, E. *The Life of the Most Honourable Knight, Sir Henry Gage, Late Governor of Oxford* (Oxford, 1645)

Whitelocke, B. *Memorials of the English Affairs* (London, 1682)

Editions of Primary Sources

Bell, R. (ed.) *Fairfax Correspondence,* (two volumes, London, 1849)

Binns, J. (ed.) *The Memoirs and Memorials of Sir Hugh Cholmley of Whitby, 1600–1657* (Yorkshire Archaeological Society, 2000)

Carlyle, T. (ed.) *Oliver Cromwell's Letters and Speeches,* (three volumes, London, 1845)

Clark. A. (ed.) *Brief Lives, chiefly of contemporaries, set down by John Aubrey, between the years 1669 and 1696* (two volumes, London, 1898)

Dore, R.N. (ed.) *The Letter Books of Sir William Brereton* (two volumes, Lancashire and Cheshire Record Society, 1984–90)

Ede-Borrett, S.L. (ed.) *The Letters of Nehemiah Wharton* (Wollaston, 1983)

Firth, C.H. (ed.) *The Life of William Cavendish, Duke of Newcastle* (London, 1886)

Firth, C.H. (ed.) *The Journal of Joachim Hane* (Oxford, 1896)

Firth, C.H. (ed.) *The Lives of William Cavendish, Duke of Newcastle and of his wife Margaret, Duchess of Newcastle* (London, 1907)

Firth, C.H. (ed.) *The Memoirs of Edmund Ludlow 1625–1672* (two volumes, London, 1698)

Chadwyck-Healey (ed.) *Bellum Civile: Hopton's Narrative of His Campaign in the West (1642–44) and Other Papers* (Somerset Record Society, 18, 1902)

Loftus, J. and P.H. Hardacre (eds.) *Colonel Joseph Bampfield's Apology: written by himself 1685* (London, 1993)

Loftus, J. (ed.) *The Memoirs of Anne, Lady Halkett and Ann, Lady Fanshawe* (Oxford, 1979)

Long, C.E. (ed.) *Richard Symonds: Diary of the Marches kept by the Royal army during the Great Civil War* (Camden Society, 1859)

I.G. Philip (ed.) *The Journal of Sir Samuel Luke* (3 volumes, Oxfordshire Record Society, 1950)

J. Roe (ed.) *Military Memoir of Colonel John Birch* (Camden Society, 1873)

H.G. Tibbutt (ed.) *The Letter Books of Sir Samuel Luke: 1644–45* (Historical Manuscripts Commission JP4, HMSO, 1963)

M. Toynbee (ed.) *Official Papers of Captain Henry Stevens, Wagon-master general to King Charles I, November 1643 – December 1644* (Oxfordshire Record Society, 1961)

Warburton, E.G.B. (ed.) *Memoirs of Prince Rupert and the Cavaliers,* (three volumes, London, 1849)

Webb, T.W. and J. (eds.) *Military Memoir of Colonel John Birch* (Camden Society, 1873)

The Journal of the House of Commons

The Journal of the House of Lords

Original News Journals

Certaine Informations from Severall parts of the Kingdom (London, 16 January 1643 – 22 February 1644)

Certaine Speciall and Remarkable Passages from Both Houses of Parliament (London, 16–26 August 1642)

A Continuation of Certaine Speciall and Remarkable Passages (London, 8 October 1642 – 16 June 1643)

England's Memorable Accidents (London, 12 September 1642 – 16 January 1643)

The Kingdomes Weekly Intelligencer (London, 27 December 1642 – 21 July 1646)

Mercurius Aulicus (Oxford, 1 January 1643 -7 September 1645)

Mercurius Britanicus (London, 5 September 1643 – 18 May 1646)

Mercurius Civicus, London's Intelligencer (London, 4 May 1643 – 10 December 1646)

Mercurius Rusticus (Oxford, 22 August 1642 – 25 March 1646)

The Parliament Scout (London, 20 June – 2 January 1646)

A Perfect Diurnal of the Passages in Parliament (London, 5 September 1642 – 19 June 1643)

A Perfect Diurnal of some Passages in Parliament (London, 26 June 1643 – 7 July 1645)

Perfect Occurrences of Parliament (London, 24 May 1644 – 6 March 1645)

Speciall Passages and Certain Information from Severall Places (London, 23 August 1642 – 3 January 1643)

The Spie (London, 23 January – 25 June 1644)

True Informer (London, 23 September 1643 – 22 February 1645)

Printed Pamphlets

E.126 [39] *A True Relation of the skirmish at Worcester* (London, 1642)

E. 124 [26] *An Exact and True Relation of the Dangerous and bloody Fight, Between His Majesties Army, and the Parliaments Forces, neer Kineton in the County of Warwick, the 23 of this instant October* (London, 1642)

E. 124[4] *Exceeding Joyfull Newes from the Earl of Stamford, the Lord Wharton, and the Lord Kymbolton* (London, 21 October 1642)

E. 126[38] Fiennes, N. *A Most True and an Exact Relation of both the Battels fought by His Excellency and His Forces against the bloudy Cavaliers* (London, 9 November 1642)

E.127 [18] *Prince Robert's Disguises* (London, 16 November 1642)

Anon, *A Particular relation of the action before Cirencester* (Oxford, 1643)

E. 100[6] *A Most Miraculous and Happy Victory* (London, 1643)

E.102 [17] *A True Relation of The Proceedings of the Cornish Forces under the command of the Lord Mohune and Sir Ralph Hopton; A Famous Victorie obtained by Sir William Waller against the Lord Herbert* (London, 1643)

E. 97[2] *The Victorious and Fortunate Proceedings of Sir William Waller* (London, 12 April 1643)

E. 100[5] *The last Intelligence from his Excellency his Quarters at Reading, since the surrendering of the town* (London, 27 April 1643)

E. 69[2] *A True Relation of the late Battell neere Newbery* (London, 26 September 1643)

E. 69[15] *A True and Exact Relation of the Marchings of the Two Regiments of Trained Bands of the City of London, being the Red and the Blew Regiments* (London, 2 October 1643)

E. 70[10] *A True Relation of the late Expedition of His Excellency, Robert Earle of Essex for the Relief of Gloucester With the Description of the Fight at Newbury* (London, 7 October 1643)

E. 78[8] *A True Relation of the Whole Proceedings of Sir William Waller and his Army from 20 November to 9 December 1643* (London, 1643)

E. 78[22] *A Narration of the great victory obtained by the Parliament's forces under Sir William Waller at Alton* (London, 16 December 1643)

E. 40[9] *Winchester taken, Together with a Fuller Relation of the Great Victory obtained (through God's Providence) at Alsford, on Friday 28 March 1644* (London, 1644)

E. 38[10] *His Highnesse Prince Ruperts Raising of the Siege at Newark* (Oxford, 1644)

E. 2[14] *A more exact Relation of the late Battaile neere York, fought by the English and Scottish forces, against Prince Rupert and the Earle of New-Castle* (London, 1644)

E.54 [19] *A Full Relation of the Late Victory,* (London, 1644)

E. 54[11] *A Relation of the Good Success of the Parliaments Forces* (London, 1644)

E. 2[1] *A Continuation of True Intelligence from the English and Scottish Forces in the North, 16 June – 10 July* (London, 1644)

E. 51[11] *Hulls managing of the Kingdoms cause or, a brief Historicall Relation of the Severall Plots and Attempts against Kingston upon Hull* (London, 18 June 1644)

E. 53[18] *An Exact and full Relation of the last Fight, Between the Kings Forces and Sir William Waller* (London, 5 July 1644)

E. 284[9] *An Exact Relation of the raising of the siege, and relieving of the town of Taunton* (London, 1645)

E. 284[11] *A Great Victory obtained against the Enemy, at the raising of the Siege from before Taunton* (London, 1645)

E. 288[28] *A more exact and perfect Relation of the great Victory obtained by Parliament's Forces under the command of Sir Thomas Fairfax* (London, 1645)

E. 288[21] *A True Relation of a Great Victory obtained by Sir Thomas Fairfax* (London, 1645)

E. 288[22] *A True Relation of a Victory obtained over the King's forces, by the army of Sir Thomas Fairfax* (London, 1645)

E. 288[27] *Letters from the Right Honourable Sir Thomas Fairfax, Lieut. Gen. Cromwell and the committee residing in the army* (London, 1645)

E. 319[22] *Powtheram Castle at Exeter, Taken by Sir Thomas Fairfax* (London, 31 January 1646)

PRINTED SECONDARY SOURCES

Adair, J. *Roundhead General: The Campaigns of Sir William Waller* (Stroud, 1997)

Adair, J. Cheriton, *1644: The Campaign and the Battle* (Kineton, 1973)

Ashley, M. *Cromwell's Generals* (London, 1954)

Ashley, M. *Rupert of the Rhine* (London, 1976)

Atkin, M. *Cromwell's Crowning Mercy: The Battle of Worcester 1651* (Stroud, 1998)

Aubrey, P. *Mr Secretary Thurloe, Cromwell's Secretary of State 1652–1660* (London, 1990)

Barratt, J. *Sieges of the English Civil Wars* (Barnsley, 2009)

Barwick, P. *The Life of John Barwick* (London, 1728)

Birken, W.J. 'The Royal College of Physicians and its support of the Parliamentary Cause in the English Civil War', *Journal of British Studies* (Volume 23, No. 1, 1983)

Capp, B. *Cromwell's Navy: The Fleet and the English Revolution 1648–1660* (Oxford, 1989)

Carlton, C. *Going to the Wars: The Experience of the British Civil War 1638–1651* (London, 1992)

Carpenter, S.D.M. *Military Leadership in the English Civil Wars, 1642–1651: 'The Genius of this Age'* (London, 2005)

Carte, T. *General History of England* (London, 1747–55)

Churchill, W.S. *The Second World War* (six volumes, London, 1948–1954)

Coate, M. *Cornwall in the Great Civil War and Interregnum 1642–1660* (Oxford, 1933)

Cooke, D. *The Civil War in Yorkshire: Fairfax versus Newcastle* (Barnsley, 2004)

Cooke, D. *The Road to Marston Moor* (Barnsley, 2007)

Cottrell, L. *Enemy of Rome* (London, 1960)

Cunningham, A.B. *A Sailor's Odyssey* (London, 1951)

Cust, R. and A. Hughes (eds.) *The English Civil War* (London, 1997)

Day, J. *Gloucester and Newbury 1643: The Turning Point of the Civil War* (Barnsley, 2007)

M. and R. Dodds, *The Pilgrimage of Grace and the Exeter Conspiracy* (two volumes, London, 1915)

Donagan, B. *War in England: 1642 – 1649* (Oxford, 2008)

Edgar, F.T.R. *Sir Ralph Hopton. The King's Man in the West (1642–1652)* (Oxford, 1968)

Firth, C.H. *Cromwell's Army: A History of the English Soldier during the Civil Wars, the Commonwealth and the Protectorate* (London, 1902)

Firth, C.H. 'Clarendon's History of the Rebellion', *English Historical Review* (Volume 19, 1904)

Firth, C.H. 'The Journal of Prince Rupert's marches, 5 Sept. 1642 to 4 July 1646', *English Historical Review* (Volume 13, No. 52, 1898)

Firth, C.H. *Oliver Cromwell and the Rule of the Puritans in England* (Oxford, 1900)

Firth, C.H. 'Thomas Scot's Account of his Actions as Intelligencer during the Commonwealth', *English Historical Review* (Volume 12, No. 45, 1897)

Firth, C.H. 'Two Accounts of the Battle of Marston Moor', *English Historical Review* (Volume 5, No. 18, 1890)

Fletcher, A. and D. MacCulloch, *Tudor Rebellions* (Fifth edition, London, 2004)

Foard, G. *Naseby: The Decisive Battle* (Kent, 1995)

Fraser, A. *Cromwell: Our Chief of Men* (London, 1974)

Fraser, A. *The Weaker Vessel* (London, 1984)

Gardiner, S.R. *History of the Great Civil War 1642–1649* (four volumes, London, 1893)

Gentles, I. *The New Model Army in England, Ireland and Scotland, 1645–1653* (London, 1992)

Glow, L. 'The Committee of Safety', *English Historical Review* (Volume 80, No. 315, 1965)

Godwin, G.N. *The Civil War in Hampshire (1642–46) and the siege of Basing House* (London, 1882)

Gudgin, P. *Military Intelligence – A History* (Stroud, 1999)

Harrison, G.A. *Royalist Organisation in Gloucestershire and Bristol 1642–1645* (unpublished MA thesis, University of Manchester, 1961)

Hibbert, C. *Cavaliers and Roundheads. The English at War, 1642–1649* (London, 1994)

Hill, C. *The Century of Revolution: 1603–1714* (London, 1975)

Holmes, C. *The Eastern Association in the English Civil War* (Cambridge University Press, 1974)

Hopper, A. *Black Tom: Sir Thomas Fairfax and the English Revolution* (Manchester University Press, 2007)

Hudson, R. (ed.) *The Grand Quarrel* (Stroud, 1993)

Hutchinson, R. *Elizabeth's Spy Master: Francis Walsingham and the Secret War that Saved England* (London, 2006)

Hutton, R. 'Clarendon's History of the Rebellion', *English Historical Review* (Volume 97, No. 382, 1982)

Hutton, R. *The Royalist War Effort* (second edition, London, 1999)

Hutton, R. 'The Structure of the Royalist Party, 1642–1646', *The Historical Journal* (Volume 24, No. 3, 1981)

Kahn, D. *The Code-Breakers: The Comprehensive History of Secret Communication from Ancient Times to the Internet* (New York 1967, revised 1996)

Kenyon, J. *The Civil Wars of England* (London, 1996)

Kitson, F. *Prince Rupert: Portrait of a Soldier* (London, 1994)

Kitson, F. *Old Ironsides: The Military Biography of Oliver Cromwell* (London, 2004)

Macadam, A. *Mercurius Britanicus: Journalism and Politics in the English Civil War* (unpublished DPhil Thesis, University of Sussex, 2005)

Macaulay, C. *History of England from the Accession of James I* (London, 1763–83)

MacLachlan, T. *The Civil War in Wiltshire* (Salisbury, 1997)

MacLachlan, T. *The Civil War in Hampshire* (Salisbury, 2000)

Manning, B. *The English People and the English Revolution* (London, 1976)

Manning, B. 'The Nobles, the People and the Constitution', in T. Ashton (ed.), *Crisis in Europe 1560–1660* (New York, 1967)

Markham, C.R. *A Life of the Great Lord Fairfax* (London, 1870)

Marshall, A. *Intelligence and Espionage in the Reign of Charles II, 1660–1685* (Cambridge, 1994)

Miller, A.C. *Sir Richard Grenville of the Civil War* (London, 1979)

Morrah, P. *Prince Rupert of the Rhine* (London, 1976)

Nevitt, M. *Women and the Pamphlet Culture of Revolutionary England 1640–1660* (Aldershot, 2006)

Newman, P.R. *Royalist Officers in England and Wales, 1642–1660* (New York, 1981)

Nicholas, D. *Mr Secretary Nicholas (1593–1669): His Life and Letters* (London, 1955)

Oldmixon, J. *Critical History of England* (London, 1724)

Ollard, R. *This War without an Enemy: A History of the English Civil Wars* (London, 1976)

Parritt, B.A.H. *The Intelligencers: The story of British Military Intelligence up to 1914* (Ashford, 1971)

Parry, R.H. *The English Civil War and After: 1642–1658* (London, 1970)

Parsons, D. *The Diary of Sir Henry Slingsby* (London, 1836)

Peddie, J. *Hannibal's War* (Stroud, 1997)

Phillips, J. R. *Memoirs of the Civil War in Wales and the Marches, 1642–1646* (London, 1874)

Plowden, A. *Women all on Fire The Women of the English Civil War* (Stroud, 1998)

Purkiss, D. *The English Civil War: A People's History* (London, 2006)

Reese, P. *Cromwell's Masterstroke: Dunbar 1650* (Barnsley, 2006)

Reid, S. *All the King's Armies: A Military History of the English Civil War 1642–1651* (Kent, 1998)

Richardson, R.C. *The English Revolution Revisited* (London, 1991)

Richardson, R.C. *The Debate on the English Revolution* (Manchester, 1998)

Roberts, K. and J. Tincey, *Edgehill 1642* (Oxford, 2001)

Rogers, H.C.B. *Battles and Generals of the Civil War 1642–1651* (London, 1961)

Rose-Troup, F. *The Western Rebellion of 1549* (London, 1913)

Roy, I. *The Royalist Army in the First Civil War* (unpublished DPhil thesis, University of Oxford, 1963)

Roy, I. 'The Royalist Council of War', *Bulletin of the Institute of Historical Research* (Volume 35, 1962)

Royle, T. *Civil War: The Wars of the Three Kingdoms 1638–1660* (London, 2004)

Sarkar, D. *The Battle of Powicke Bridge* (Worcester, 2007)

Scott, C., A. Turton and E.G. von Arni, *Edgehill: The Battle Reinterpreted* (Barnsley, 2004)

Sharp, C. (ed.) *The Rising in the North: The 1569 Rebellion* (Ilkley, 1975)

Sherwood, R. *The Civil War in the Midlands 1642–1651* (Stroud, 1992)

Slim, W. *Defeat into Victory* (London, 1956)

Spaulding, T.M. 'Militarie Instructions for the Cavallrie' *Journal of the American Military History Foundation* (Vol.2, No.2, 1938)

Stoyle, M.J. 'The Gear Rout: The Cornish Rising of 1648 and the Second Civil War', *Albion. A Quarterly Journal concerned with British Studies* (Volume 32, No. 1, 2000)

Stoyle, M. *Loyalty and Locality. Popular Allegiance in Devon during the English Civil War* (Exeter, 1994)

Stoyle, M.J. 'Pagans or Paragons? Images of the Cornish during the English Civil War', *English Historical Review* (Volume 111, No. 441, 1996)

Stoyle, M. *Soldiers and Strangers: An Ethnic History of the English Civil War* (Yale, 2005)

Stucley, J. *Sir Bevill Grenville and his Times* (Sussex, 1983)

Thomas, P.W. *Sir John Berkenhead, 1617–1679 A Royalist Career in Politics and Polemics* (Oxford, 1969)

Toynbee, M. and P.Young, *Cropredy Bridge 1644* (Kineton, 1970)

Underdown, D. *Revel, Riot and Rebellion* (Oxford, 1985)

Verney, F.P. *Memoirs of the Verney Family during the Civil War* (London, 1892)

Wanklyn M. and F. Jones, *A Military History of the English Civil War, 1642–1646* (London, 2005)

Wanklyn M. 'A General Much Maligned. The Earl of Manchester as Army Commander in the Second Newbury Campaign', *War in History* (Volume 14, Number 2, 2007)

Wanklyn, M. *Decisive Battles of the English Civil War* (Barnsley, 2006)

Wanklyn, M. *The Warrior Generals: Winning the British Civil Wars, 1642–1652* (New Haven and London, 2010)

Wedgwood, C.V. *The Thirty Years' War* (London, 1938)

Wedgwood, C.V. *The Great Rebellion: The King's Peace 1637–1641* (London, 1955)

Wedgwood, C.V. *The Great Rebellion: The King's War 1641–1647* (London, 1958)

Wenham, P. *The Great and Close Siege of York 1644* (Kineton, 1970)

Whitehead, J. *Cavalier and Roundhead Spies: Intelligence in the Civil War and Commonwealth* (Barnsley, 2009)

Willis-Bund, J.W. *The Civil War in Worcestershire* (Birmingham, 1905)

Wilson, J. *Fairfax: A Life of Thomas, Lord Fairfax, Captain-General of all the Parliament's Forces in the English Civil War, Creator and Commander of the New Model Army* (London, 1985)

Worden, B. *Roundhead Reputations. The English Civil Wars and the Passions of Posterity* (London, 2001)

Worden, B. *The English Civil Wars 1640–1660* (London, 2009)

Wood, A.A. *Athenae Oxoniensis* (Oxford, 1721)

Woolrych, A. *Battles of the English Civil War* (London, 1961)

Wroughton, J. *An Unhappy Civil War: The Experiences of Ordinary People in Gloucestershire, Somerset and Wiltshire 1642–1646* (Bath, 1999)

Young, P. *Edgehill 1642* (first printed in 1967, first reprint Moreton-in-Marsh, 1995)

Young, P. *Marston Moor 1644* (Moreton-in-Marsh, 1970)

Young, P. *Naseby 1645* (London, 1985)

Young, P. and W. Emberton, *The Cavalier Army: Its Organisation and Everyday Life* (London, 1974)

Young, P. and R. Holmes, *The English Civil War: A Military History of the Three Civil Wars 1642–1651* (London, 1974)

Index